THE LONDON PUB

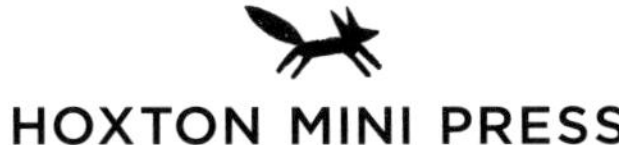

HOXTON MINI PRESS

ABOUT HOXTON MINI PRESS

Hello. Hoxton Mini Press is a small publisher from east London. We want to bring unusual photography to a wide audience; arty books should be beautiful (but they needn't be big or expensive). Books are no longer just about information. They are objects in their own right: things to collect and own and inspire. Thank you for supporting us.

www.hoxtonminipress.com

VINTAGE BRITAIN

A series celebrating the recent history of
these isles through rather nice photography.

BOOK ONE
The East End in Colour
1960–1980

BOOK TWO
The Isle of Dogs

BOOK THREE
Dog Show 1961–1978

BOOK FOUR
Paradise Street

BOOK FIVE
The East End in Colour
1980–1990

BOOK SIX
London Underground
1970–1980

BOOK SEVEN
Hackney Archive

BOOK EIGHT
Butlin's Holiday Camp 1982

BOOK NINE
London 1977–1987

BOOK TEN
London in the Snow

BOOK ELEVEN
A Very British Picnic

BOOK TWELVE
The London Pub

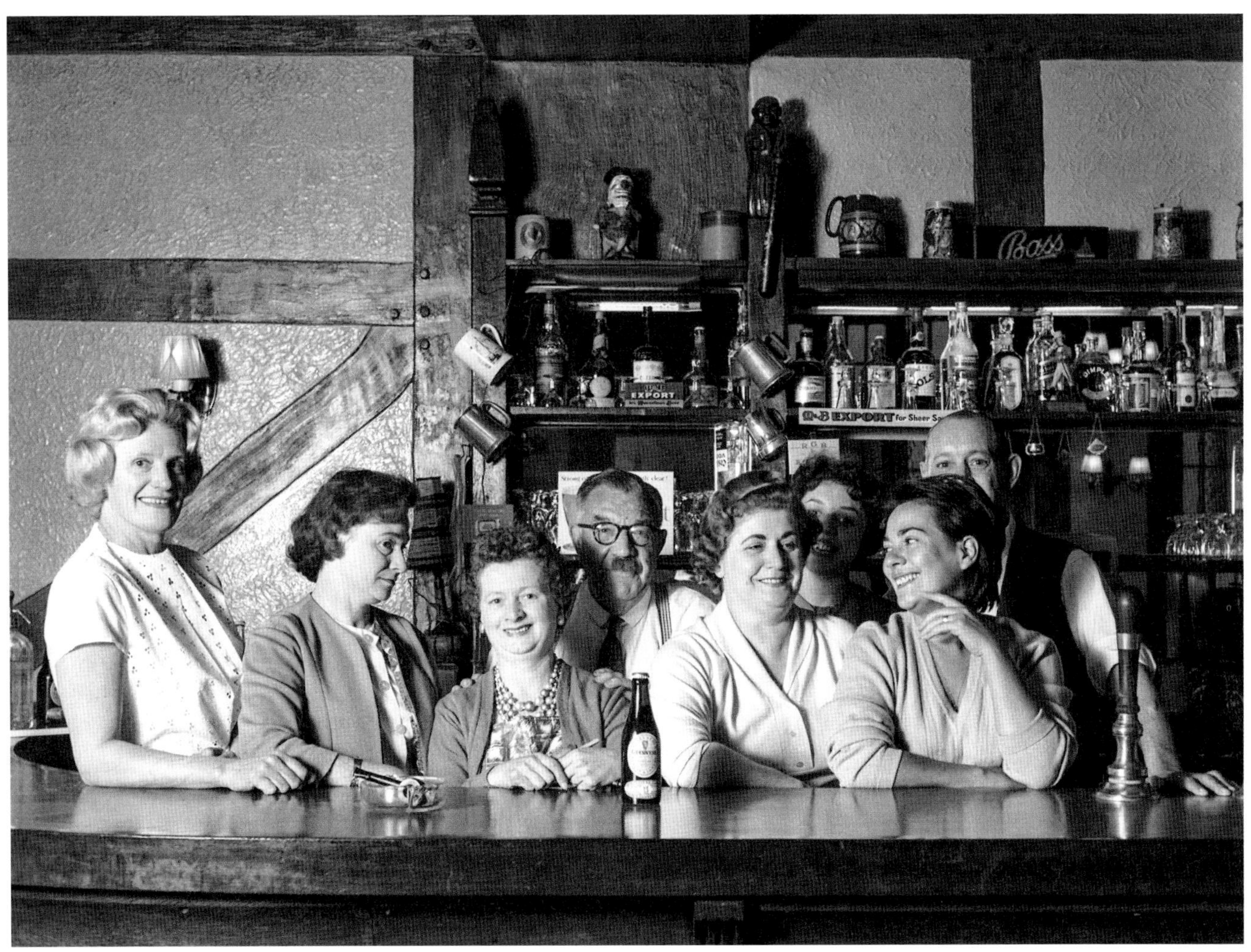

Bartenders at The George. *London, 1962*

INTRODUCTION

April 2021 was an extraordinary time for British pubs. After being forced to close by the pandemic, those with outdoor areas were allowed to partially reopen. Hardy drinkers were rewarded with a brutally cold spring. And journalists and broadcasters from around the globe descended on London in their droves.

What was it like to have pubs back? How had we survived without them? What did pubs mean to us? They were desperate to know.

Everyone in the world understood that pubs were the heartbeat of British life. No one cared that nail bars and barbers were also reopening at the same time. The pub was back. And that meant life was finally returning to normal. There was hope.

Even in the Second World War, pubs had never closed like this. During the Blitz, bombs rained on London every night. But as long as the pubs opened the following morning – even if that meant stretching a plank across a couple of beer barrels to serve as a makeshift bar amid the rubble – we weren't beaten.

Pubs are like air or water. They're so important we take them for granted, until they're gone. At this moment, we're still getting used to them being back again, and the everyday freedom to walk up to the bar and order a pint is as rewarding as that first sip.

In this context, the photographs collected here show how extraordinary our ordinary life is. As a pub geek, I came to them looking for mirrors engraved with brewery logos, old hanging signs and extinct beer brands. They're all here, in abundance. But what grabs you first are the people.

London has always been a diverse city brimming with strong characters. It breeds people with a thirst for life, and acts as a magnet for thirsty people born elsewhere. Throughout the 20th century, they made the city's pubs blaze with light and life.

Everyone is here: Pearly Kings and Queens revelling in the spontaneous subculture they have created; sailors home on leave; courting couples stealing kisses over tables full of empty glasses; sharp-suited men from the Caribbean introducing their music and dance moves to their new neighbours; old ladies holding court, staring down the myth that pubs were male-only spaces. Mick Jagger and Keith Richards prop up the bar like two blokes at the end of a hard day at the office. Suzi Quatro takes time out from being the Queen of Rock and Roll to play a game of snooker. Teddy Boys hog the jukebox while men old enough to remember the Boer War play pool. Meanwhile, dogs wait stoically at the bar, and children hover somewhat less patiently just outside the door.

If the cast is rich in its variety, so is the range of activities they enjoy. London's pubs have never been mere drinking shops. The darts is taken very seriously. A Tottenham pub becomes an art gallery dedicated to the local football team. Big men perform feats of strength. And always there is singing, the 'free and easy' where neighbours stand on stage or even a bar stool to serenade their neighbours, paving the way for future karaoke. When small televisions begin creeping onto pub walls and attracting the steady gaze of the punters, they seem to suck some of the life out of the place.

My own favourite time in a London pub is the contemplative afternoon pint. Pubs breathe out and stretch their limbs around 3pm, and that moment is repeatedly captured here. Single men contemplating love, life or loss, staring into the middle distance. The afternoon sun shafting in through high windows. As summer stifles, tables and chairs are dragged out into the street, and the music still plays.

This rich pastime of the city played out against a backdrop that tells its own story about life in London, and how it evolved during and after the huge expansion of the Industrial Revolution. Well into the 20th century, most working-class Londoners lived in warren-like slums, and drank in homely, cosy alehouses. From the middle of the 19th century, ambitious landlords built grander, more ornate premises that became known as 'gin palaces'. The disapproval of these places by the upper classes went well beyond fears of drunkenness. The same marble columns and gilded frames considered elegant in the gentlemen's clubs of St James's were decried as vulgar, gaudy 'mock' glamour when they appeared in pubs – even when created by the same craftsmen.

Pubs move more slowly than the rest of the city. By the late 20th century, gas lamps, colonnaded entrances and giant, etched mirrors were plentiful survivors from the Victorian era, and are now seen as a vital part of our architectural and cultural heritage by the descendants of those who once condemned them as a social evil.

In 1945, George Orwell wrote an essay for the Evening Standard called 'The Moon Under Water', describing his perfect pub. In reality, Orwell experts believe it was a composite of his three favourite pubs, all of which still survive around Highbury Corner: The Hen and Chickens, The Canonbury, and The Compton Arms. He celebrates their 'draught stout, open fires, cheap meals, a garden, motherly barmaids and no radio.' If it were not for his title being stolen by a pub chain (with no sense of irony), it would have made a good title for this introduction. Between them, the pubs collected here share every aspect of the perfect, idealised pub – even if none of them quite makes it on its own.

A lifetime later, what's changed about the London pub, apart from the solemnity and Brylcreem of the publican being replaced by beards and quiffs?

The wine and the food are certainly much better. I'm not sure whether the beer is or not (that would depend on whatever the latest trend in craft beer happens to be when you read this). Women can feel more comfortable generally, and the furniture is comfier for everyone.

The basic function of the pub is unchanged. But we visit much less often now that we have plasma screens, Netflix and Deliveroo, as well as Westfield, Starbucks and Vue. The pub now is an occasional treat, more desperate for our business. It's louder in every sense of the word. At its worst, it can assault all the senses, the opposite of what most people desire when they cross the threshold. At its best, it remains a unique and irreplacable social hub that adapts to fit whatever community it serves, each one subtly different from its peers.

The great thing about London's pubs is they are impossible to generalise. Scattered through the city are many that still resemble the pubs in these pages, held in time as if by some magic spell. I'm visiting one when I finish writing this. I hope you'll understand if, like Orwell, I don't break the spell by revealing where it is.

Pete Brown
London, 2022

By the 20th century, most pubs were owned by breweries. Watney's
(purveyors of the infamously bland 'Red Barrel' beer) were one of
the largest. The Baptist's Head (now closed). *Clerkenwell, 1954*

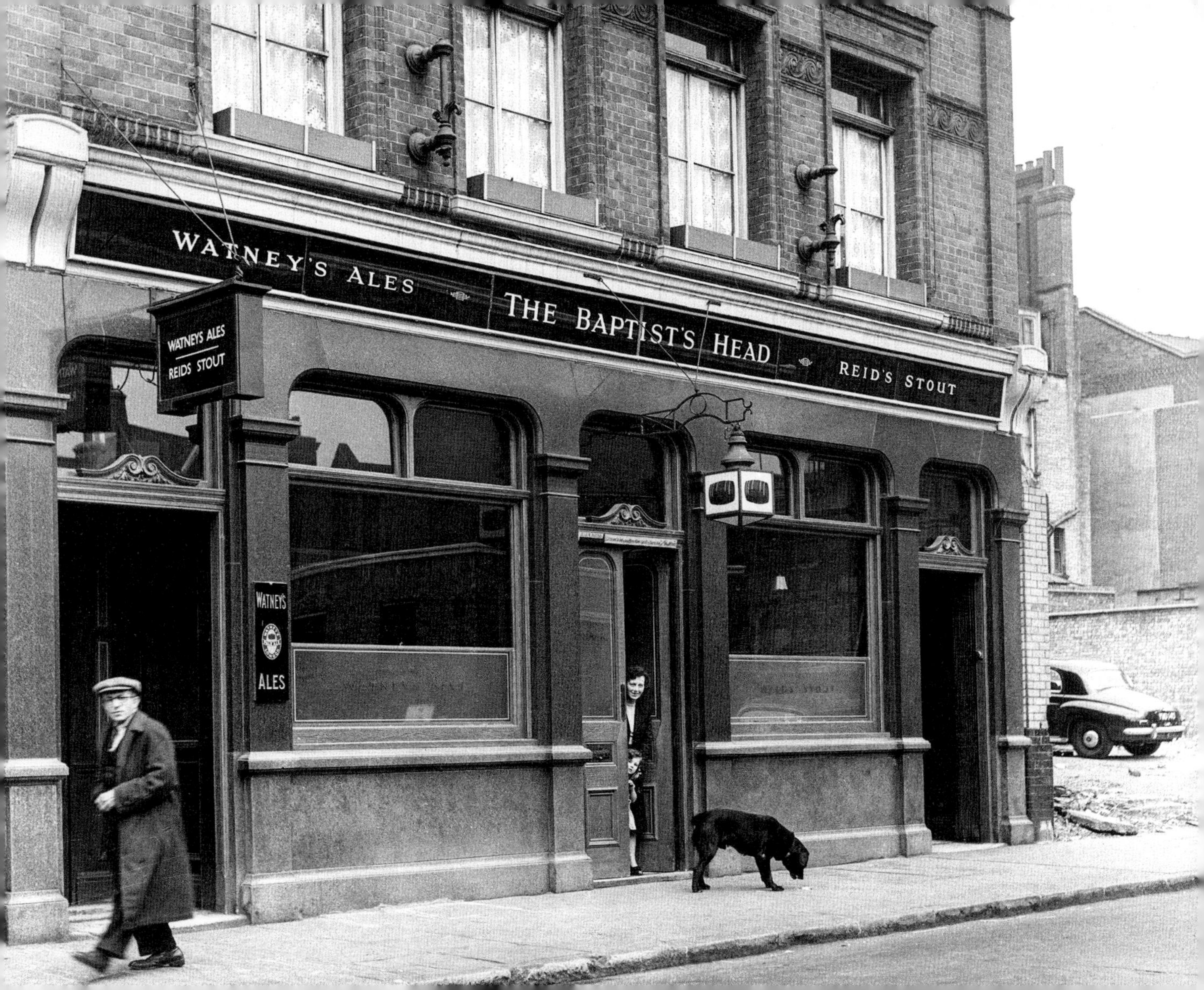
WATNEY'S ALES
THE BAPTIST'S HEAD
REID'S STOUT
WATNEYS ALES
REIDS STOUT
WATNEYS ALES

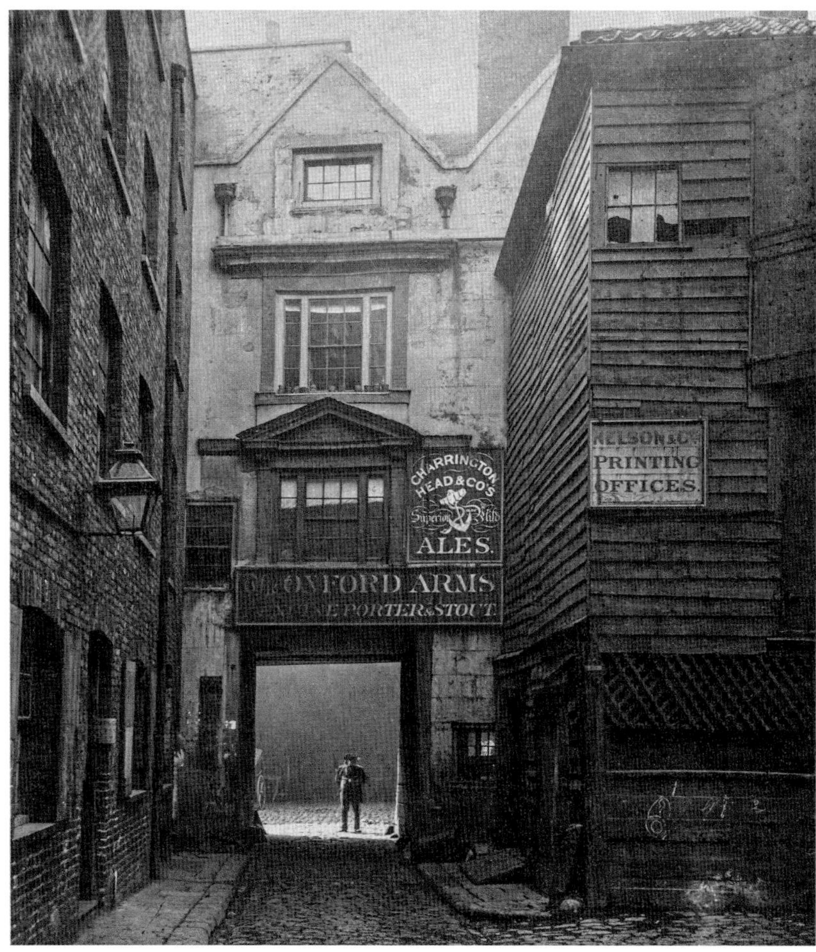

The Oxford Arms (now demolished) was one of the last galleried coaching inns. These inns provided travellers with stabling and accommodation until, almost overnight, railways made them obsolete. *City of London, 1875*

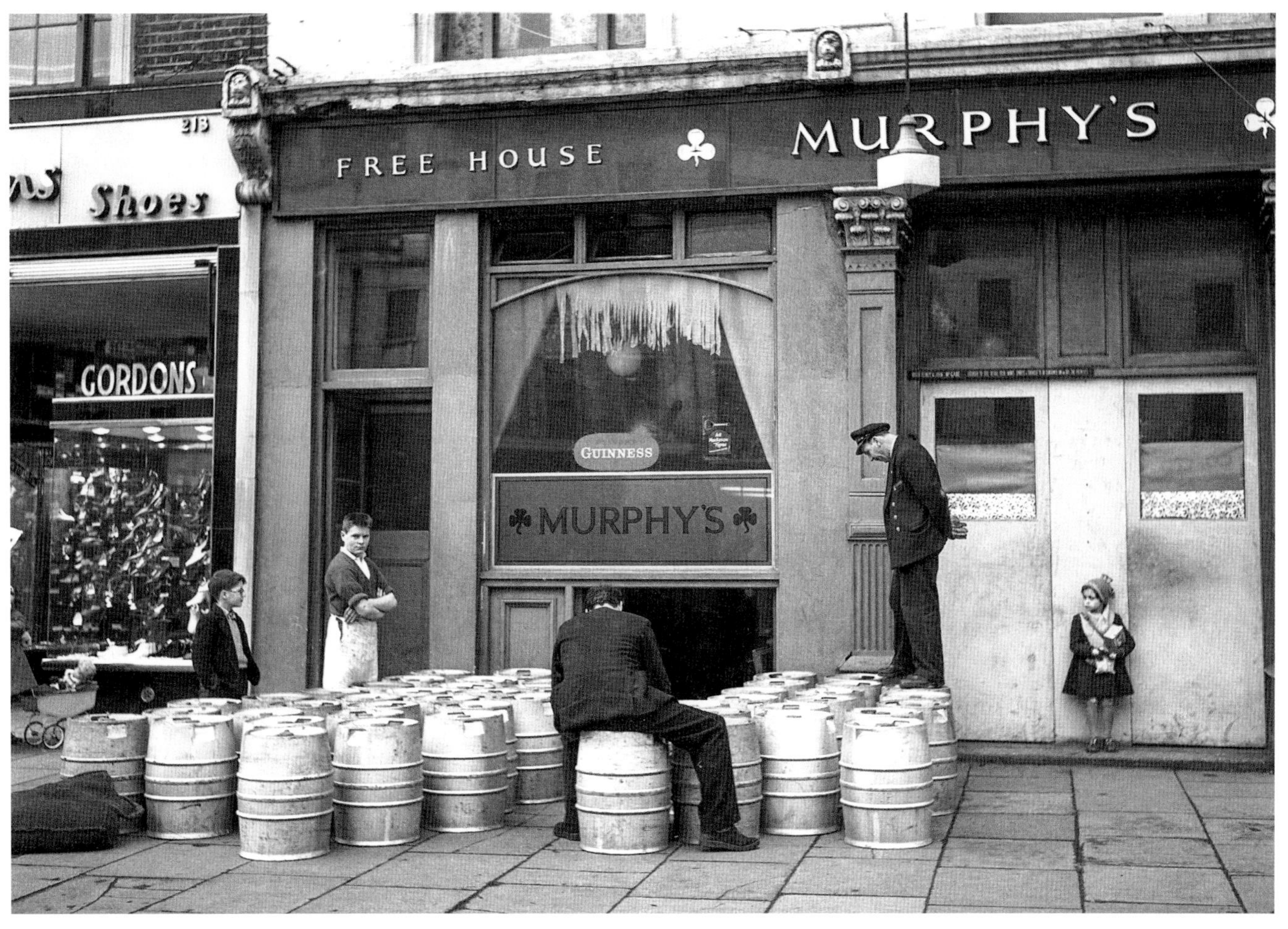

Fresh casks of beer are delivered first thing and dropped straight into the cellar from the pavement. Murphy's Free House. *London, c.1960*

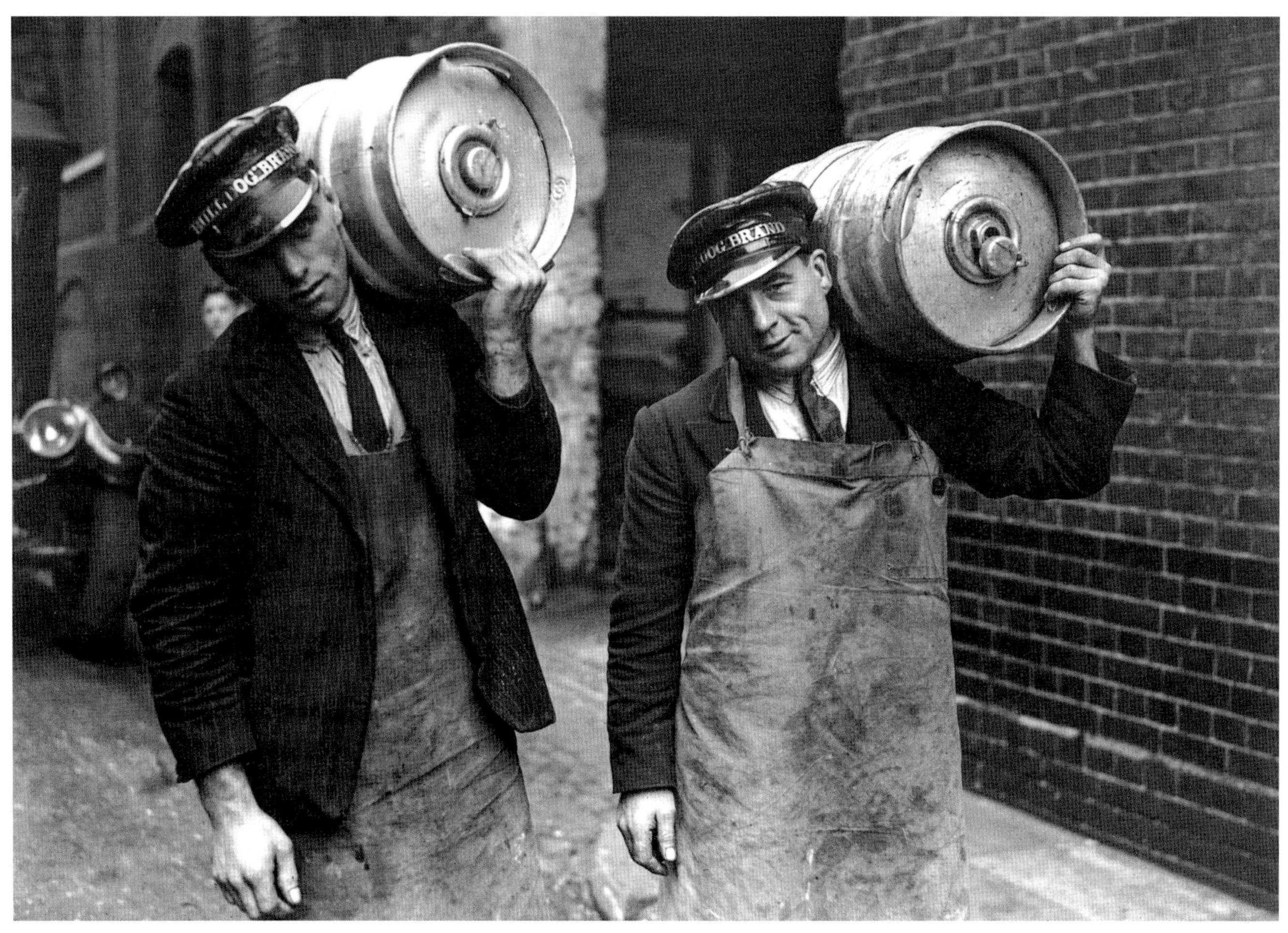

There's more to being a cellarman than hauling heavy kegs. Real ale is a fresh, live product that requires expert care. Here's an early example of pressurised kegs that made beer easier to keep and serve. *King's Cross, 1934*

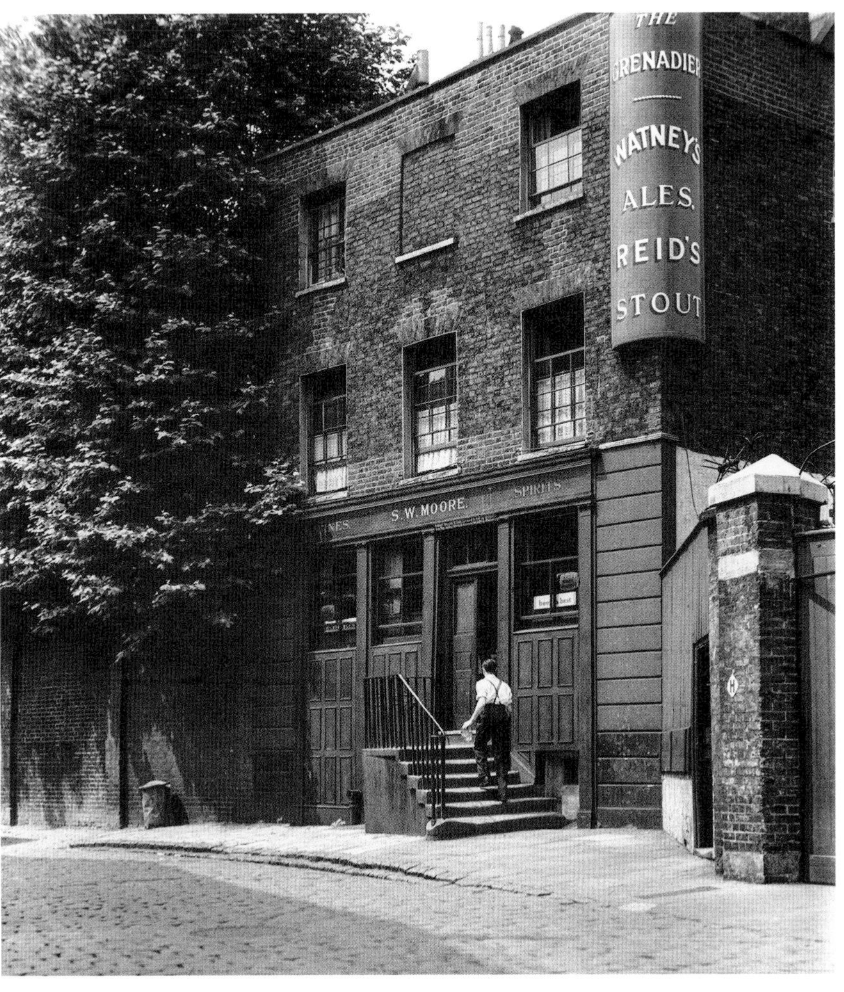

The Grenadier was named after troops serving under the Duke of Wellington, who lived nearby. This is allegedly the birthplace of the Bloody Mary. *Belgravia, c.1935*

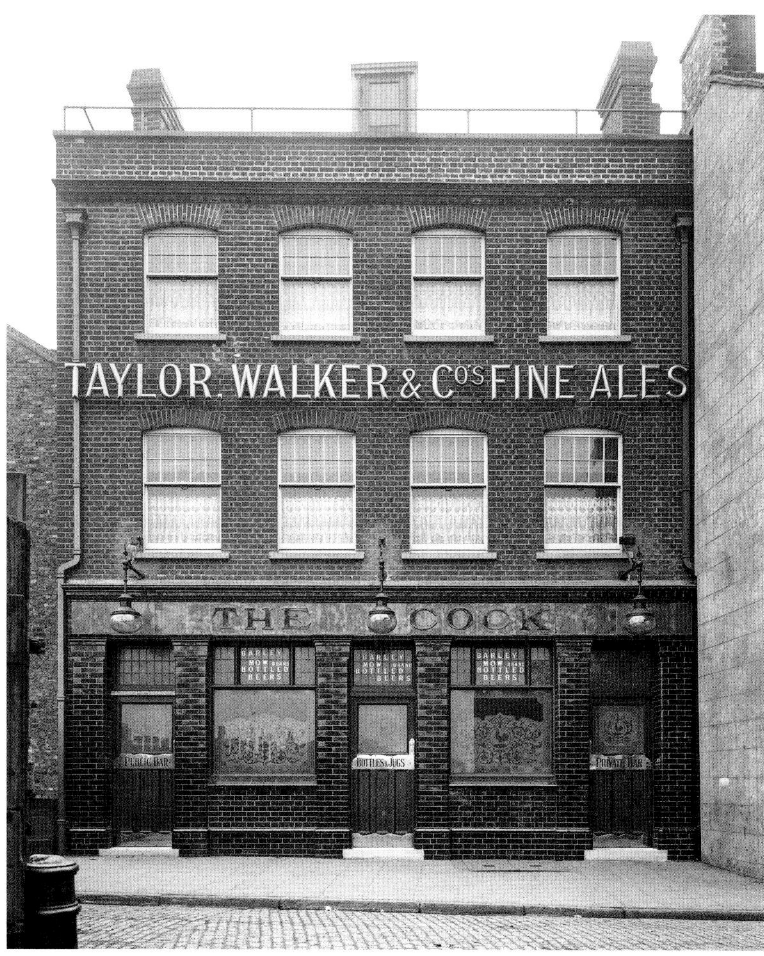

The name of the brewer was often more prominent than that of the pub, reflecting London's reputation as one of the world's great brewing cities. The Cock (now closed). *Shadwell, 1912*

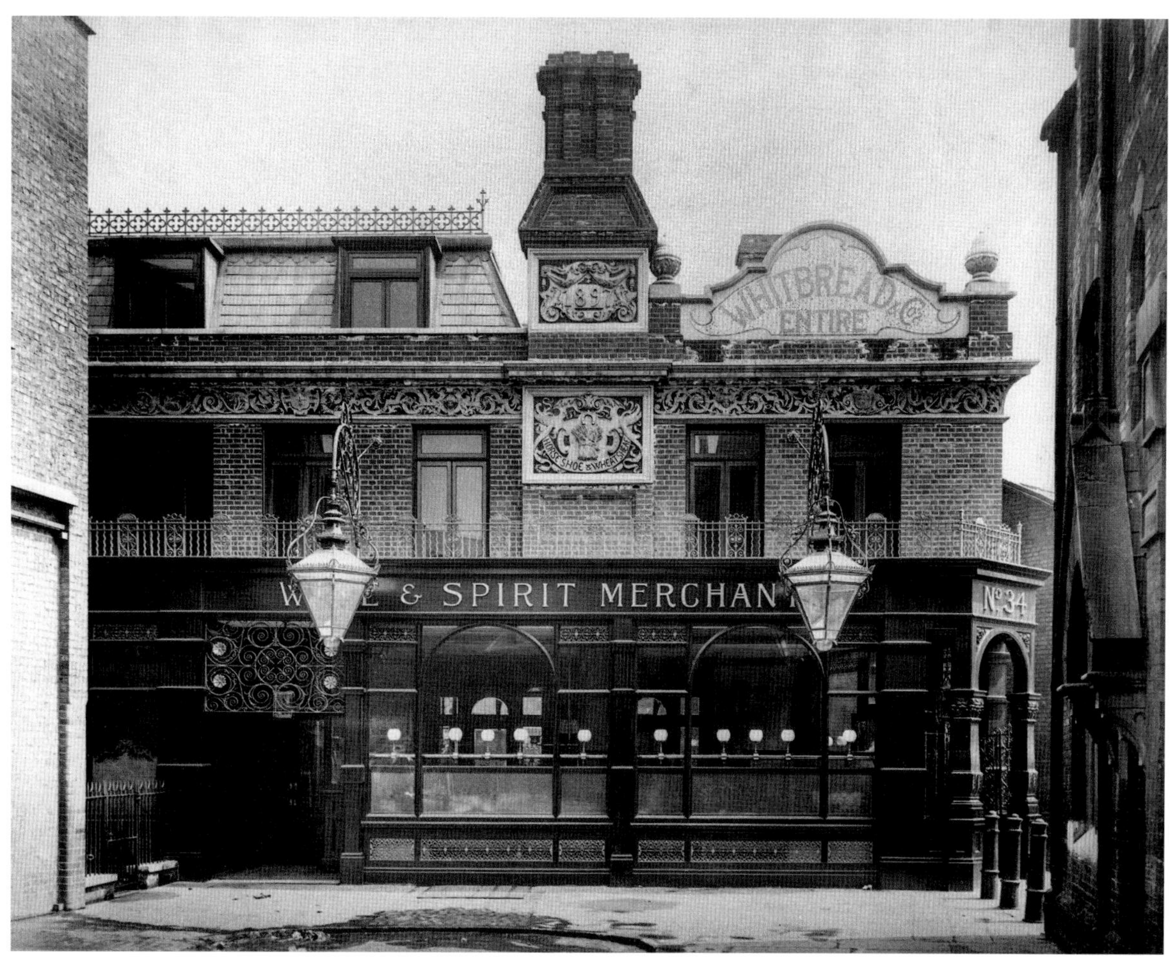

Many at the time feared that the gas lanterns outside 'gin palaces' would lure working class people in to drink, and lead to mass alcoholism. The Horseshoe & Wheatsheaf (renamed The Horseshoe Inn). *Southwark, 1898*

Morning in an east London pub. *1979*

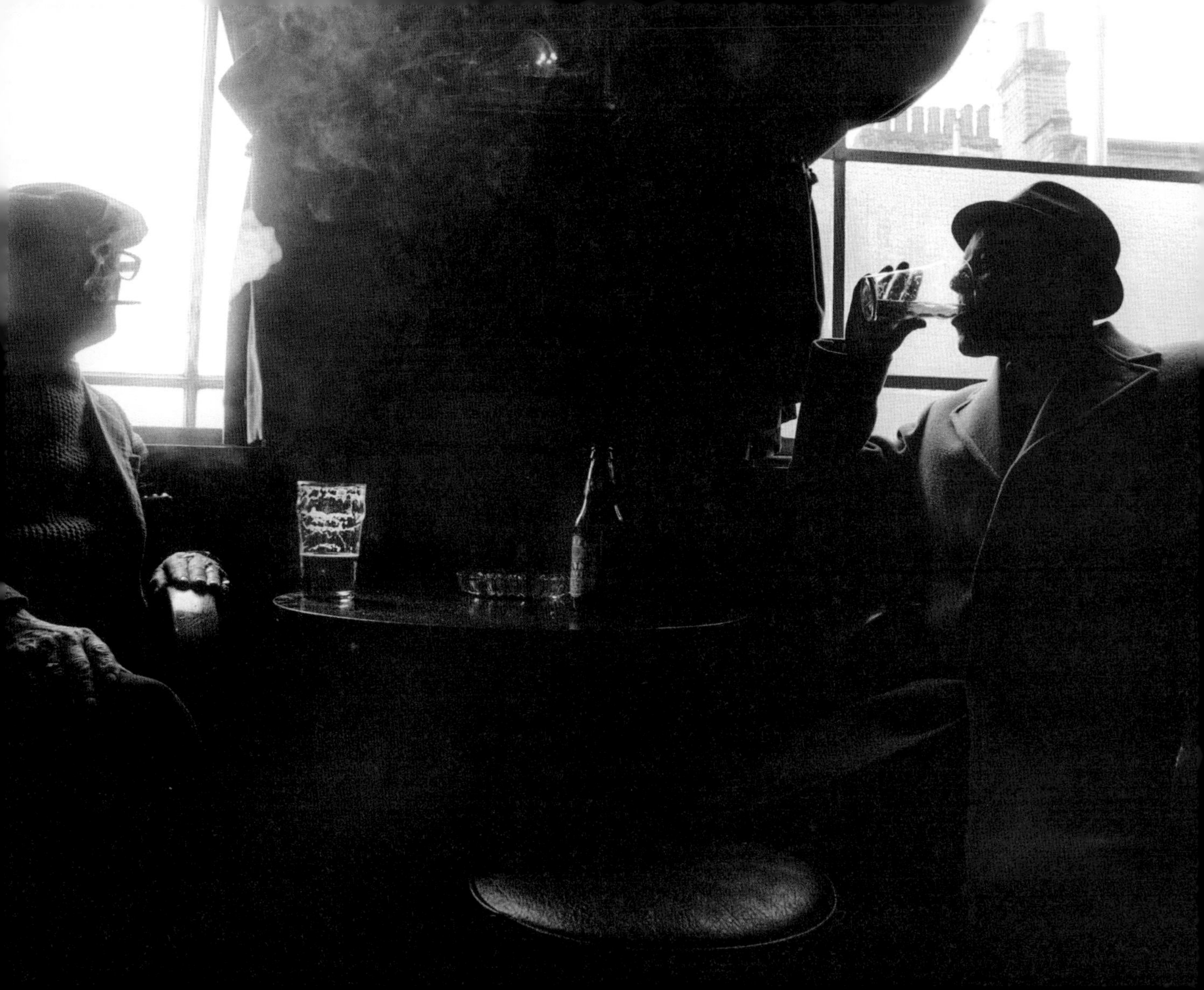

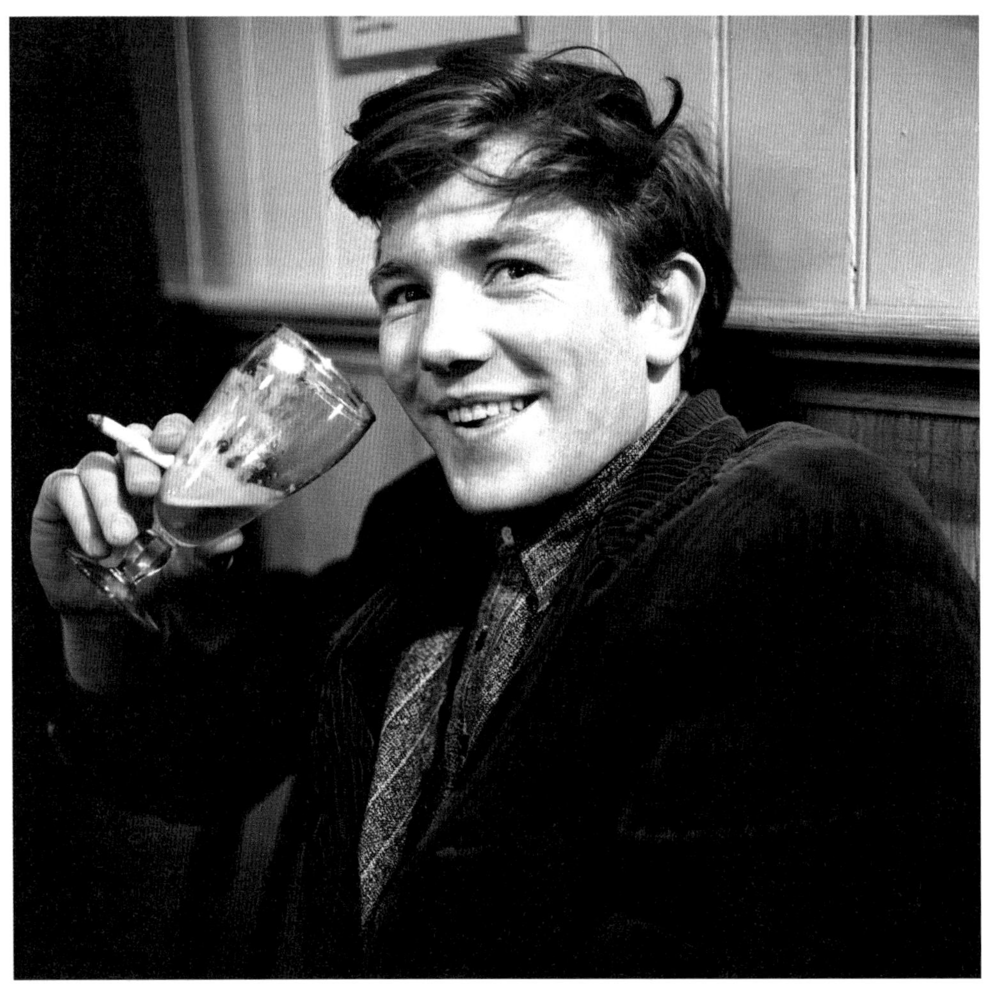

British actor Albert Finney at a pub behind the
Cambridge Theatre. *Covent Garden, 1961*

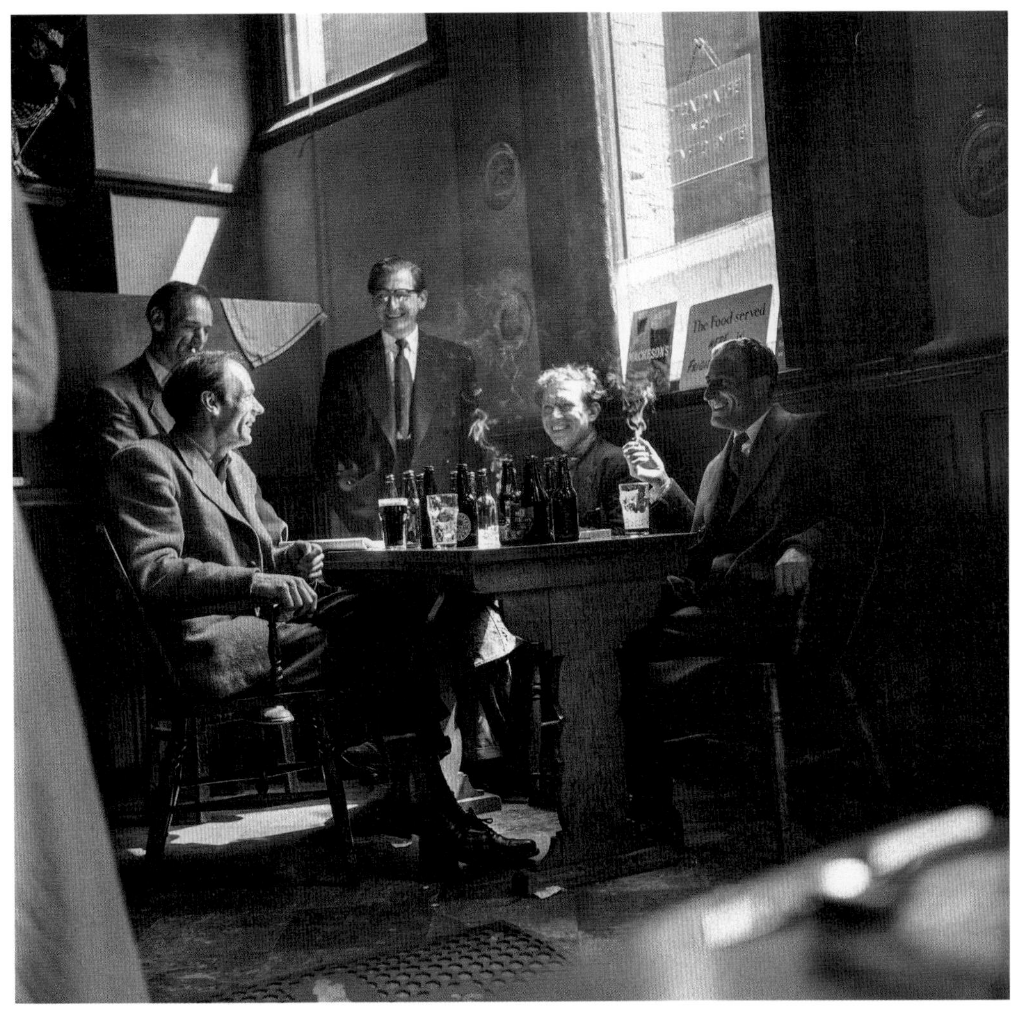

Lunch hour at The Globe near Borough Market. *Southwark, 1955*

The Blind Beggar on Whitechapel Road, where Ronnie Kray
infamously shot a rival. *East End, 1969*

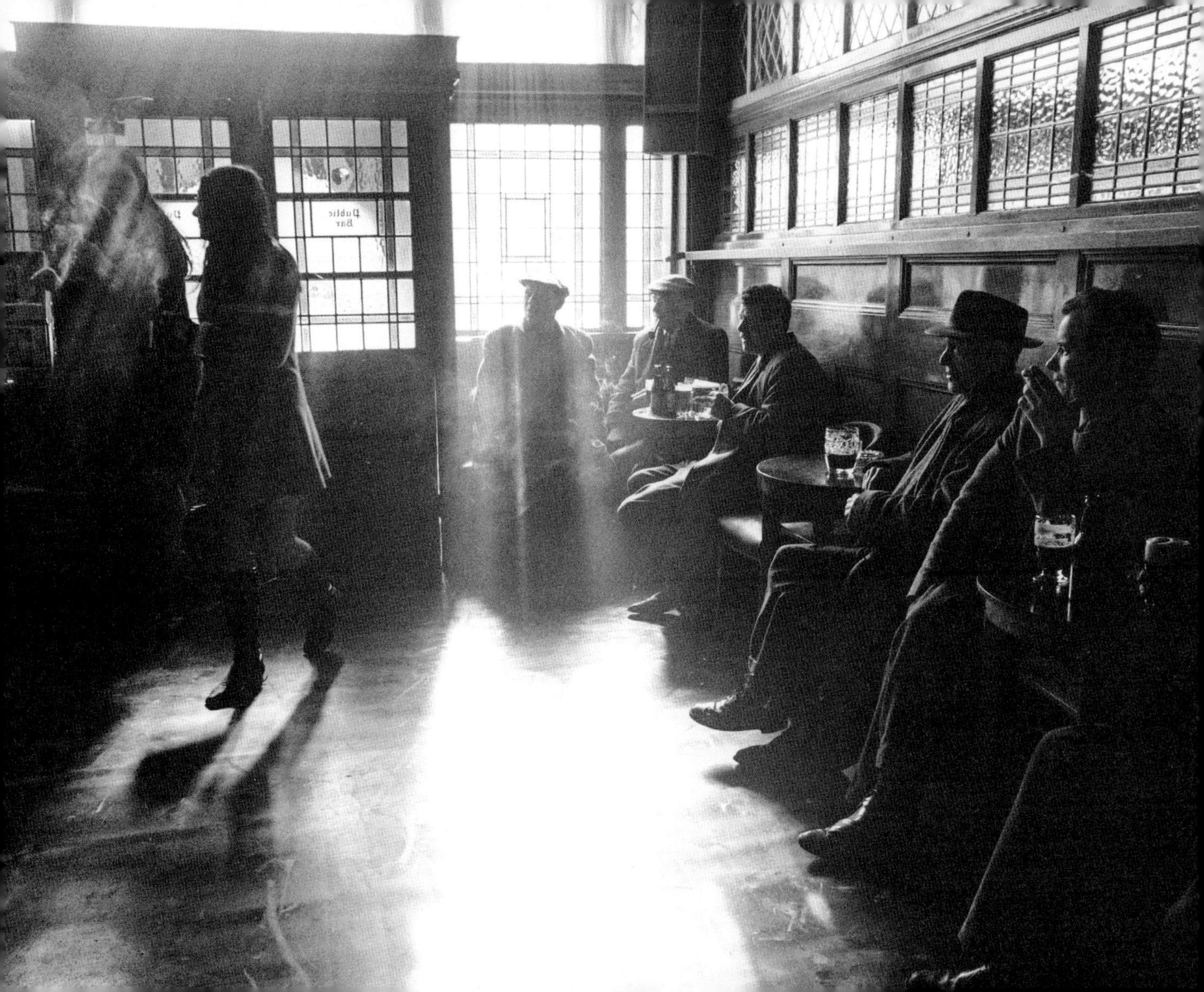

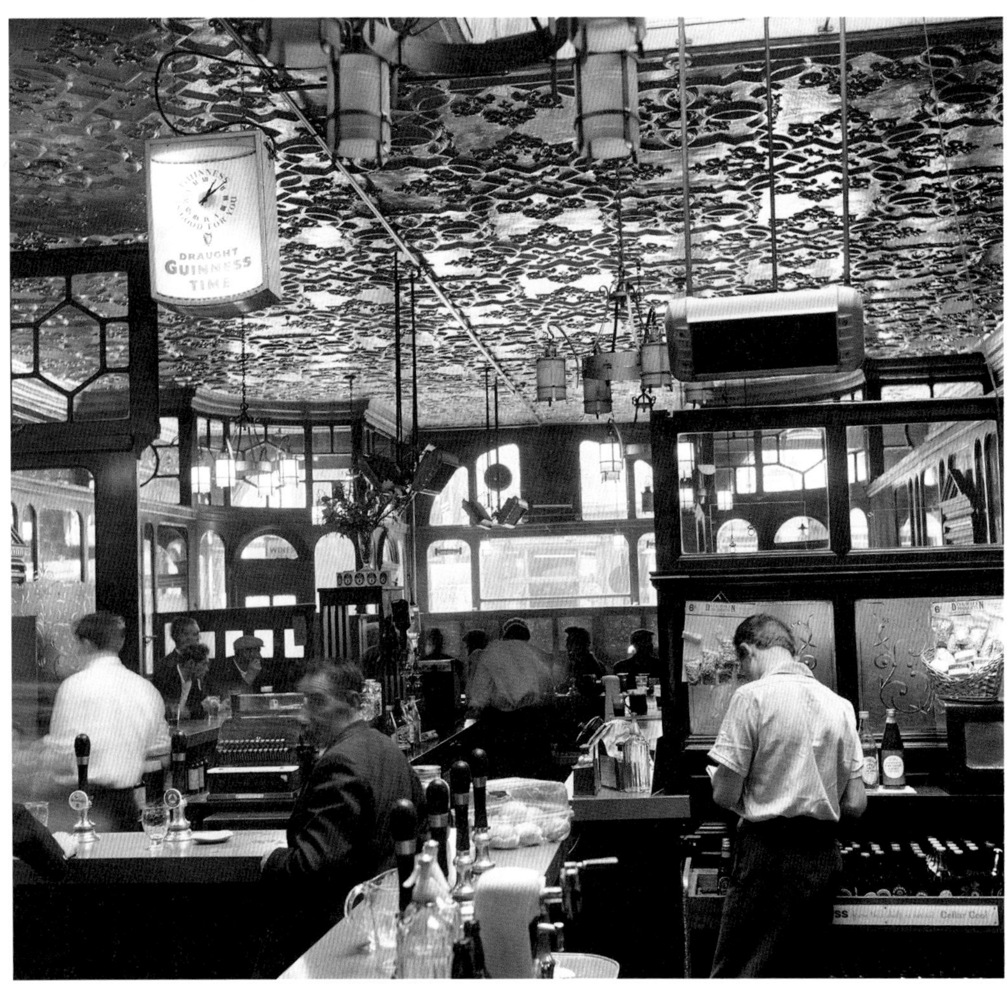

Ornate, moulded ceilings are a much loved architectural feature of 19th-century pubs that are still around today. *Edgware Road, c.1960*

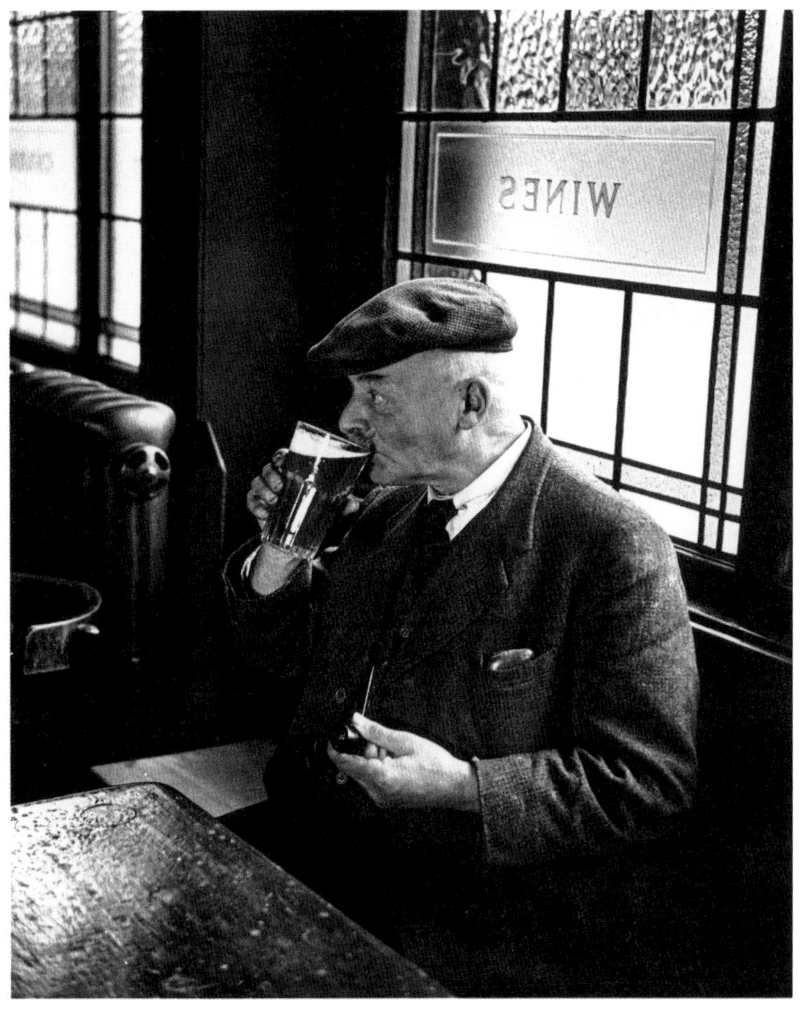

Old King's Head (now demolished). *Southwark, 1949*

A tender moment at The Colville in west London. Built as a grand hotel in 1867, in the 1950-60s it was frequented by Irish and Caribbean locals. Now, it is a gin distillery. *Notting Hill, 1969*

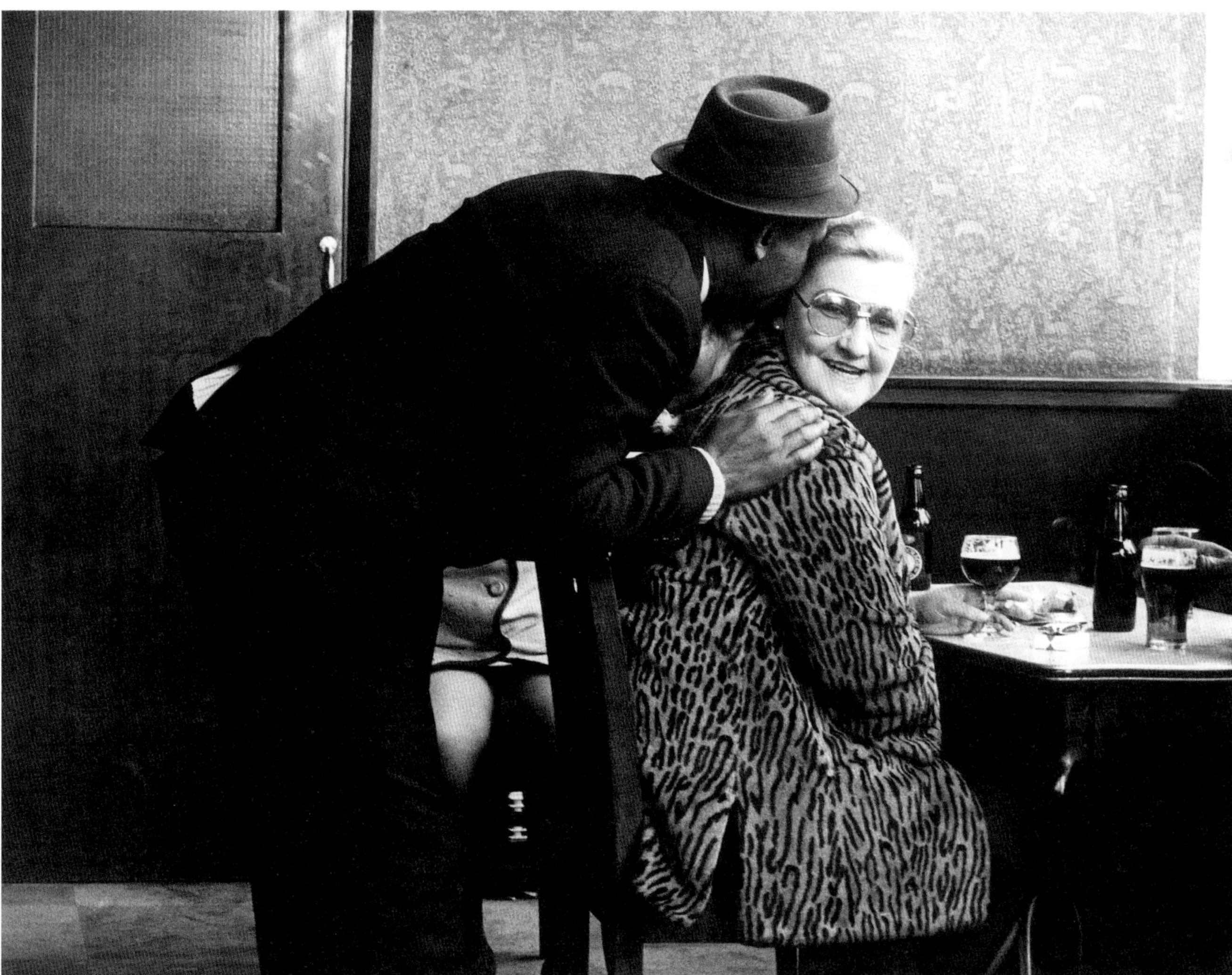

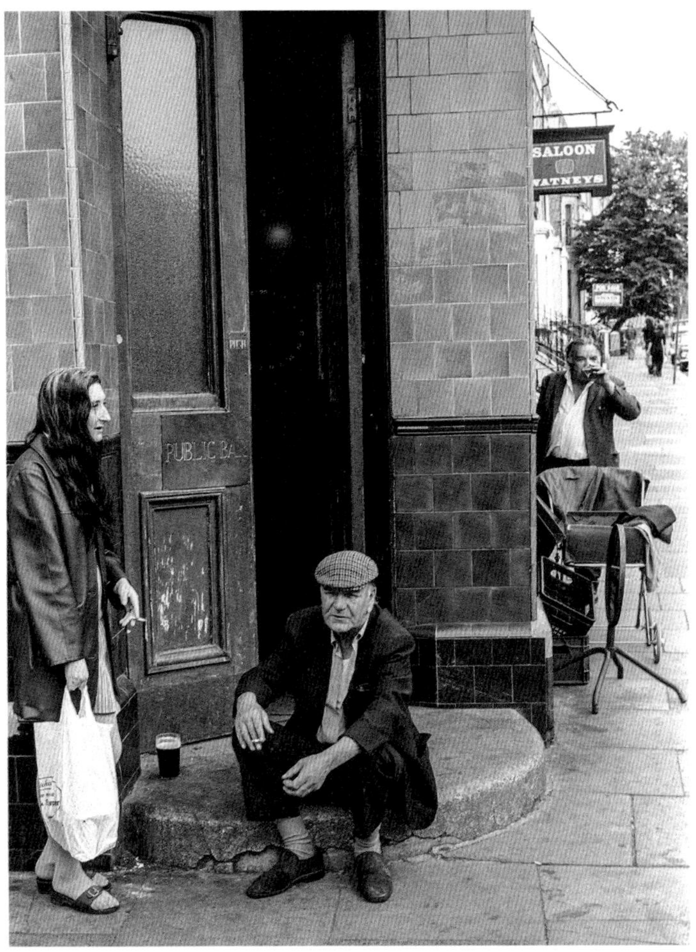

Drinking outside a pub. The saloon, signposted, was for people who wanted to pay extra to enjoy their pints in a room with carpets and comfortable seating. *South London, 1975*

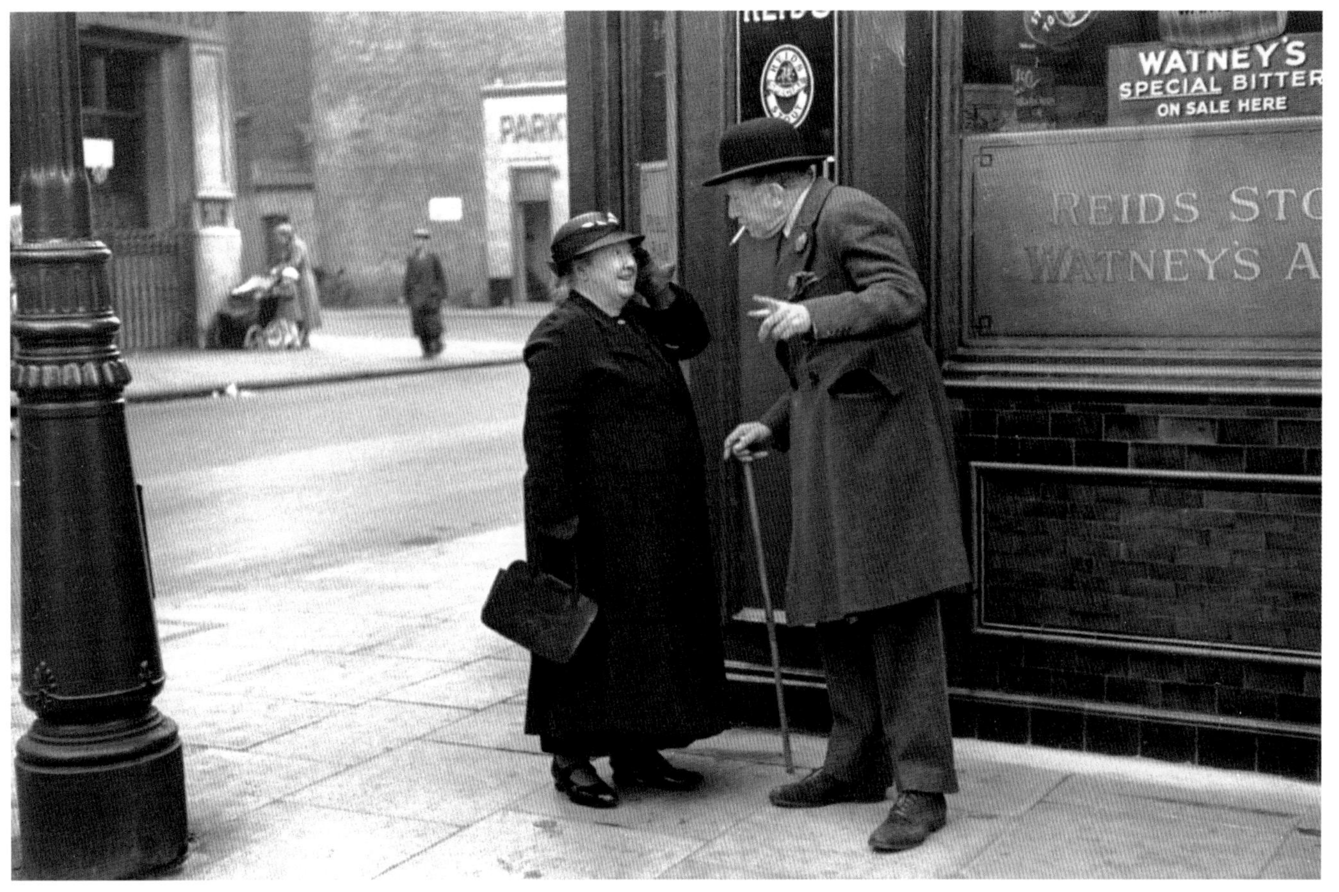

George Belcher, cartoonist for the satirical magazine
Punch, asks a woman to model for him. *London, 1938*

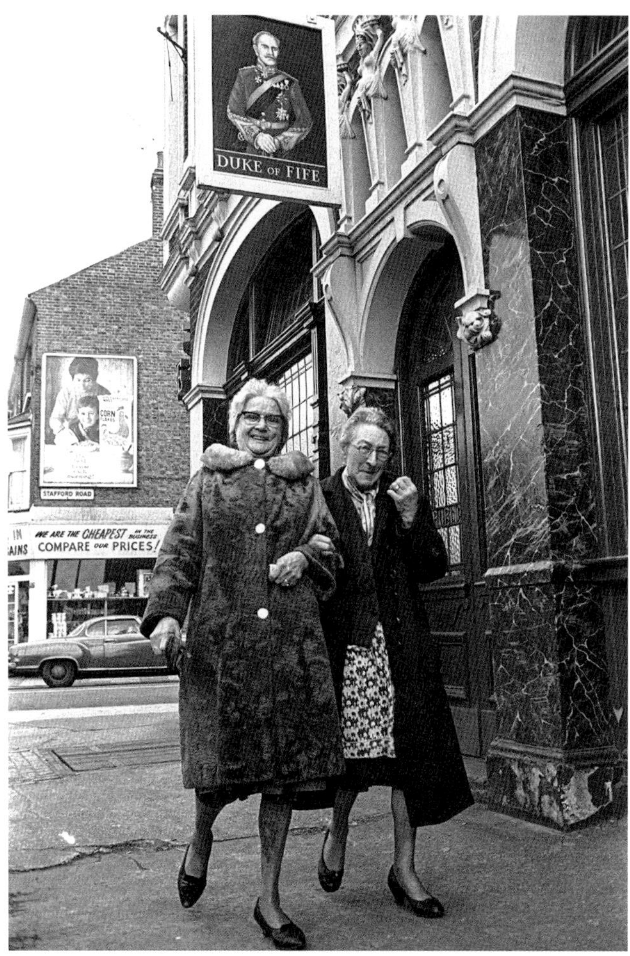

Many pubs were named after generals, often by men who served under them and opened pubs once they left the army. Duke of Fife (now closed). *Forest Gate, c.1960*

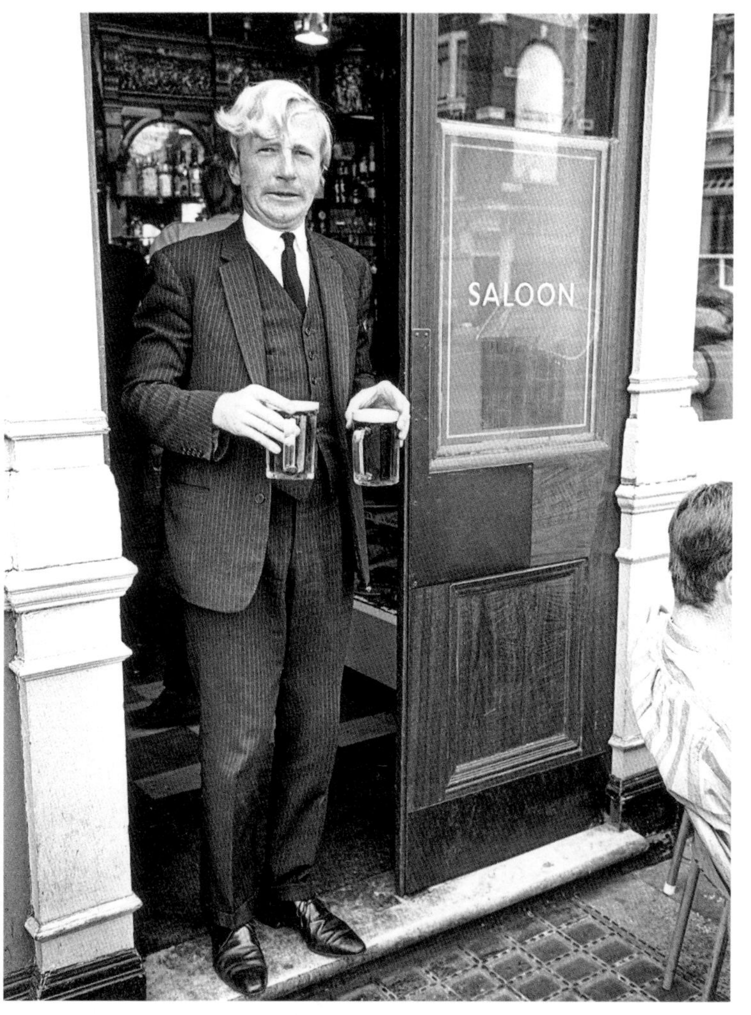

This man was definitely a saloon bar man, and proud of it. *London, 1967*

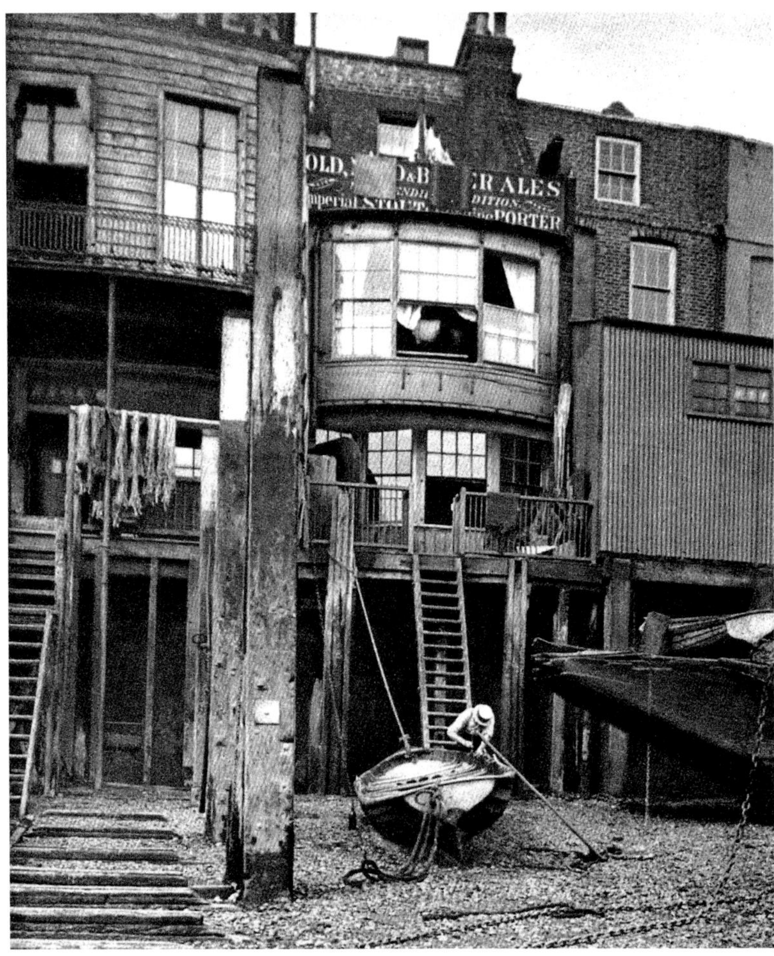

These riverside pubs are a remnant of a time when ships from all over the world passed through London's docks, along with sailors, pirates and smugglers all in need of a drink. *Limehouse, c.1927*

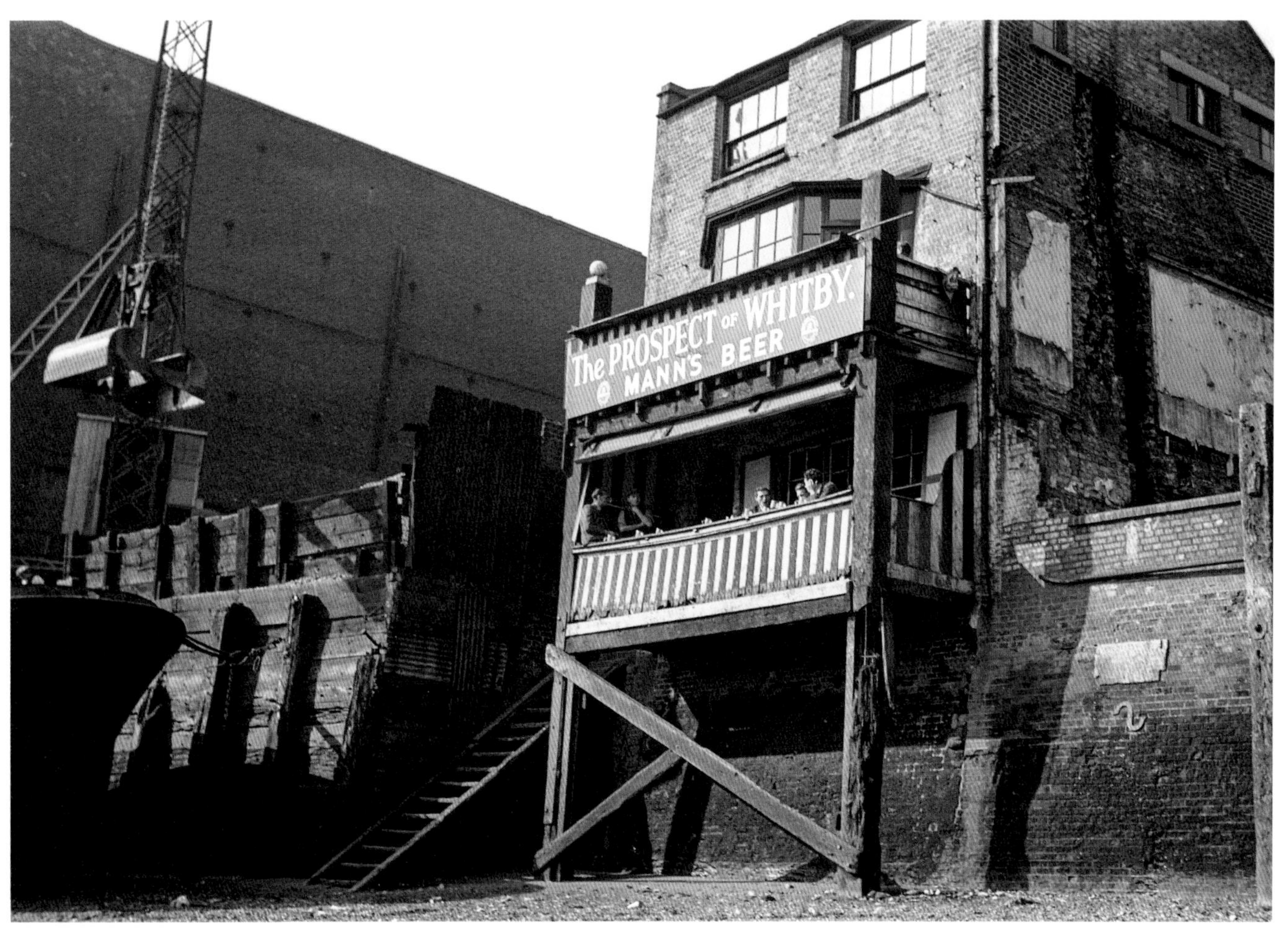

Built in 1520, The Prospect of Whitby (once known as 'The Devil's Tavern') was a favourite of 'hanging' Judge Jeffries in the 17th century, as all London tour guides will tell you. *Shadwell, c.1950*

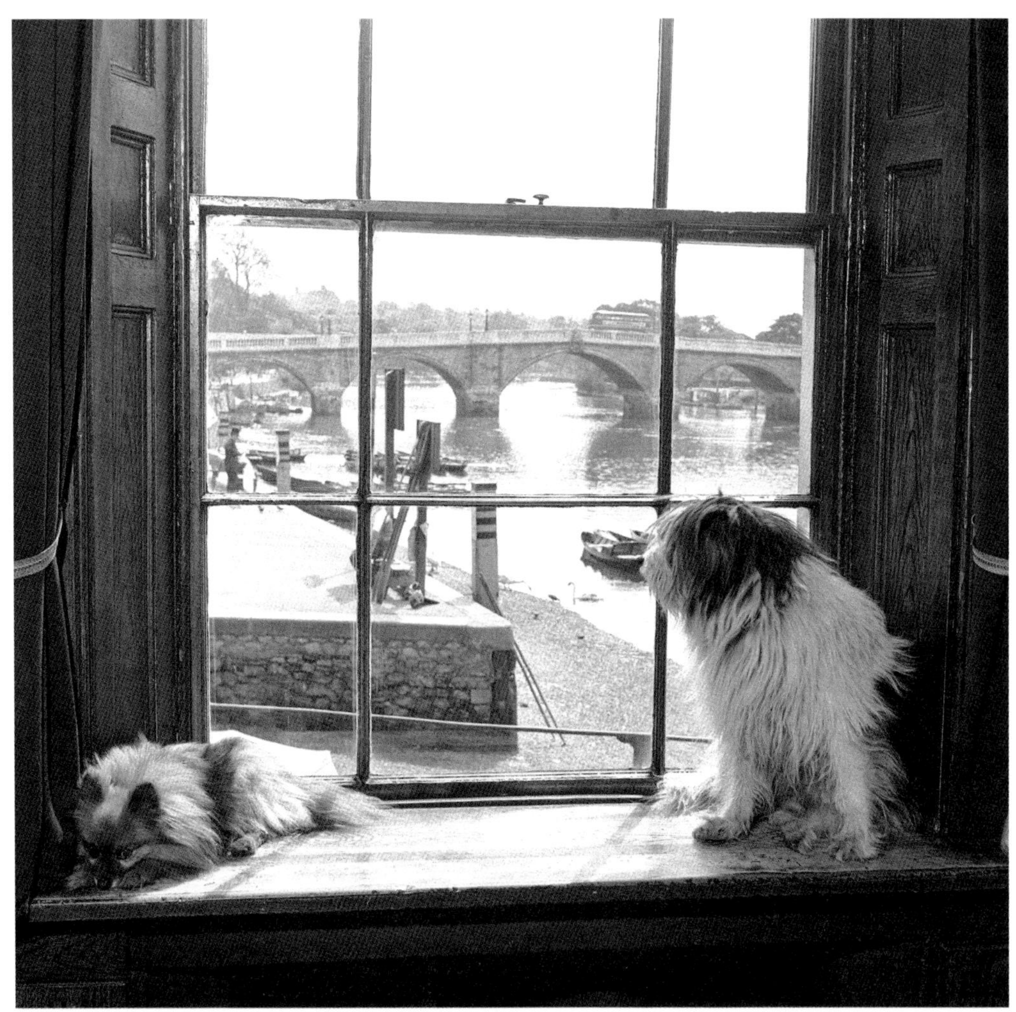

Dogs belonging to the landlady of the White Cross. *Richmond, 1954*

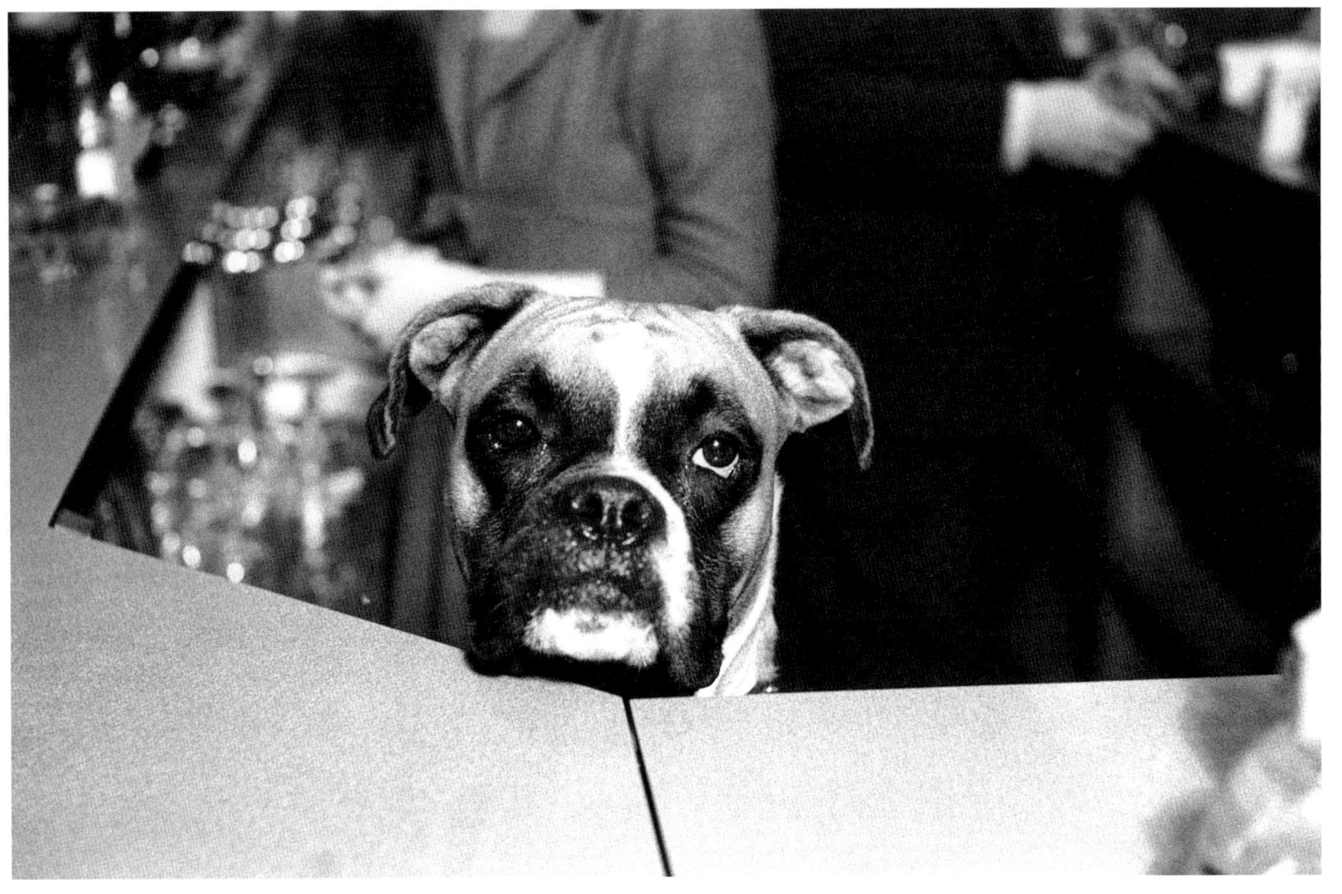

The Jolly Gardeners (now demolished). *Southwark, 1960*

Pub cats are less common than pub dogs. *Bellingham, 1939*

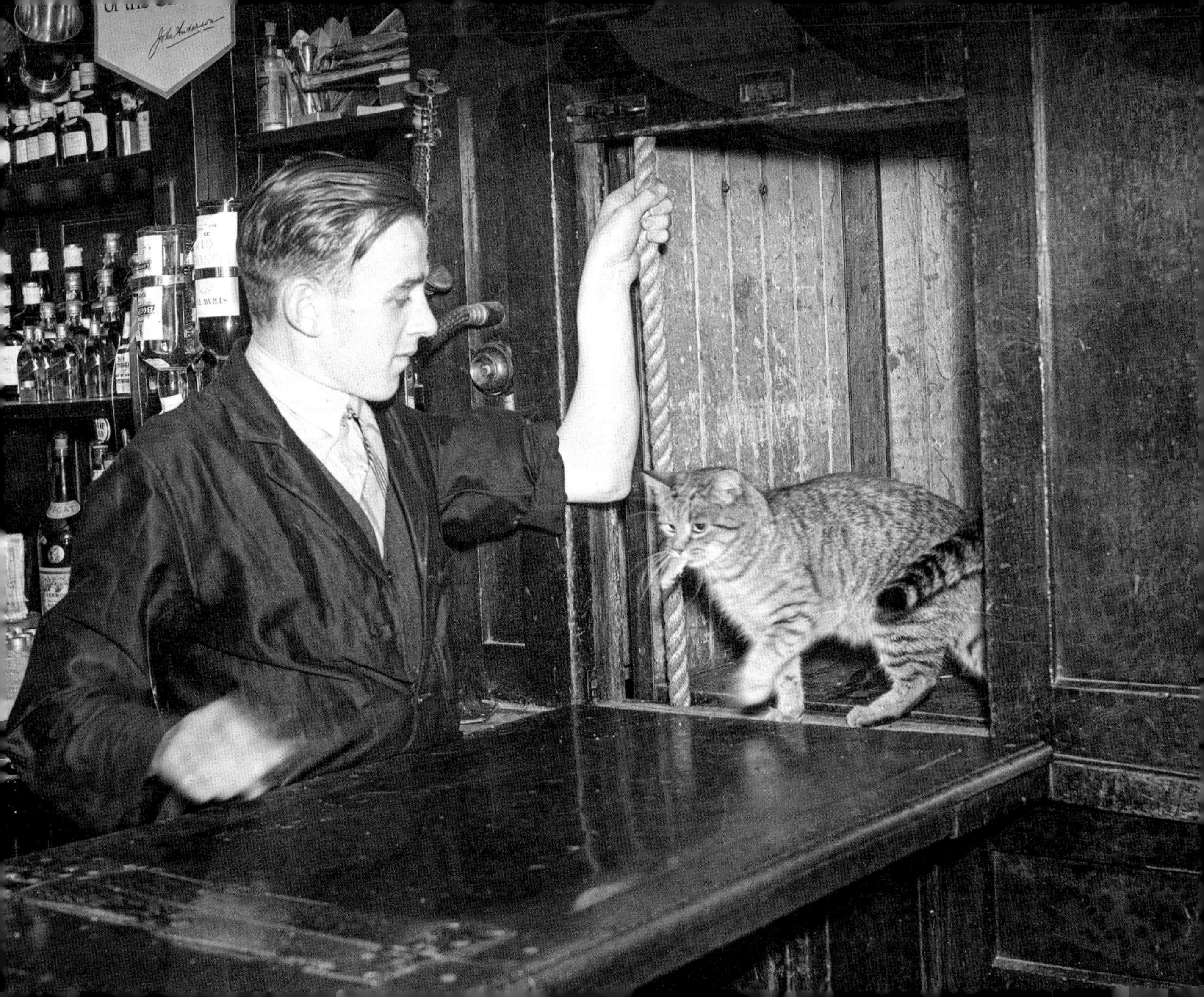

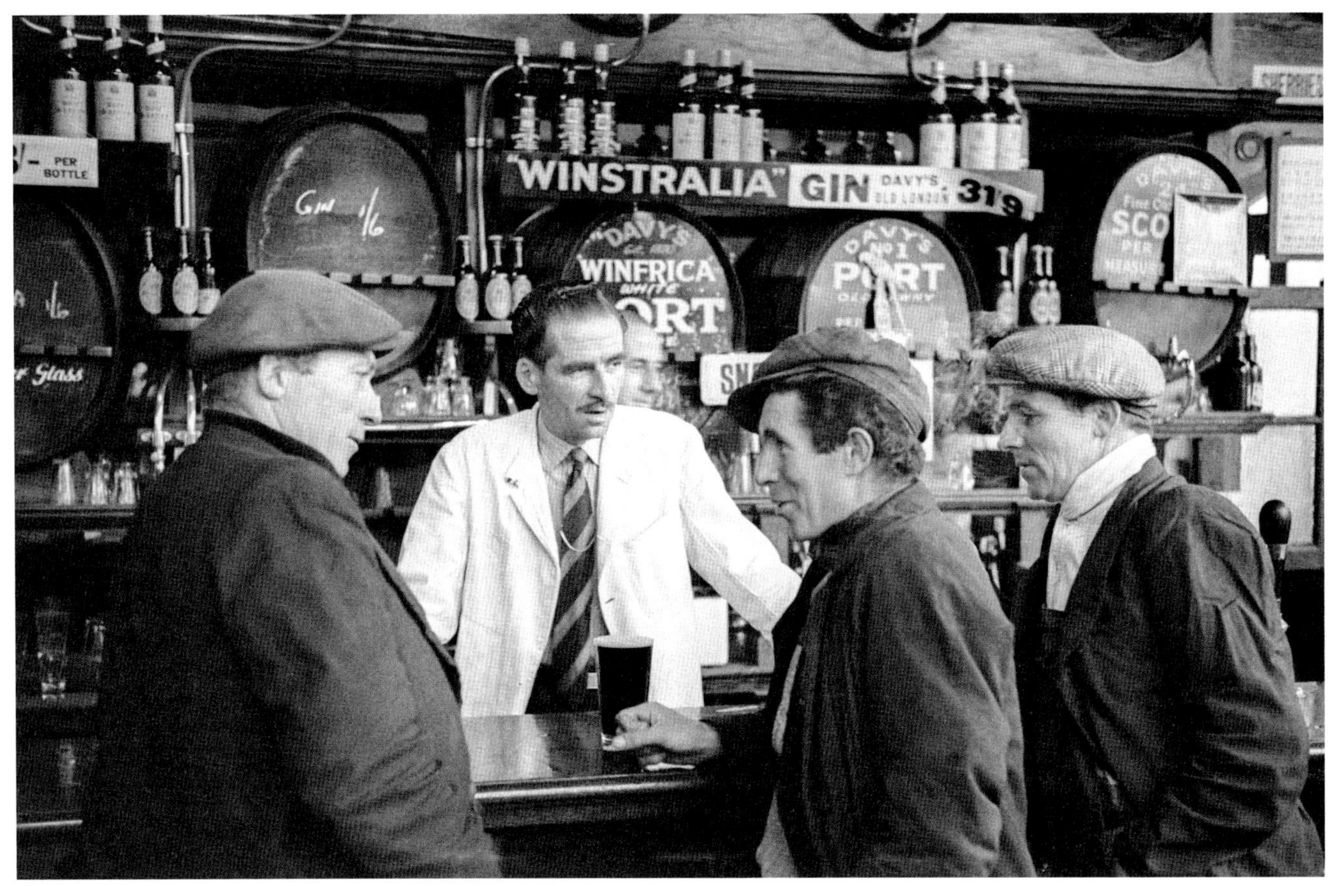

The barman's white coat and the prominence of spirits barrels in this pub recall a time when 'gin shops' sold their wares 'for medicinal purposes'. *Elephant and Castle, 1949*

SUPERIOR
OLD
IRISH &
SCOTCH
WHISKIES
CELEBRATED
DOUBLE
DIAMOND
CREAM
MARTELL
OR

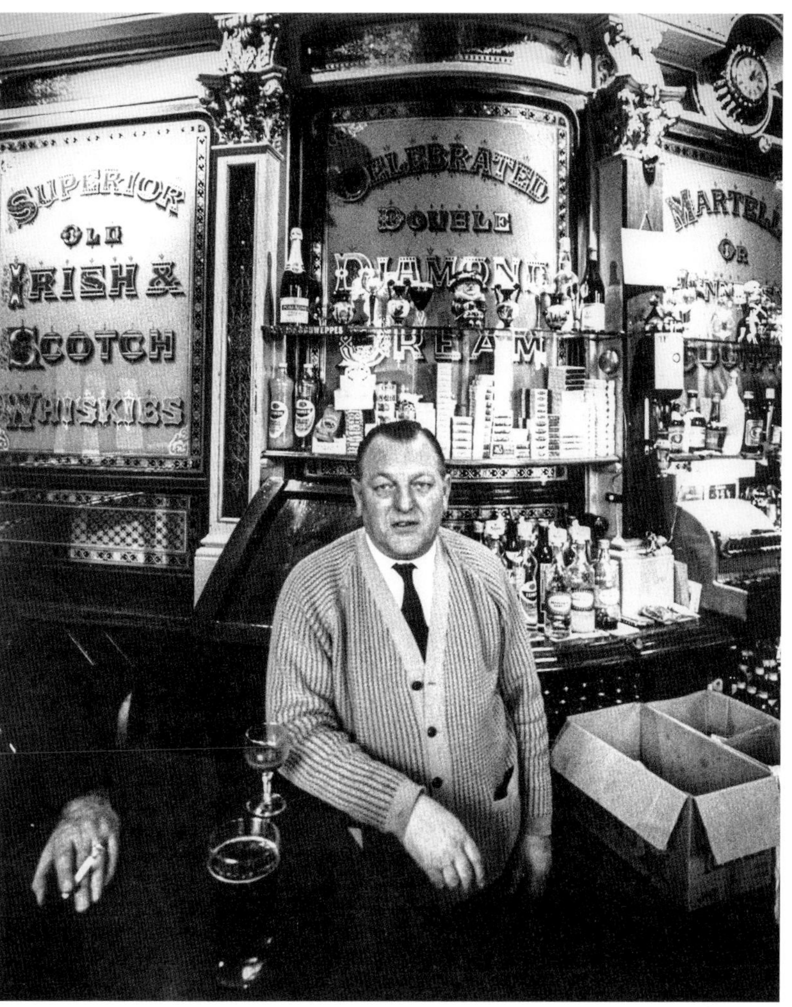

London, 1970

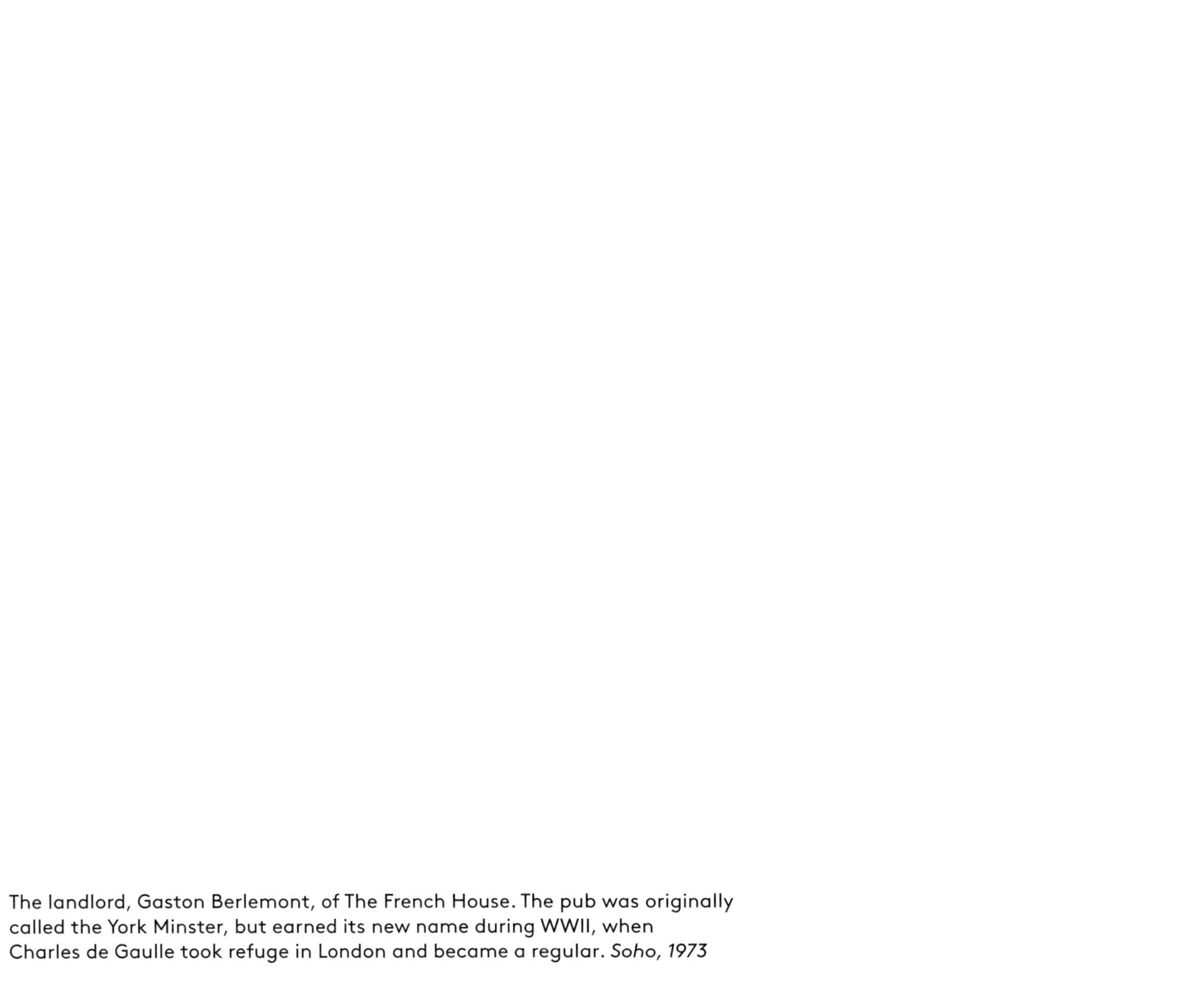

The landlord, Gaston Berlemont, of The French House. The pub was originally called the York Minster, but earned its new name during WWII, when Charles de Gaulle took refuge in London and became a regular. *Soho, 1973*

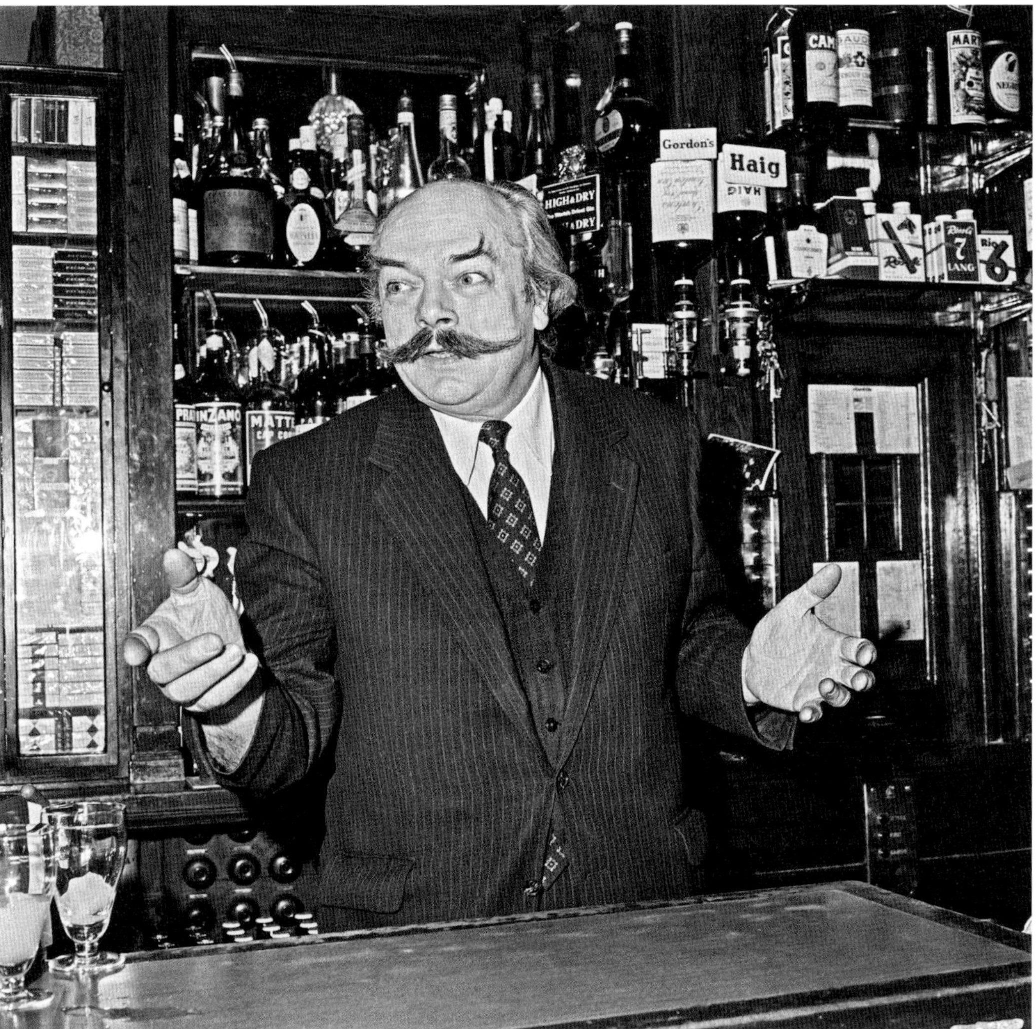

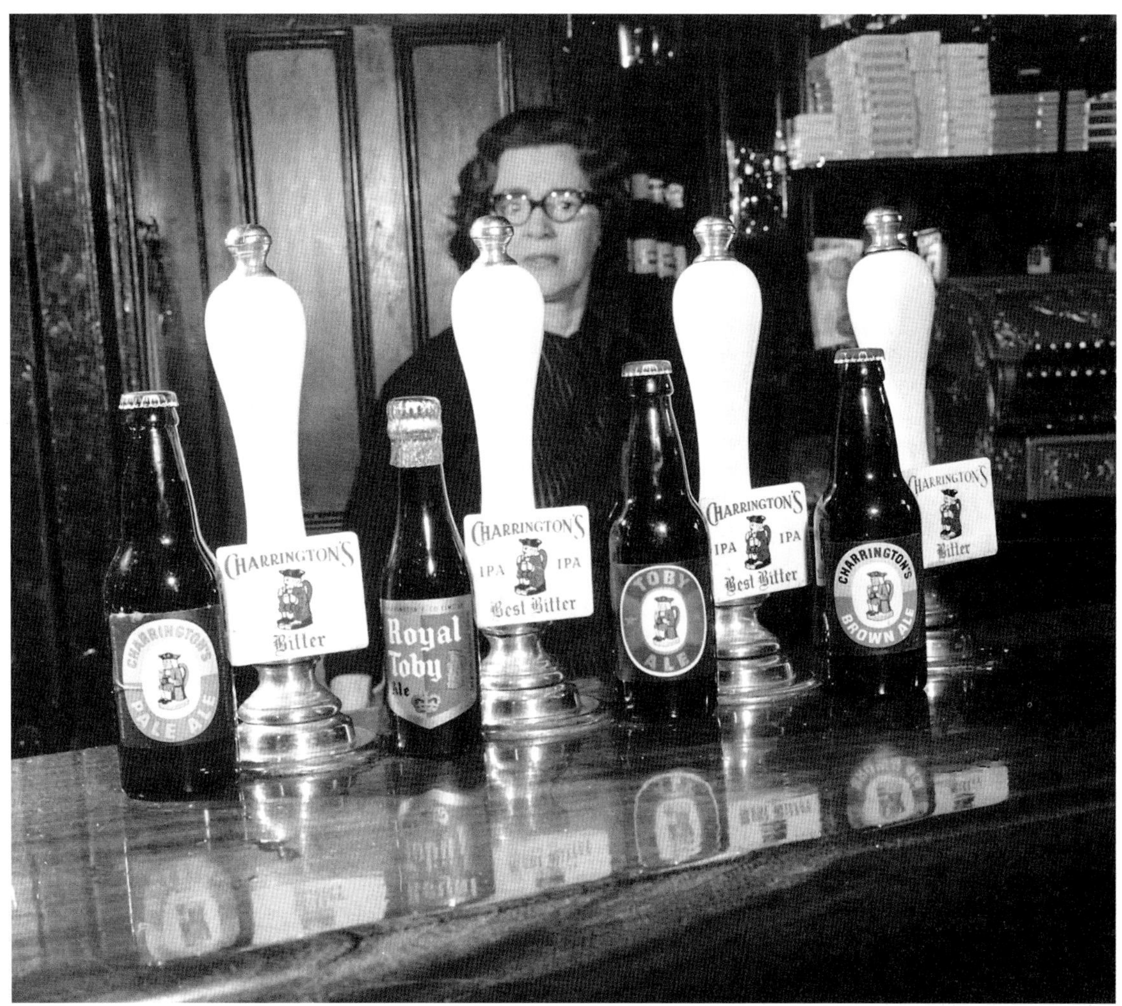

A Charrington Brewery pub. *London, 1961*

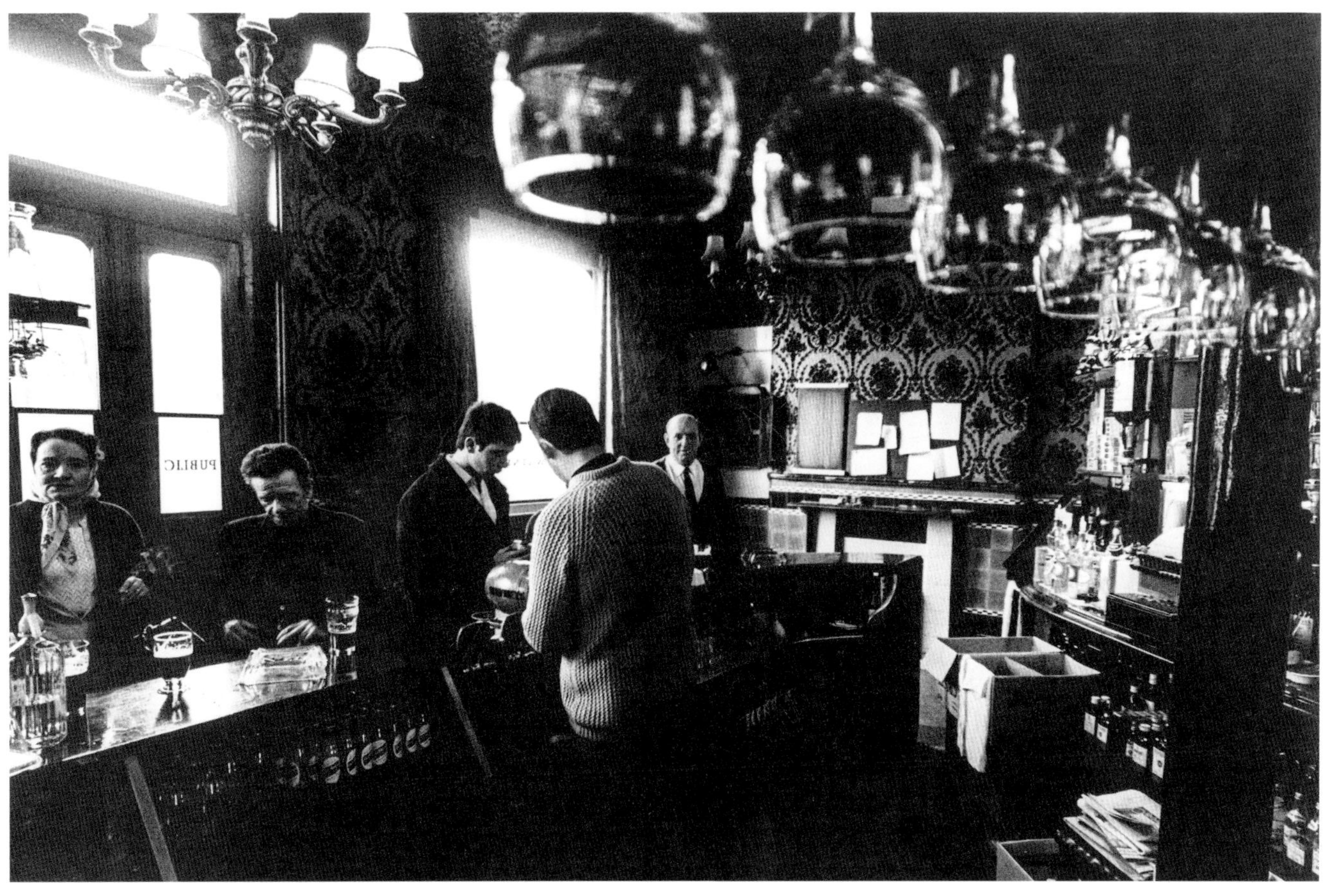

London, 1970

London, c.1950

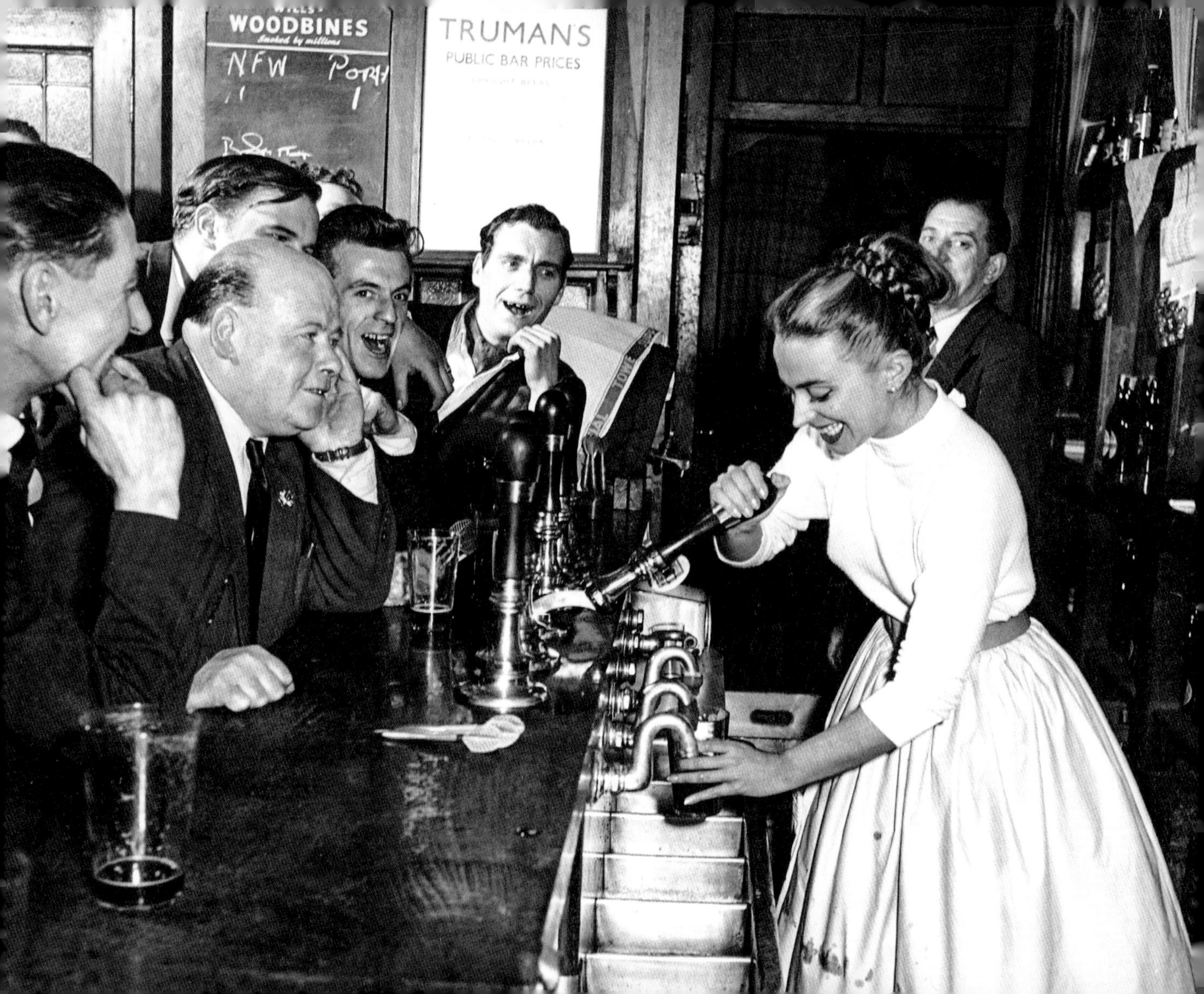

WILLS
WOODBINES
Smoked by millions
NFW   Port
TRUMAN'S
PUBLIC BAR PRICES

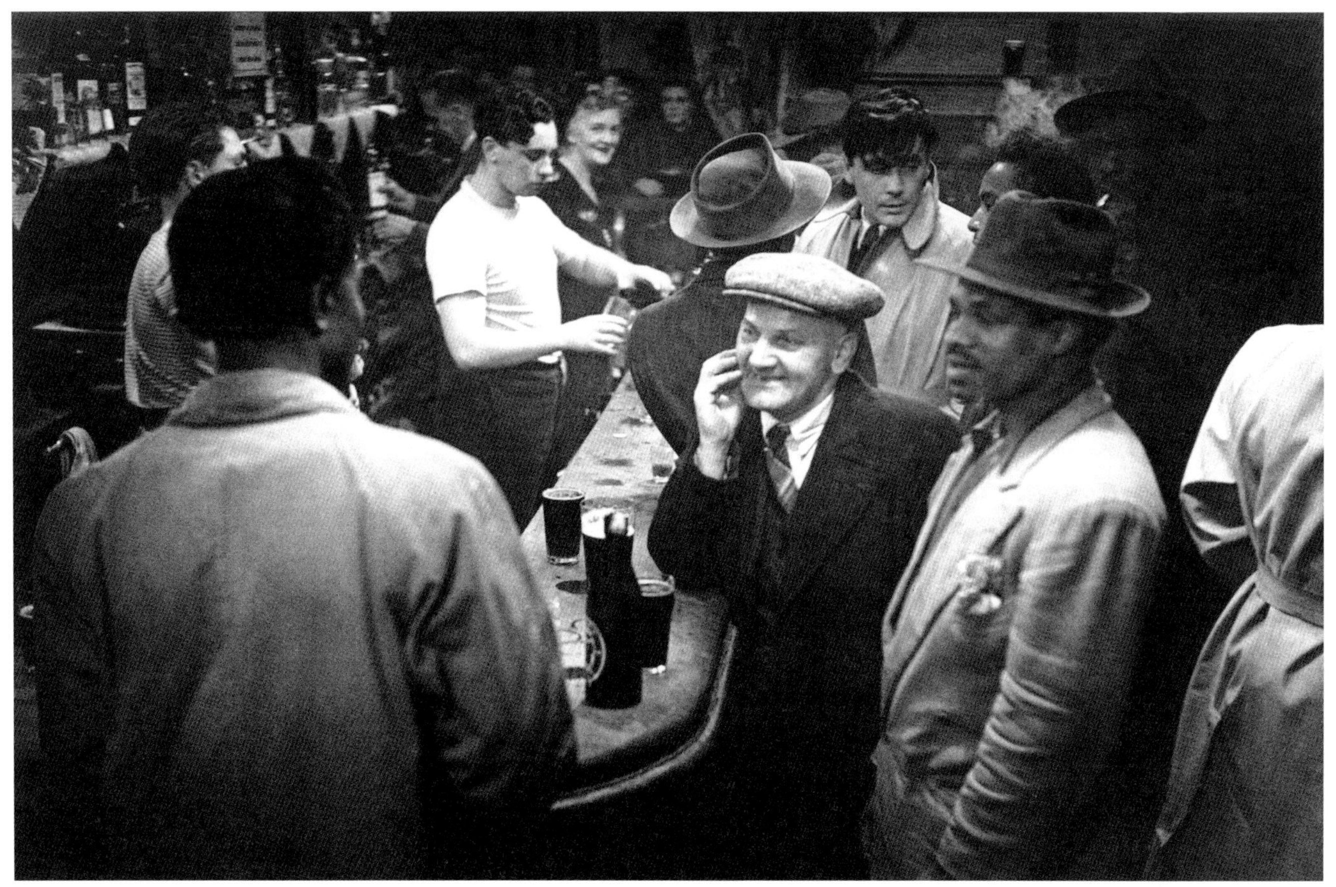

Stepney, 1949

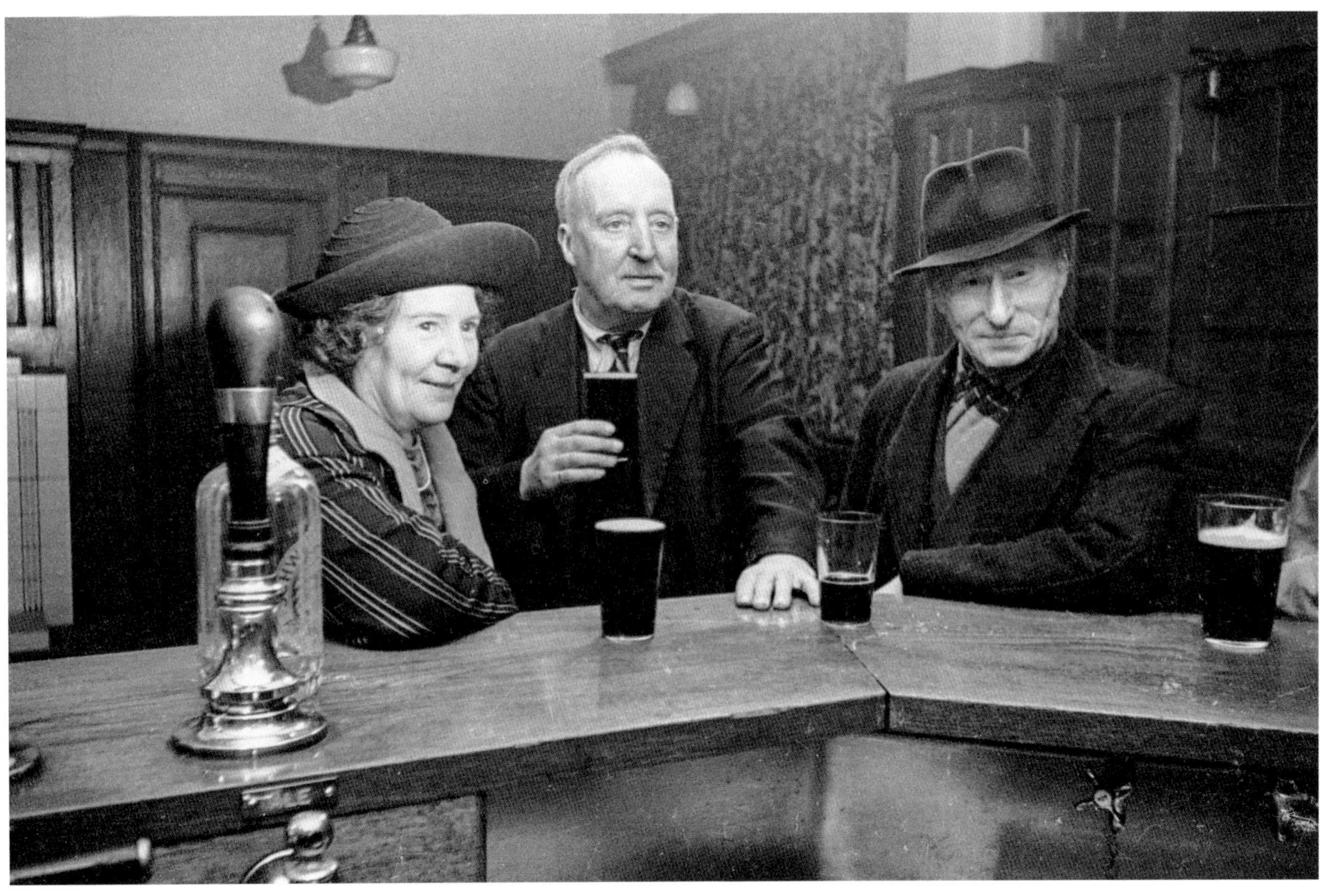

The Freemason's Arms. *Hampstead, 1943*

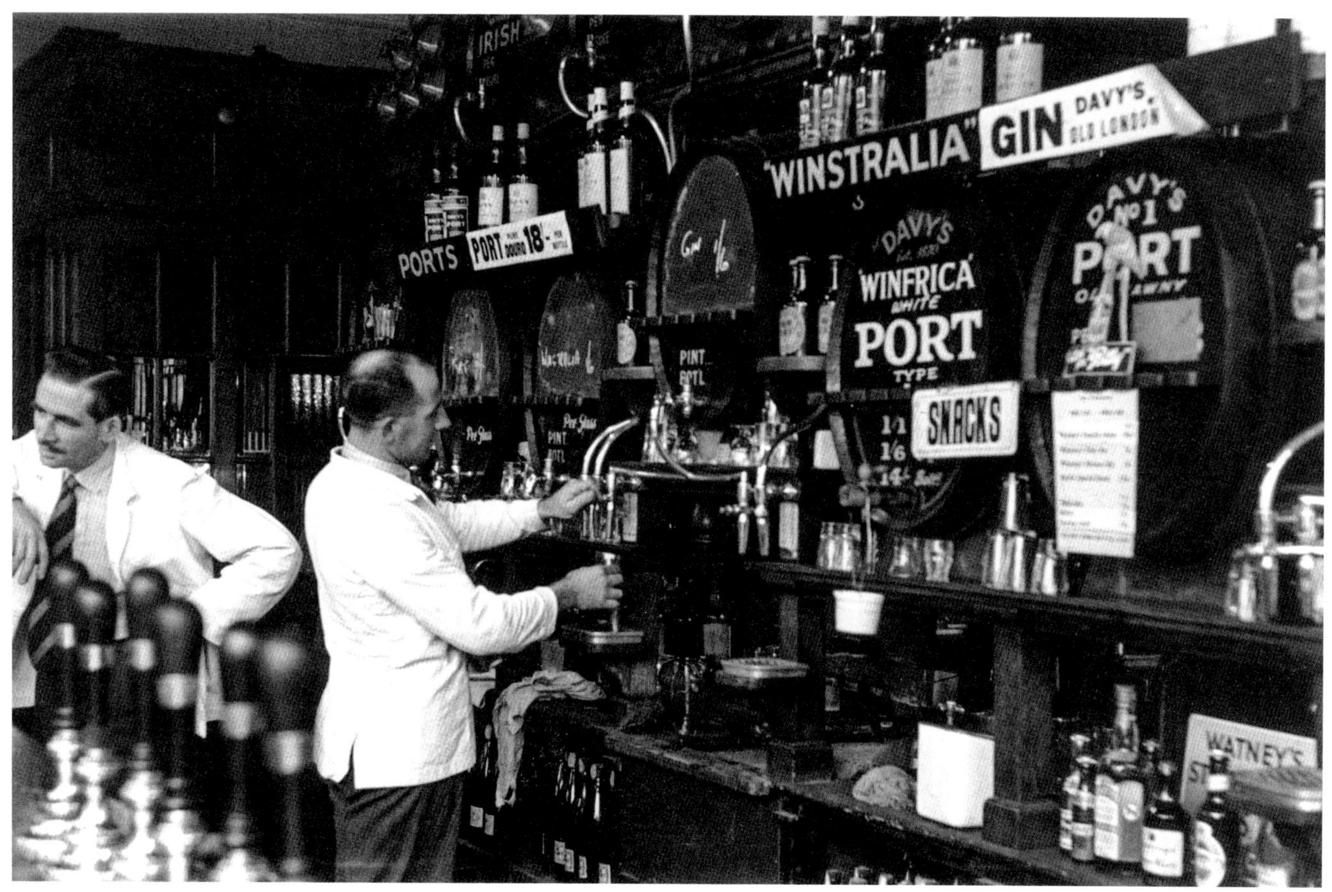

Elephant and Castle, 1949

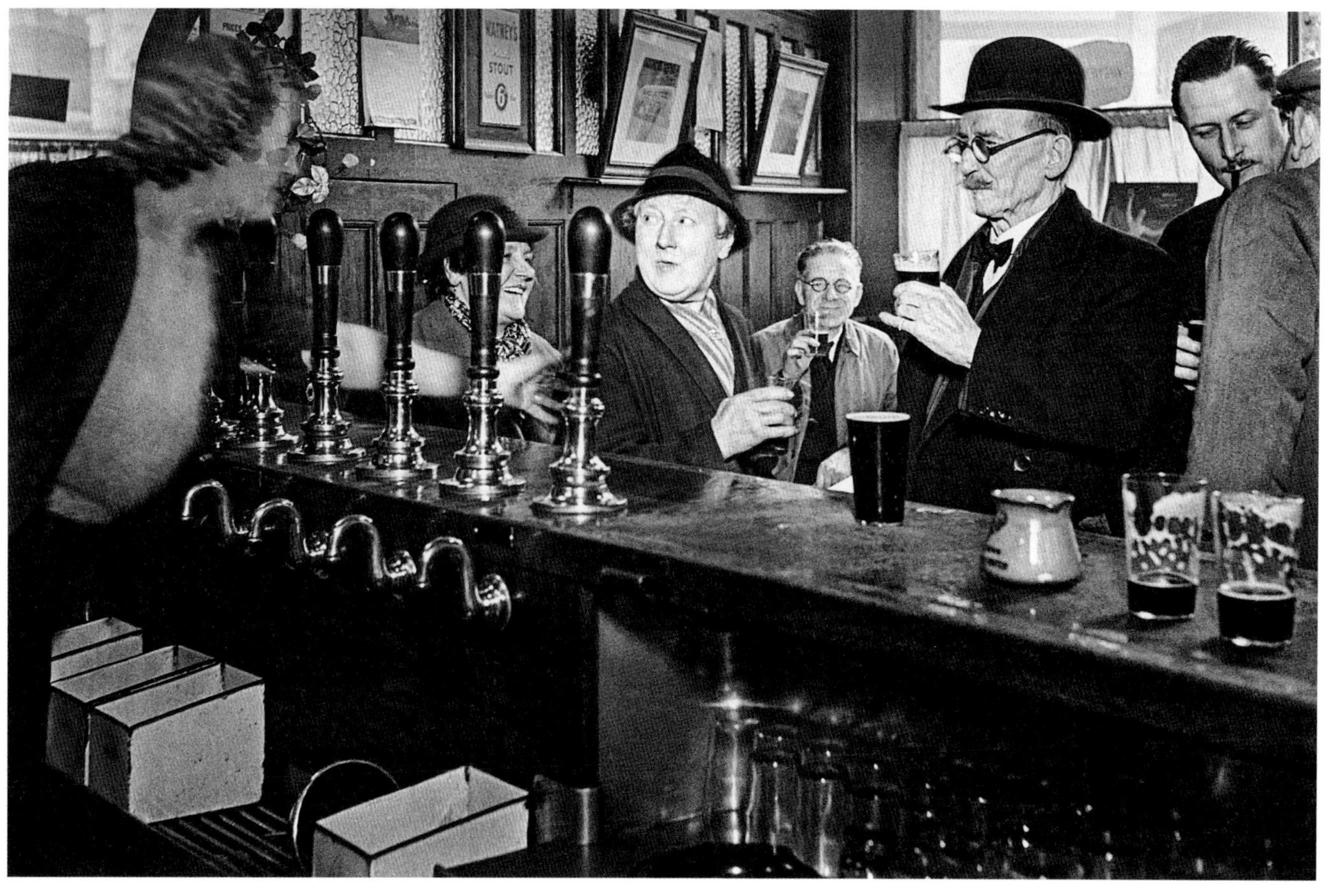

The barmaid, Alice, of The Crooked Billet
(now demolished) talks to regulars. *Aldgate, 1939*

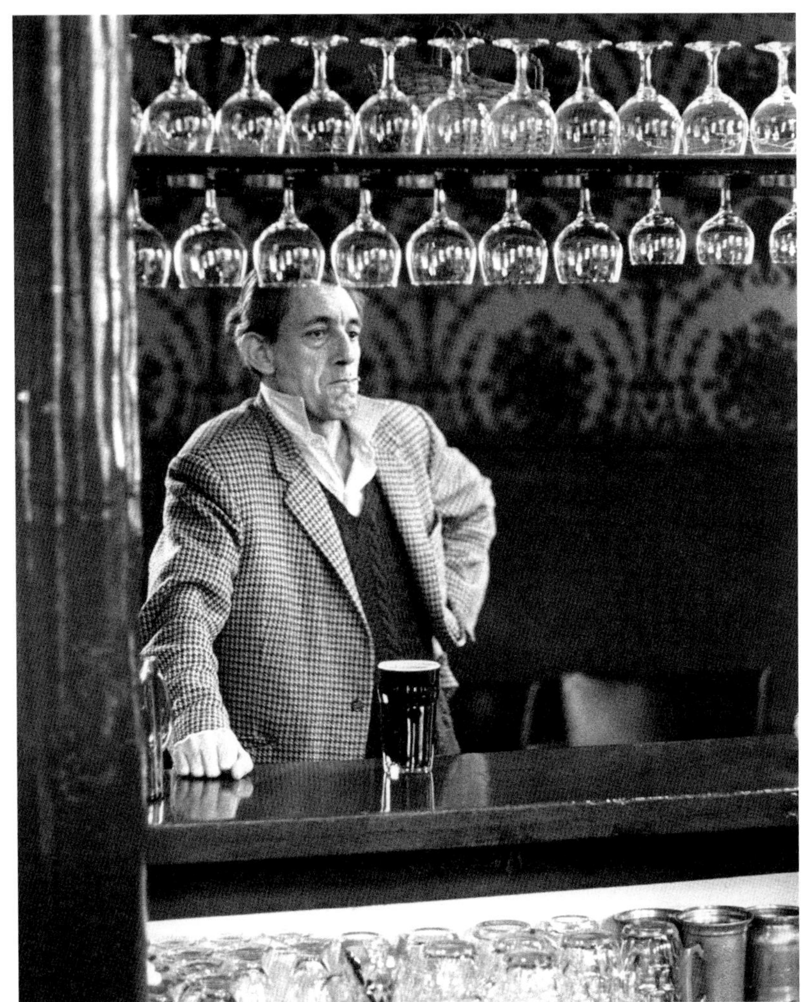

London, c.1970

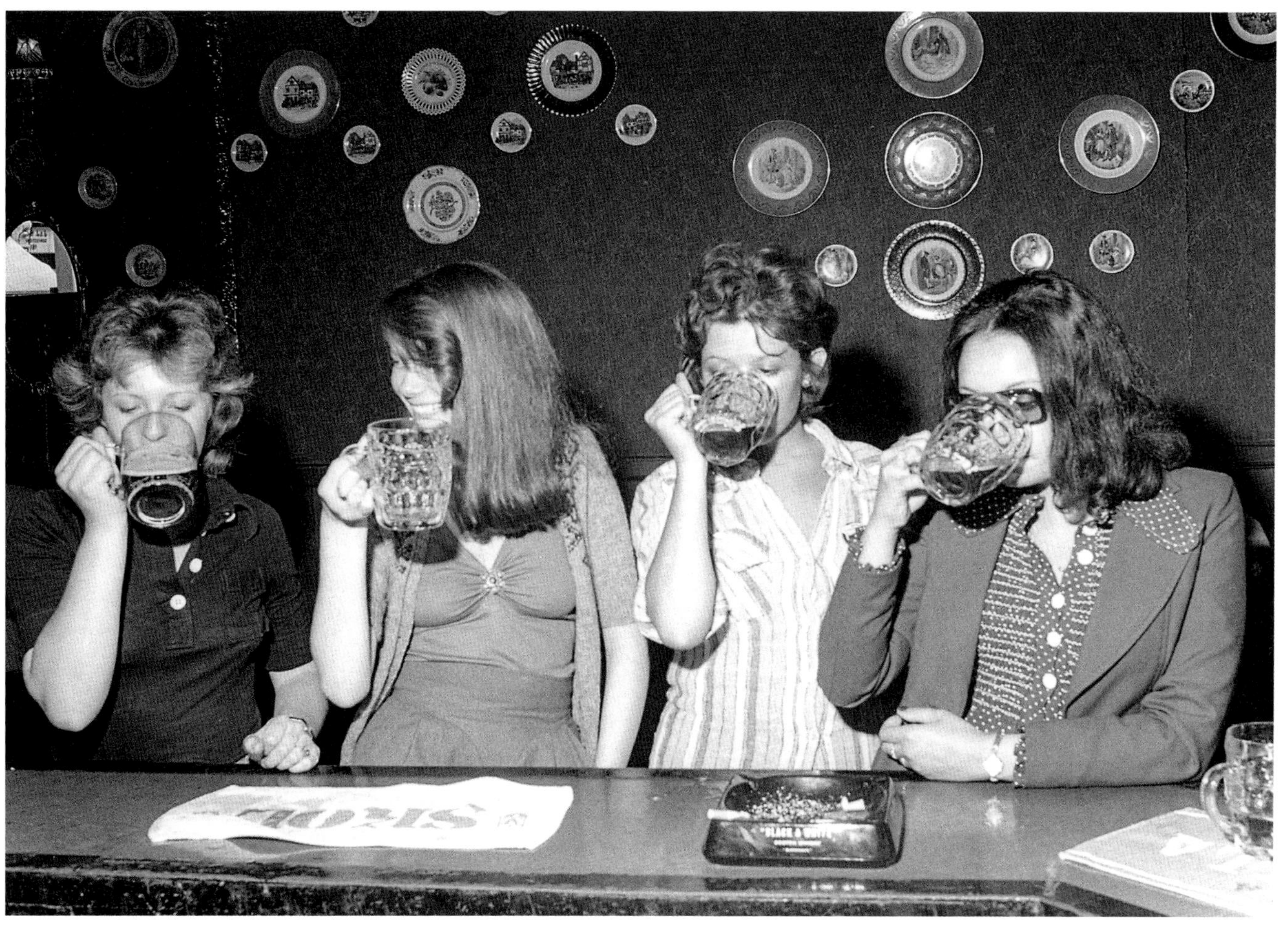

When women gained financial independence, pubs began to see them as a source of custom in their own right. Lager was originally advertised specifically as a beer for women. *London, 1975*

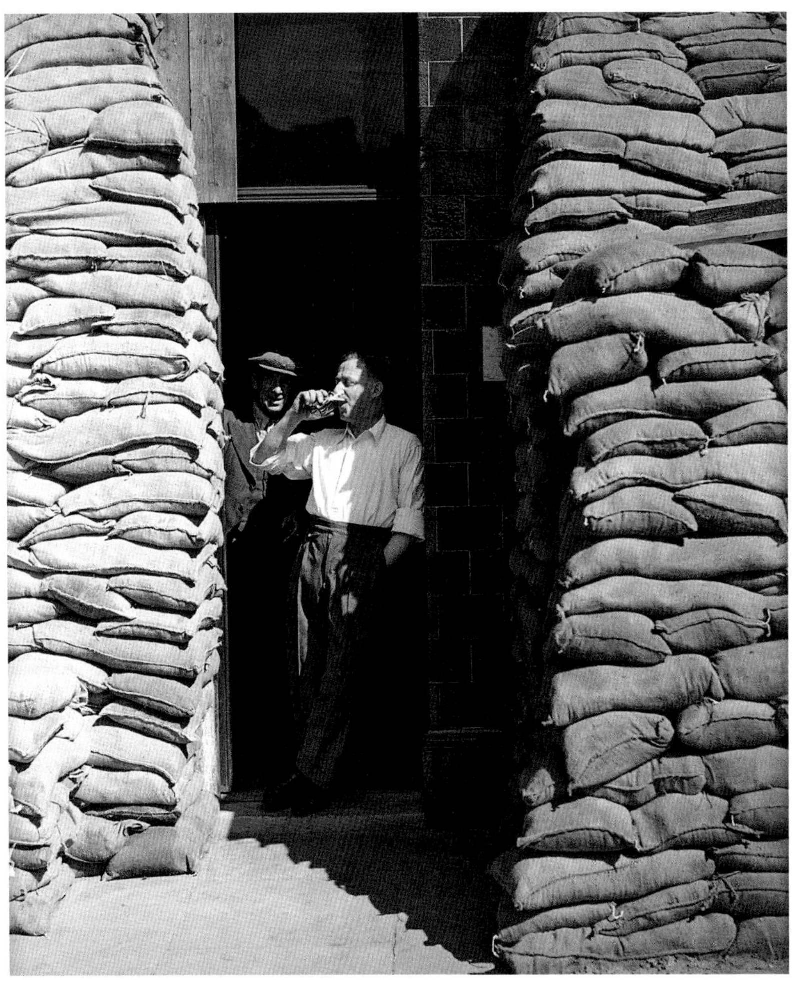

During WWII, beer was never rationed and pubs were given no extra restrictions. Churchill believed they were vital to morale. *London, 1939*

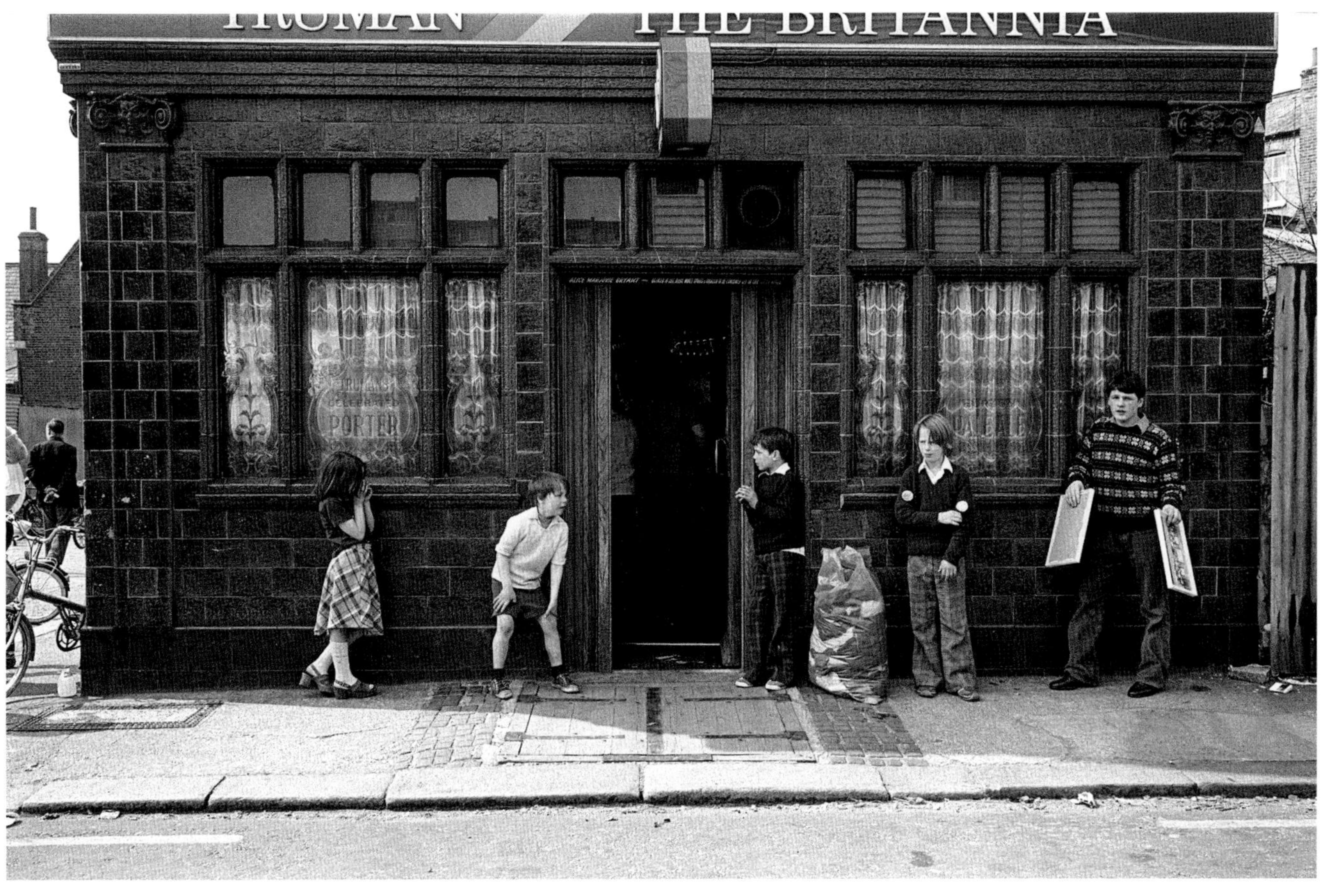

The Britannia (now closed). *Bethnal Green, 1979*

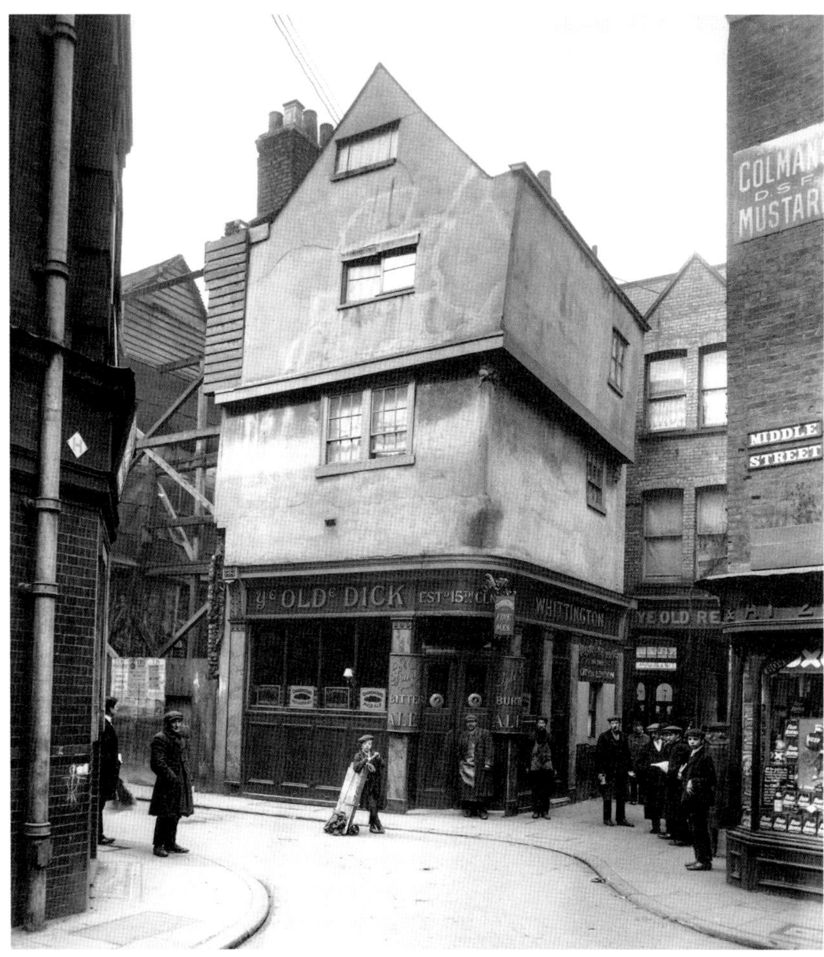

Ye Old Dick Whittington was built as a house in the 16th century. It survived the Great Fire of London and eventually became a pub before being demolished as part of 'slum clearance' in 1916. *City of London, c.1900*

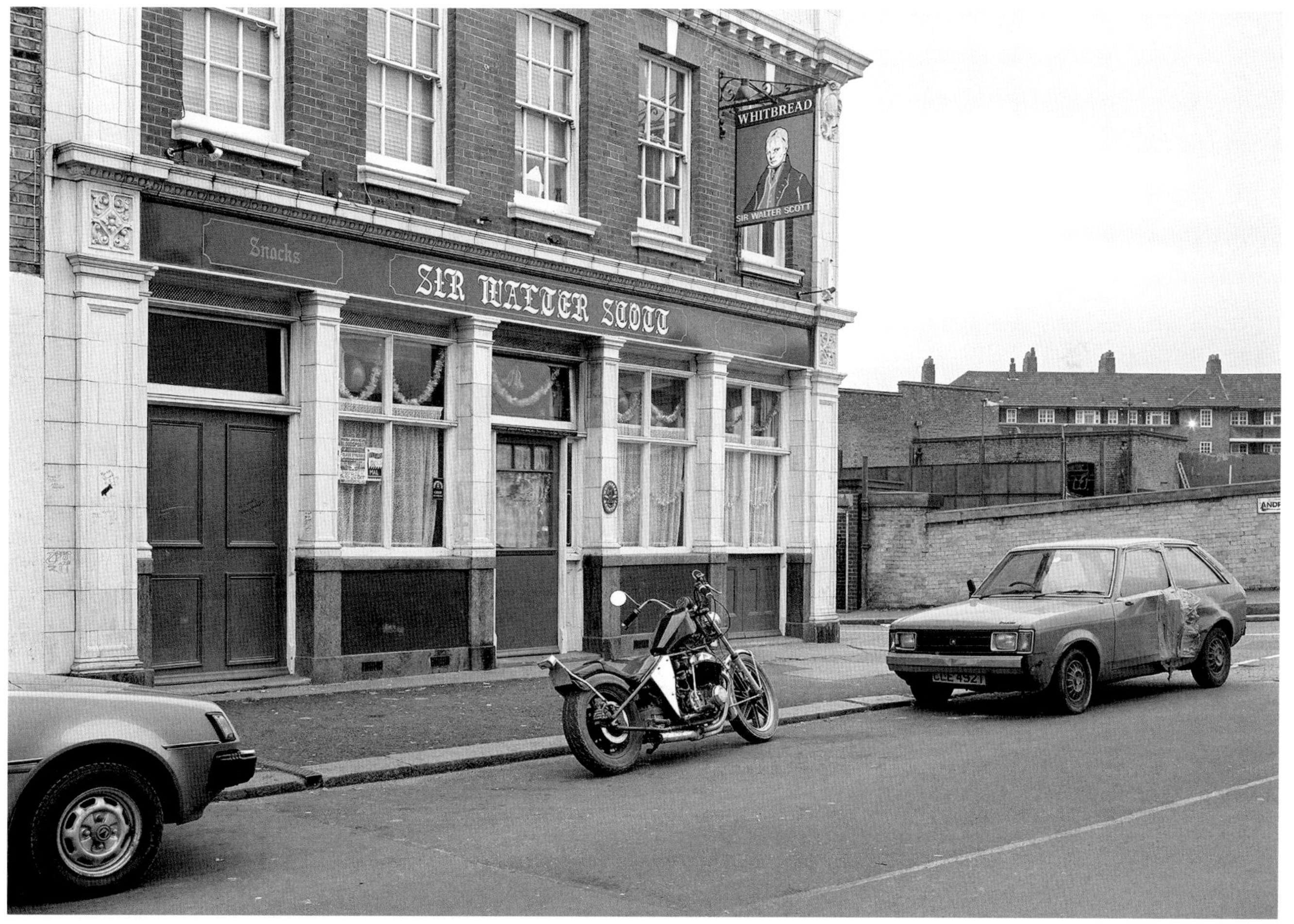

Sir Walter Scott (now closed). *Hackney, 1985*

The beer garden is a long-standing part of pub tradition,
dating back to the Middle Ages when a village green would
invariably have a pub right next to it. *West London, 1964*

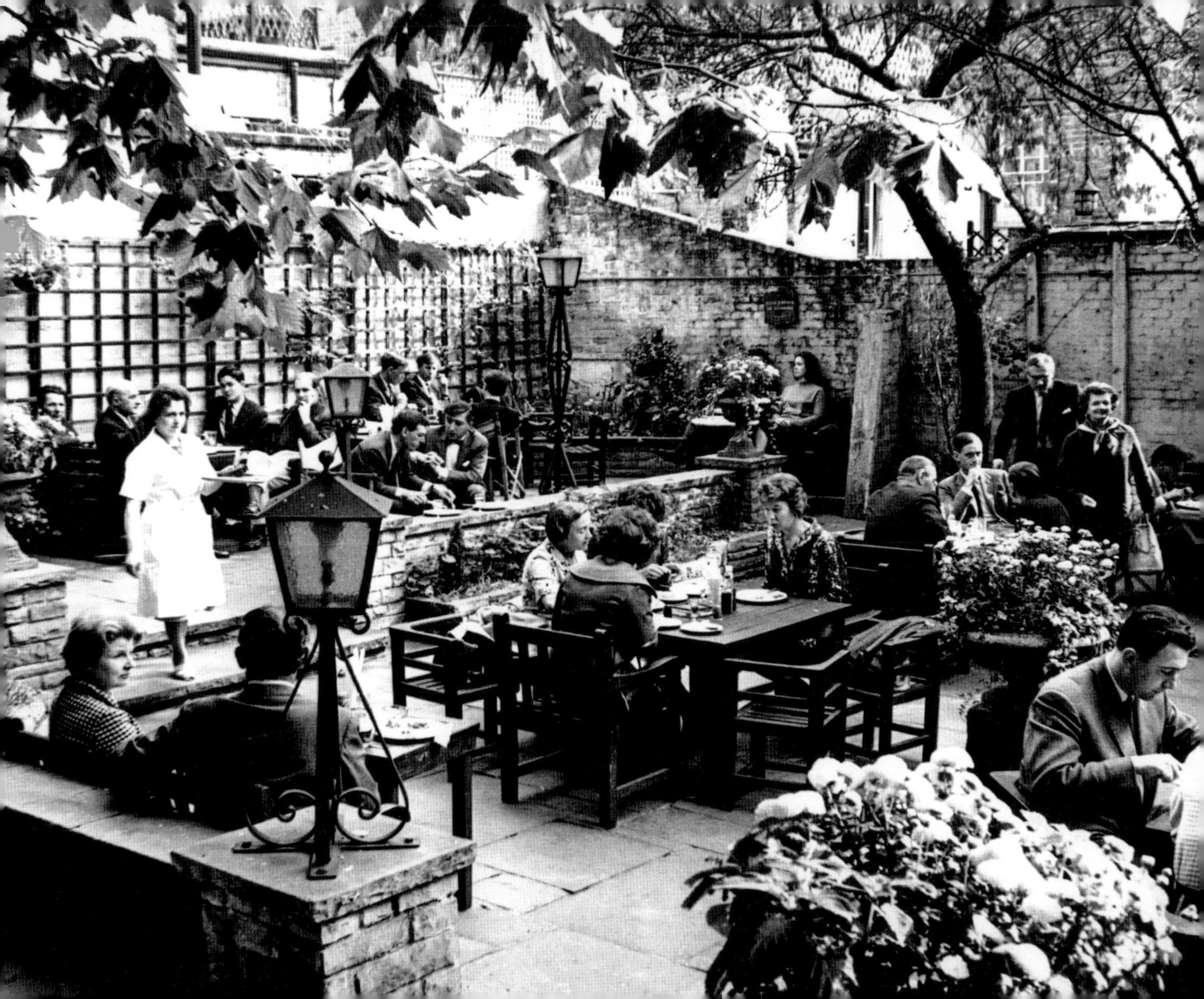

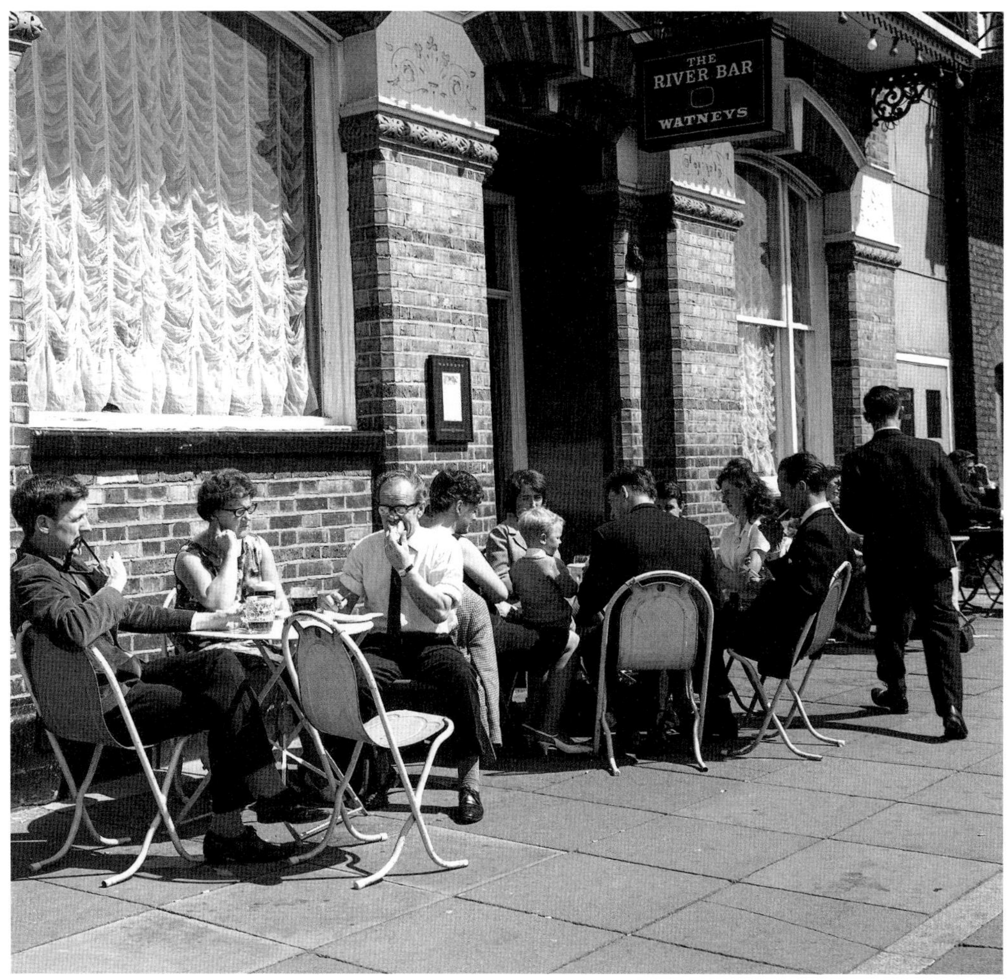

On sunny days, al fresco drinking has always been a feature
of the right kind of pub. *Hammersmith, c.1950*

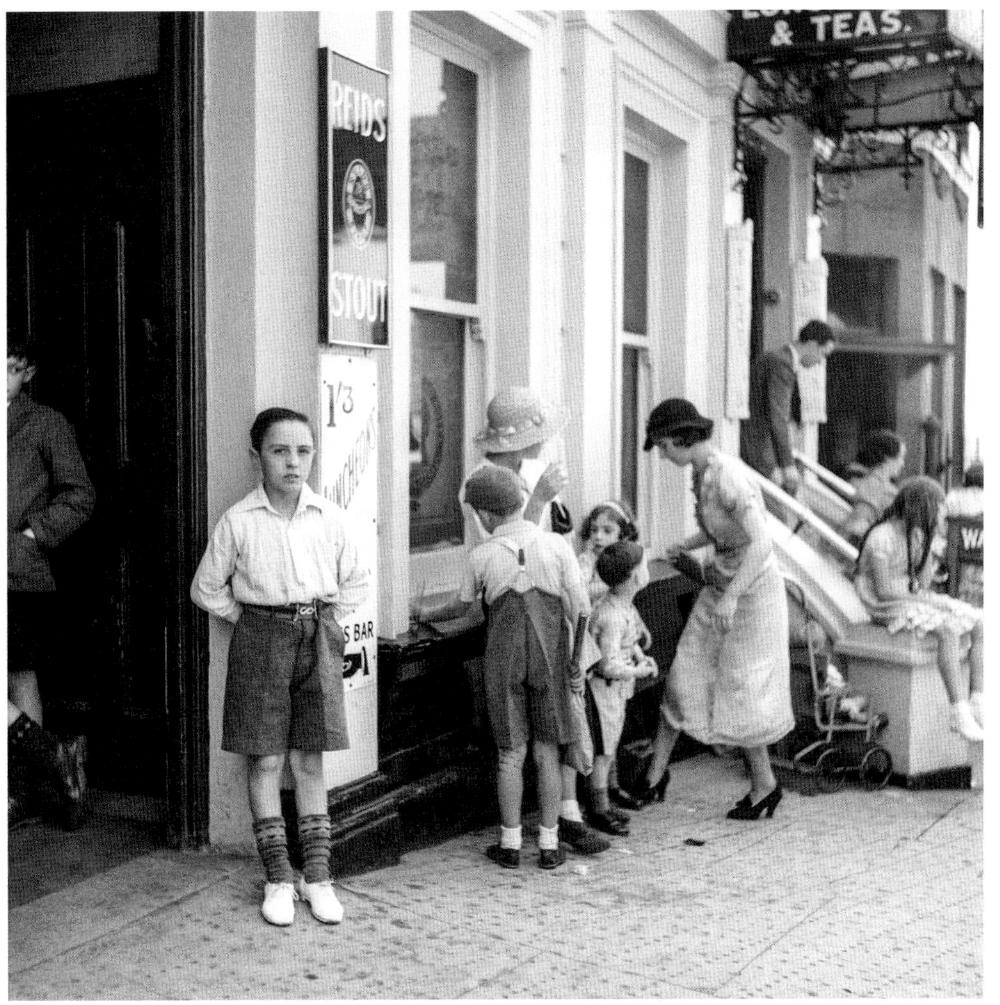

London, 1947

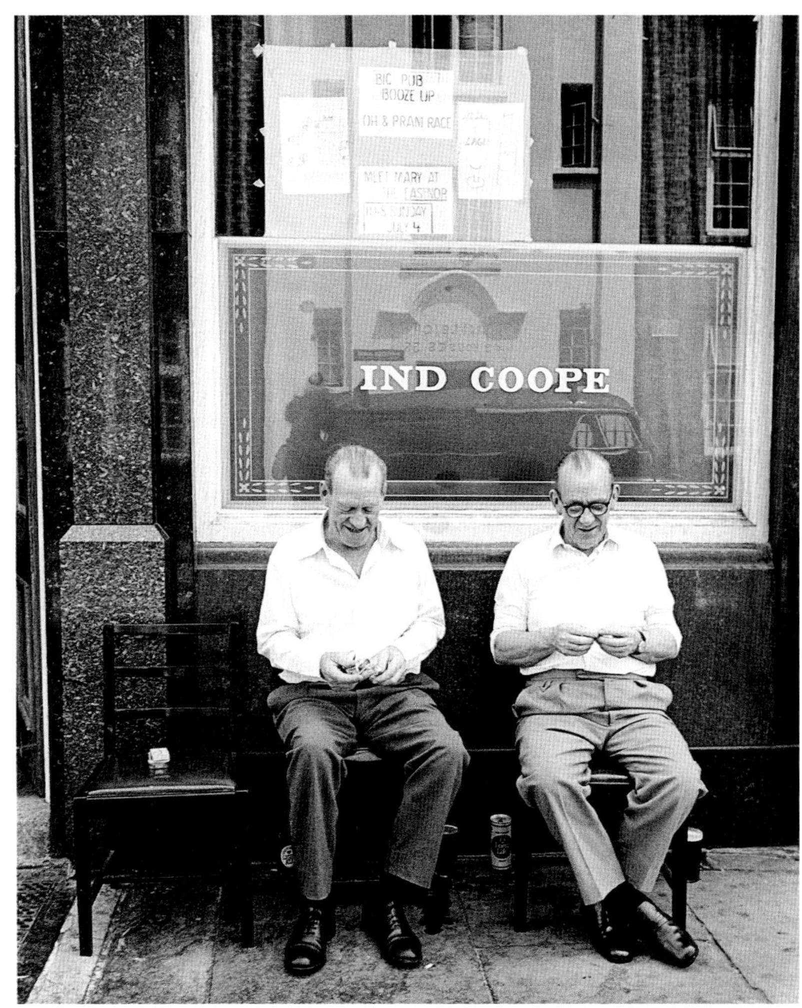

St Pancras, 1977

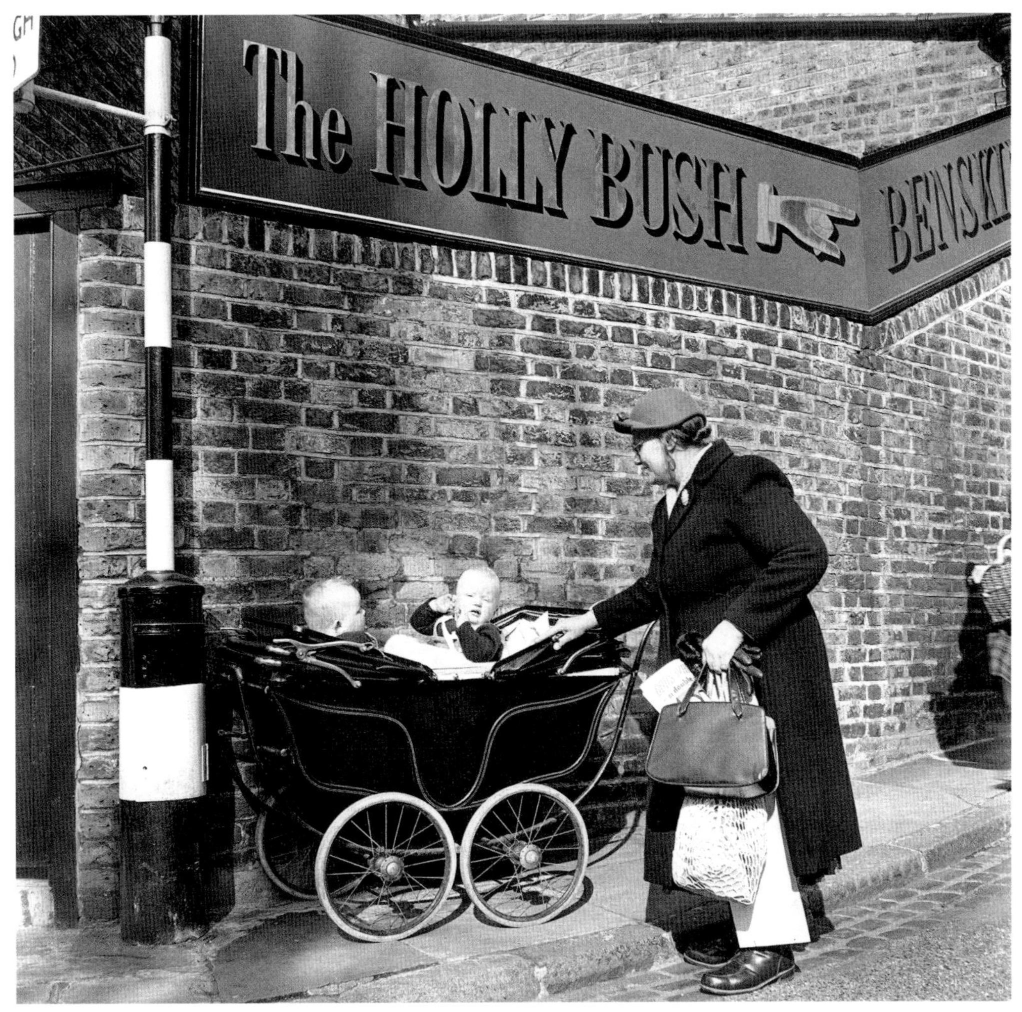

Near The Holly Bush. *Hampstead, 1954*

The Kenton Arms faces west on a junction, like the prow
of a ship, so it is often flooded with light. *Hackney, 1986*

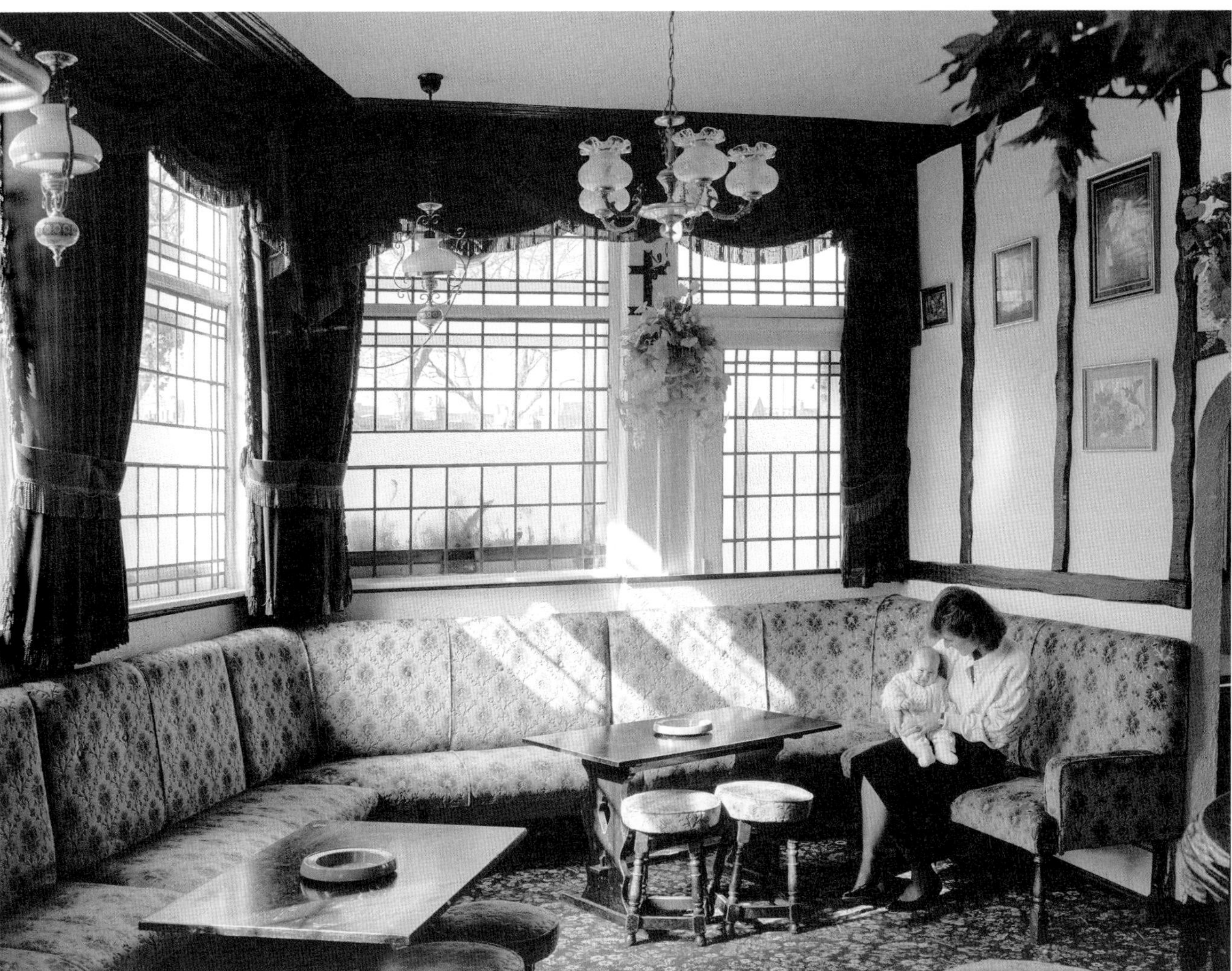

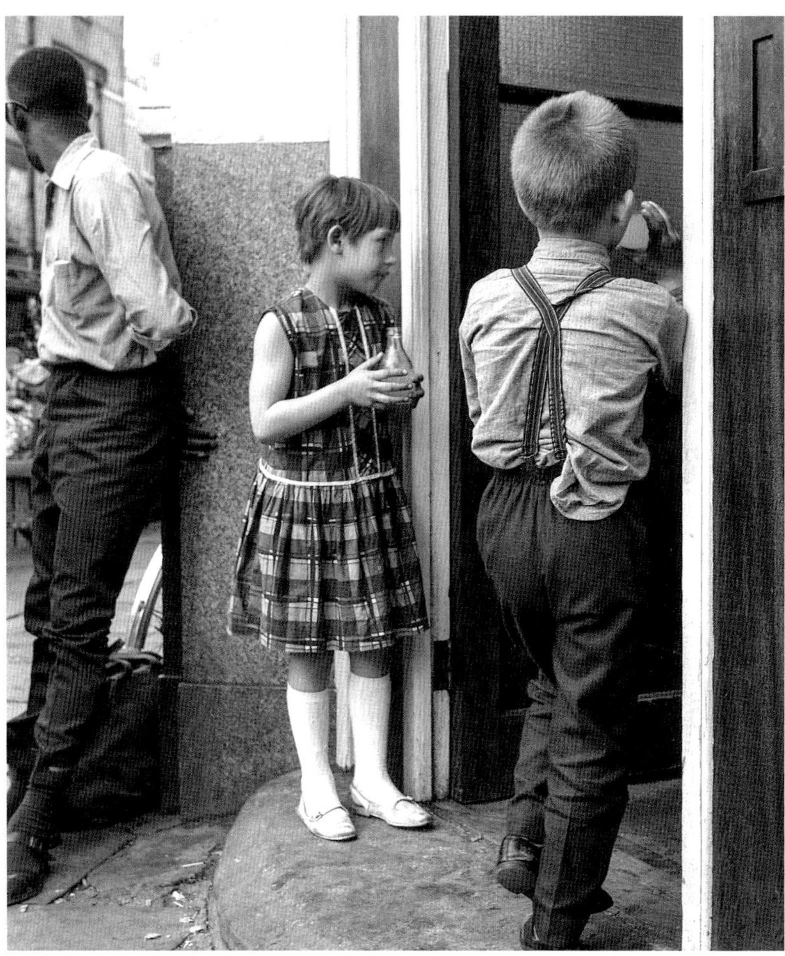

Before the 21st century, individual pubs had greater discretion about whether they allowed children on the premises or not. The Colville (now closed). *Notting Hill, 1967*

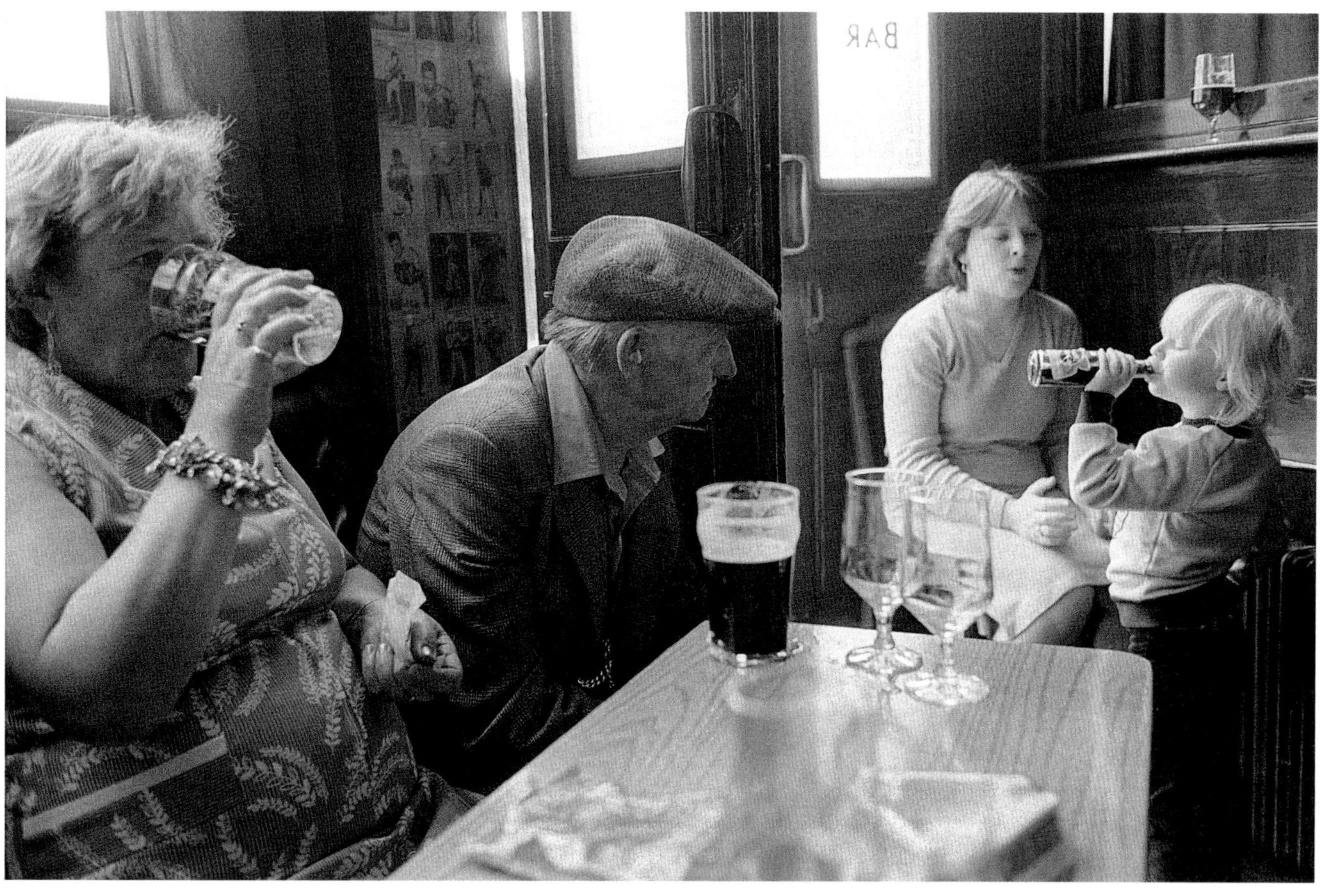

The Birdcage. *Bethnal Green, 1979*

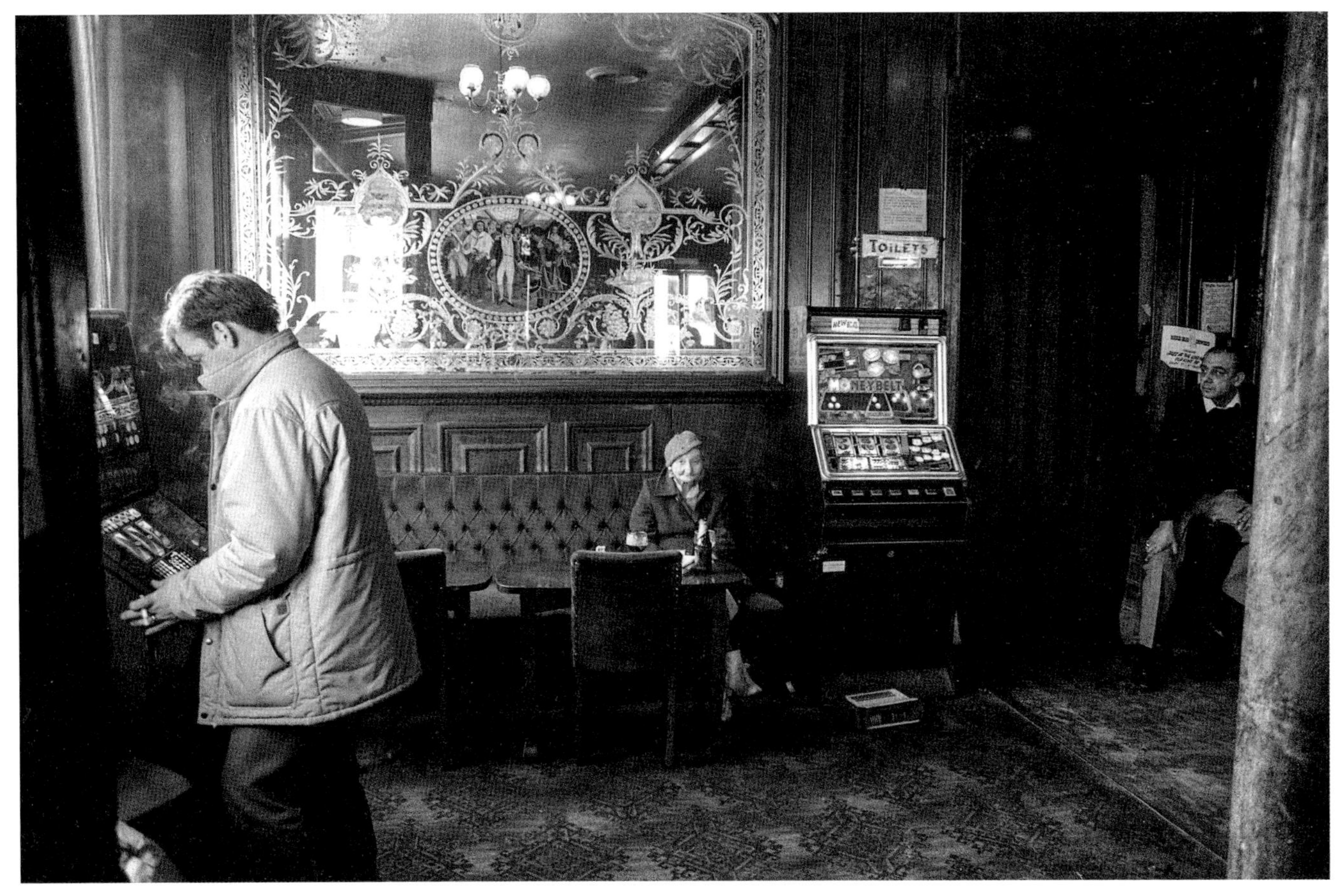

Laws on gambling were relaxed in the 1960s, allowing fruit machines to be introduced to pubs for the first time. The Lord Nelson. *Southwark, 1987*

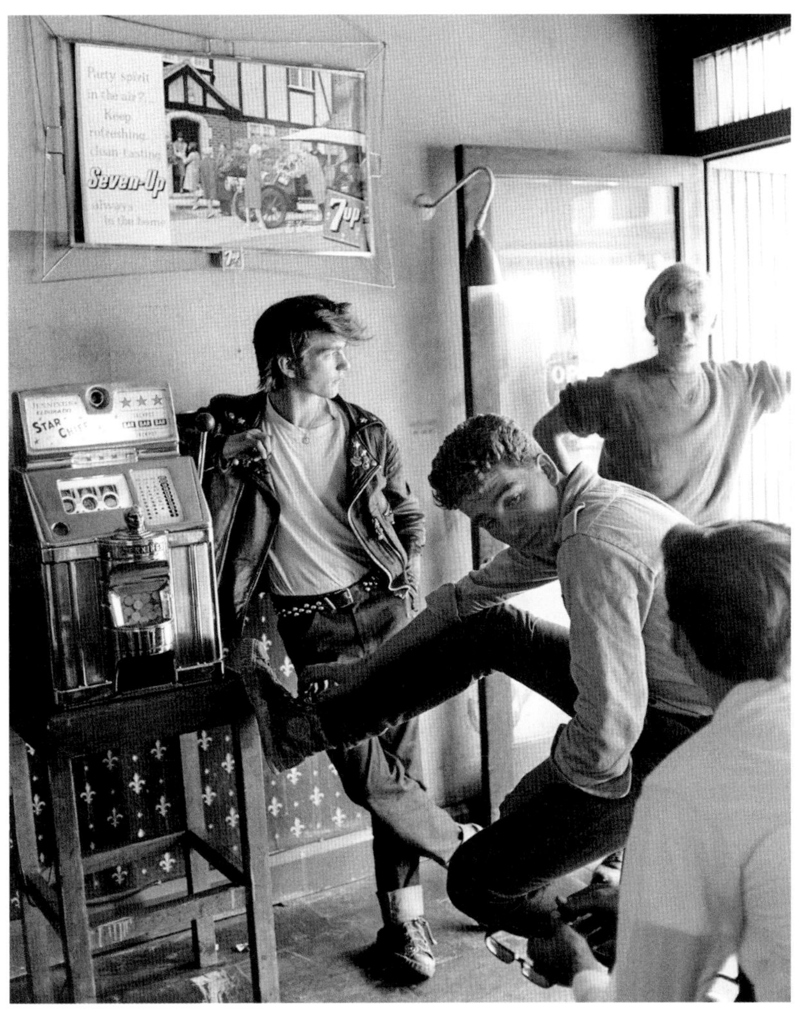

A biker gang at a pub. *London, 1964*

Pubs have always been a place to pass the time, not just to drink.
Dominoes and card games are a way to spend an afternoon and,
for some, a way of life. *East End, c.1960*

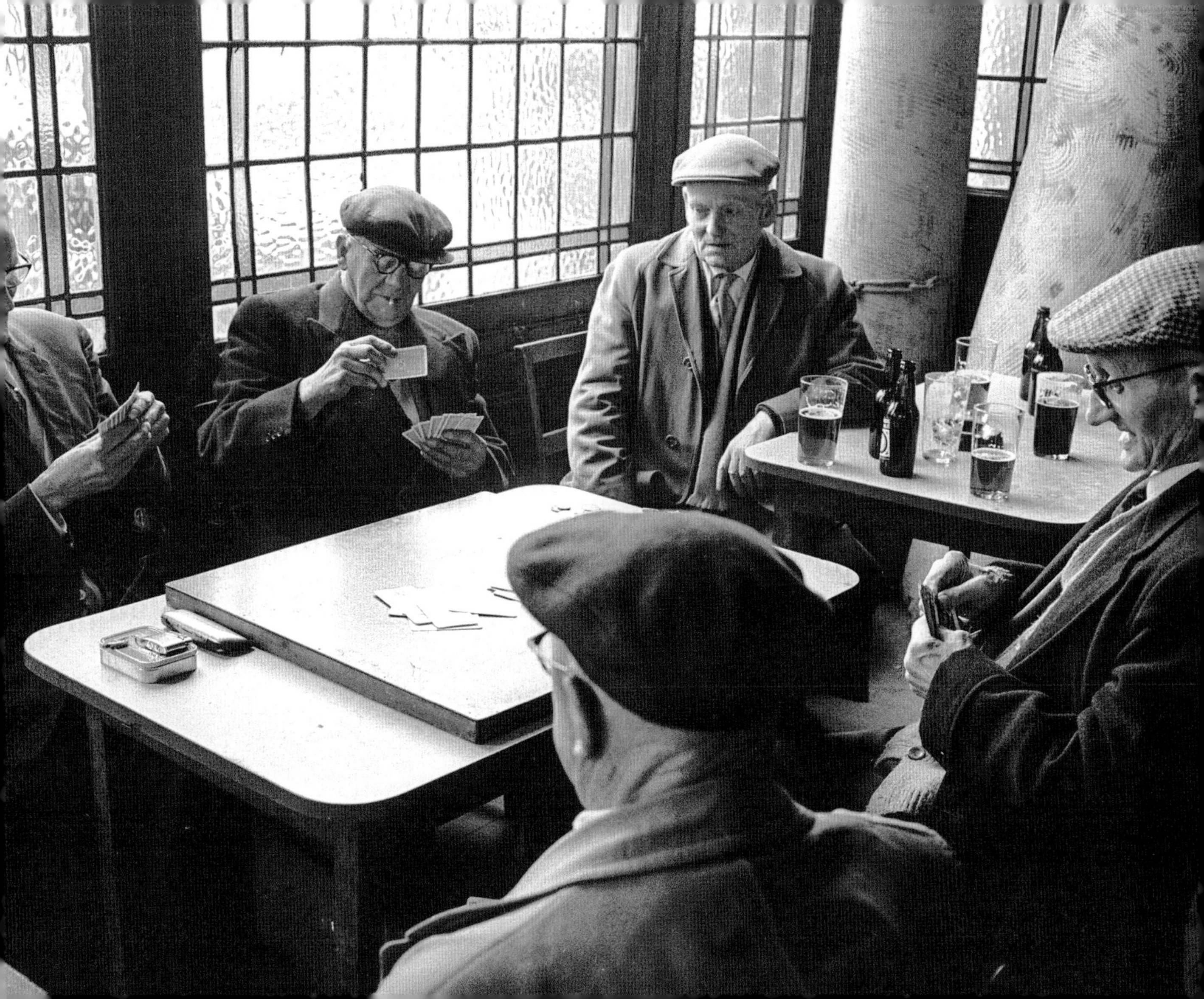

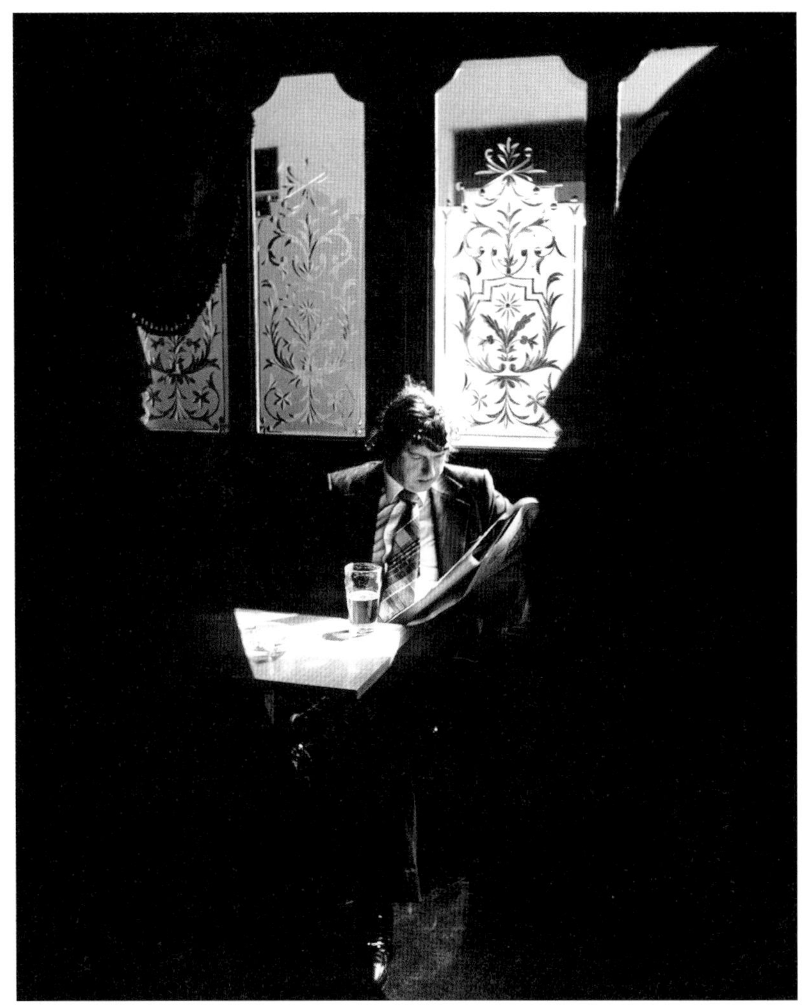

Soho, 1981

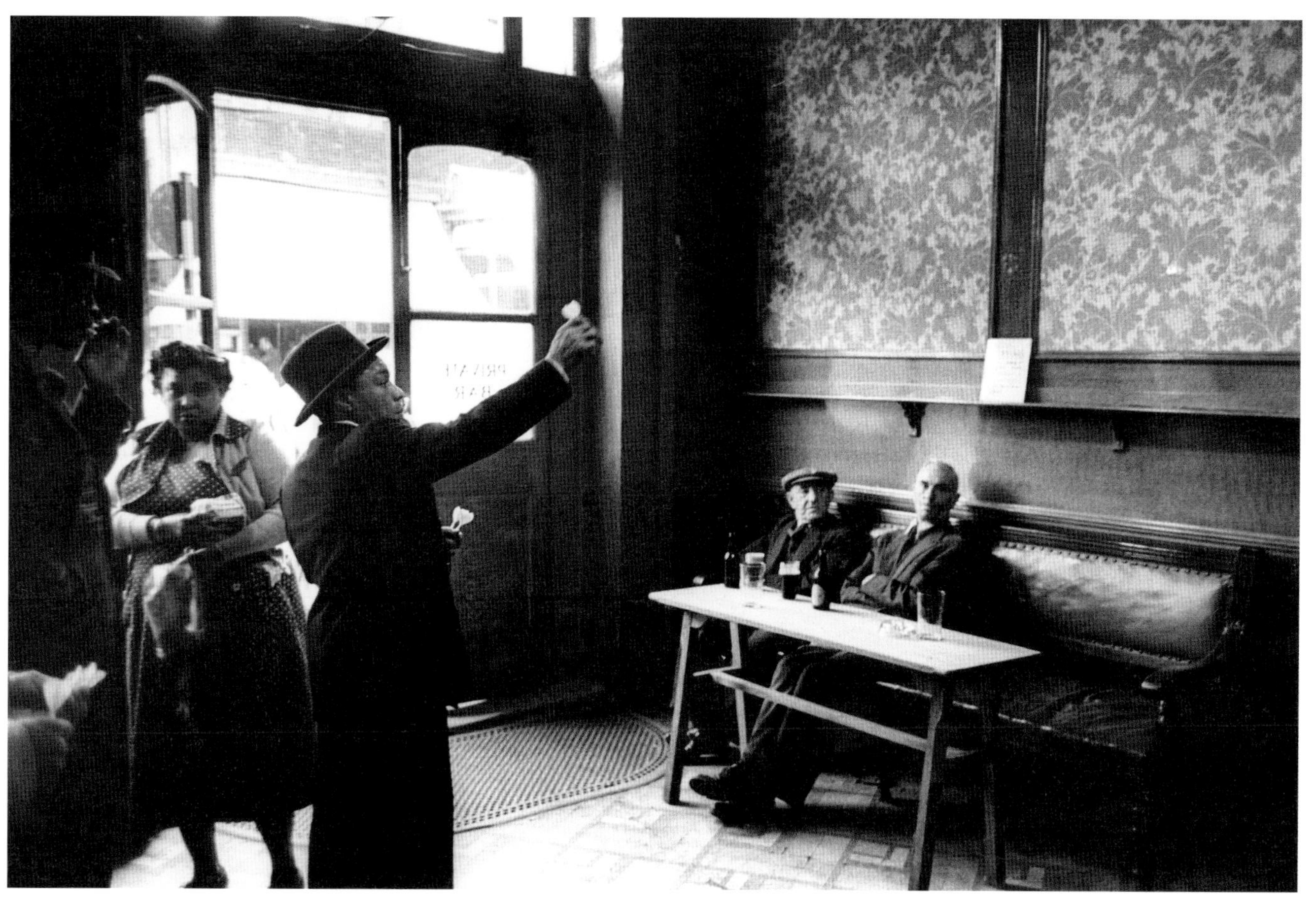

The game of darts emerged in pubs in the 19th century. Originally using cross-sections of a tree trunk, the board is now more sophisticated, but still reflects its origins. *Brixton, 1952*

A Czech proverb states that if a government raises the price of beer, it will fall. As the poster near the window shows, price hikes were not popular in the UK either. *Brick Lane, 1979*

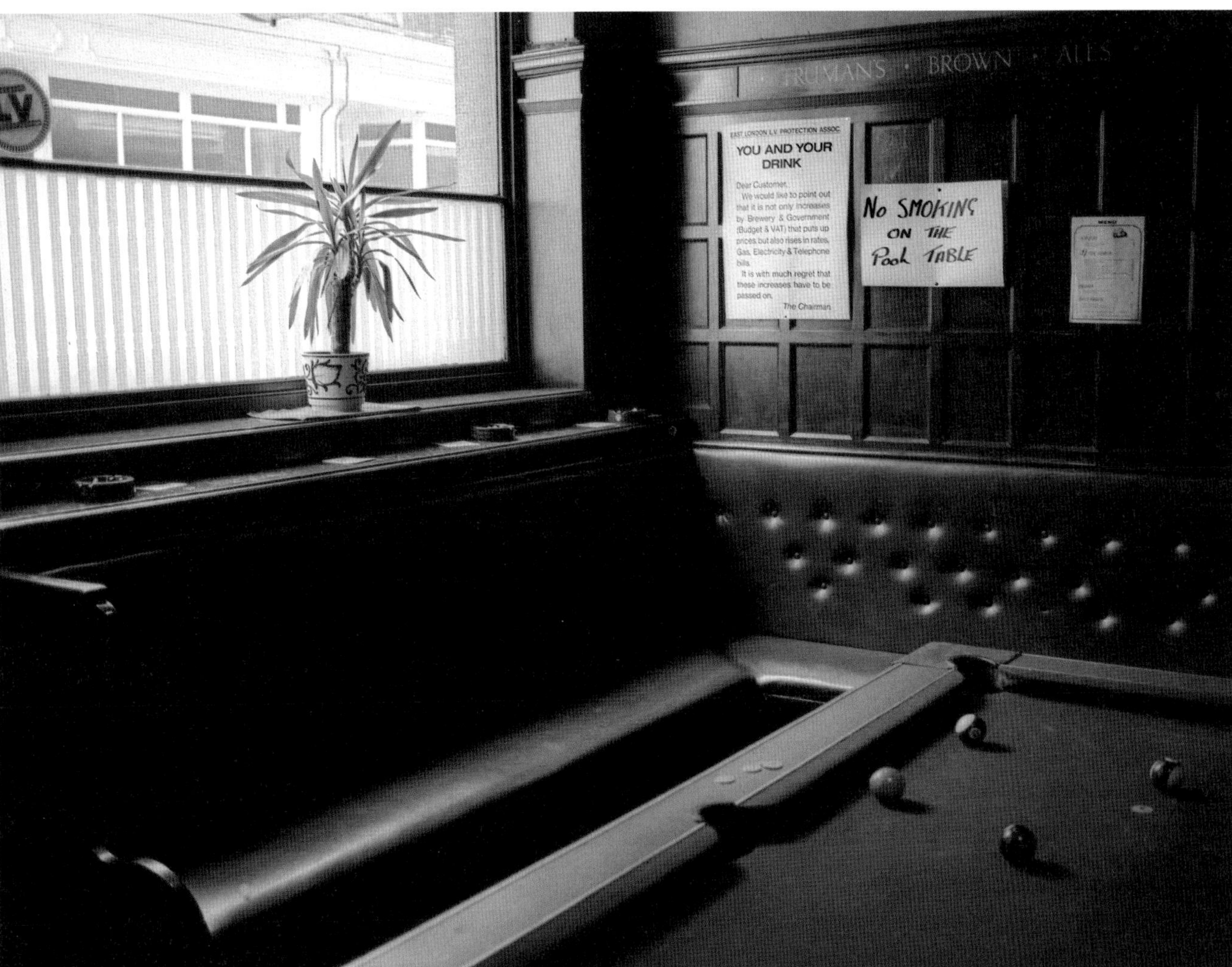
TRUMANS · BROWN · ALES
EAST LONDON L.V. PROTECTION ASSOC
YOU AND YOUR DRINK
Dear Customer,
We would like to point out that it is not only increases by Brewery & Government (Budget & VAT) that puts up prices but also rises in rates, Gas, Electricity & Telephone bills.
It is with much regret that these increases have to be passed on.
The Chairman
No SMOKING ON THE Pool TABLE

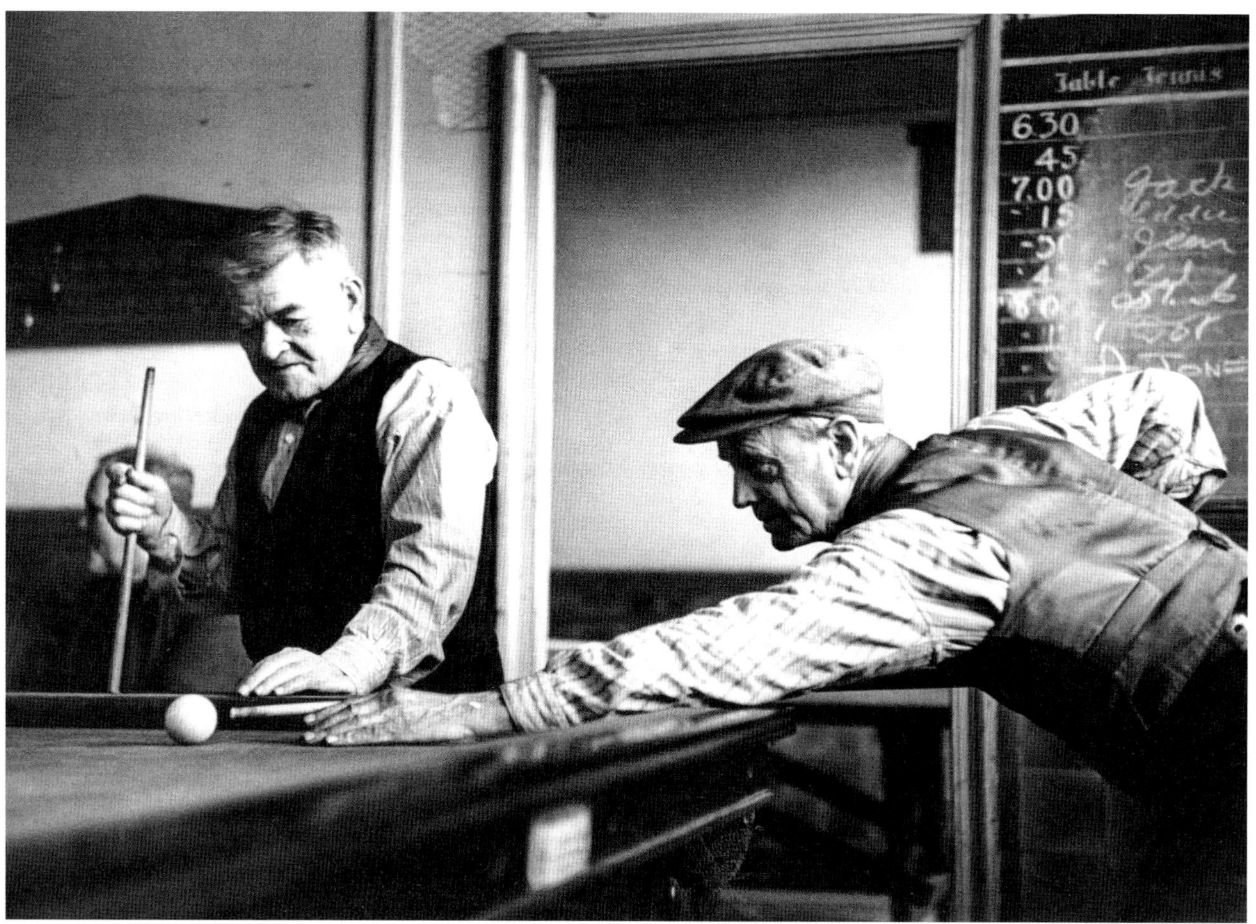

Snooker and billiards have long been popular sports, but the tables were too big for most pubs. Pool, which uses smaller tables, came over from the US and conquered British pubs in the 20th century. The Grandfathers' Club. *Elephant and Castle, 1949*

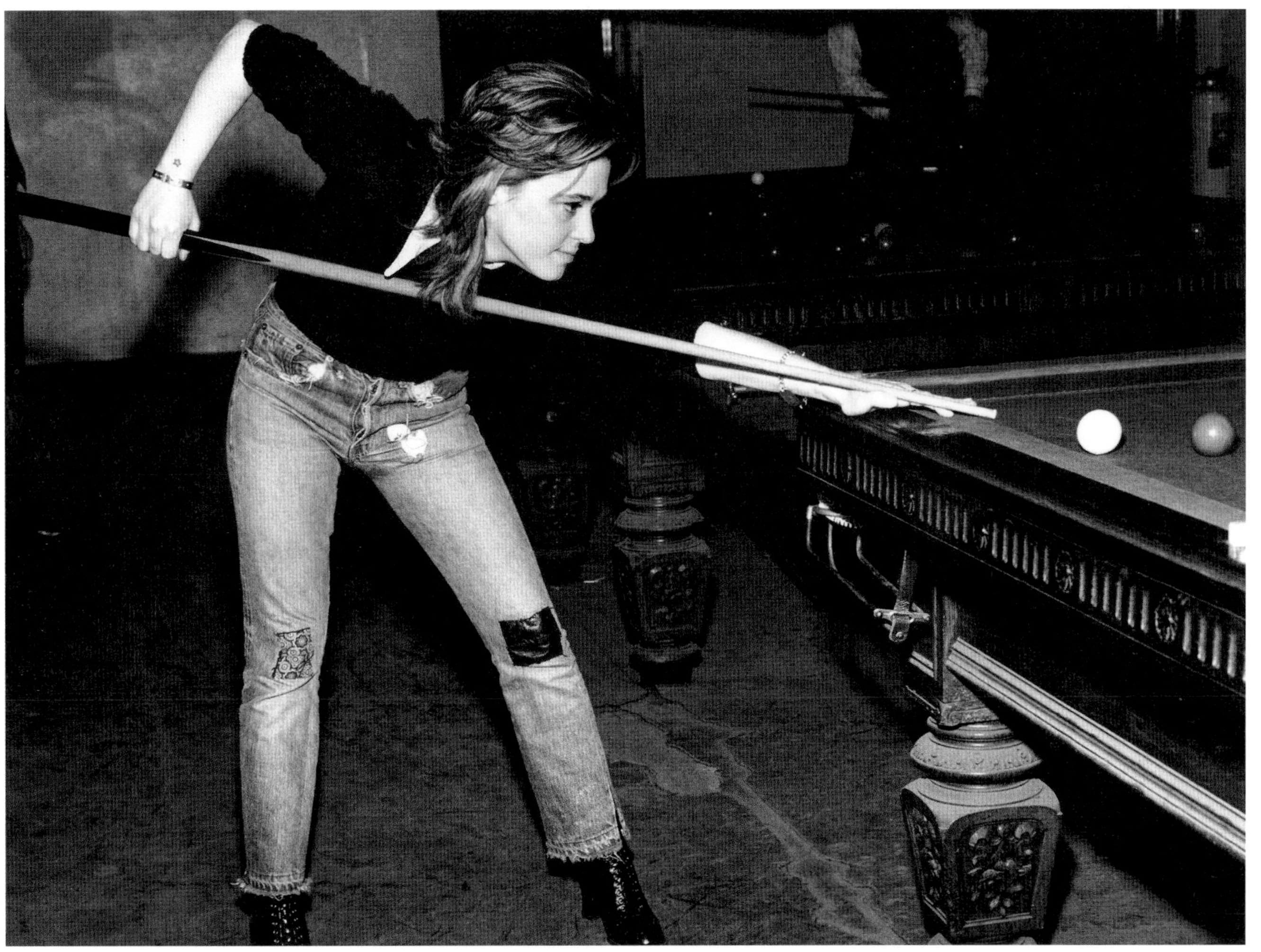

Suzi Quatro playing snooker at The Marlborough. *Soho, 1973*

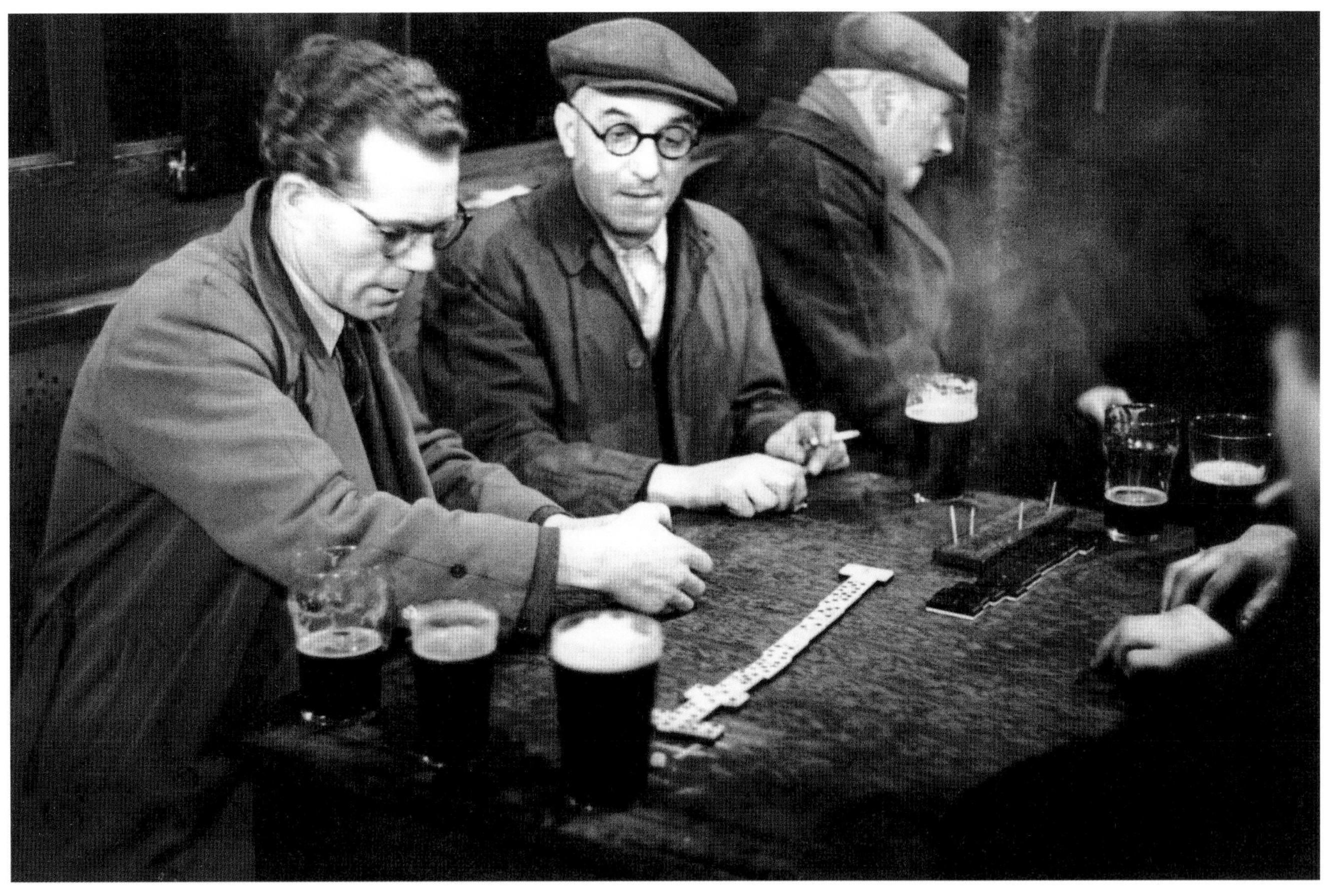

The game of dominoes stretches back to 13th-century China, and arrived in Europe via Italy in the 18th century. Once it found its way into the British pub, it never left. *Elephant and Castle, 1949*

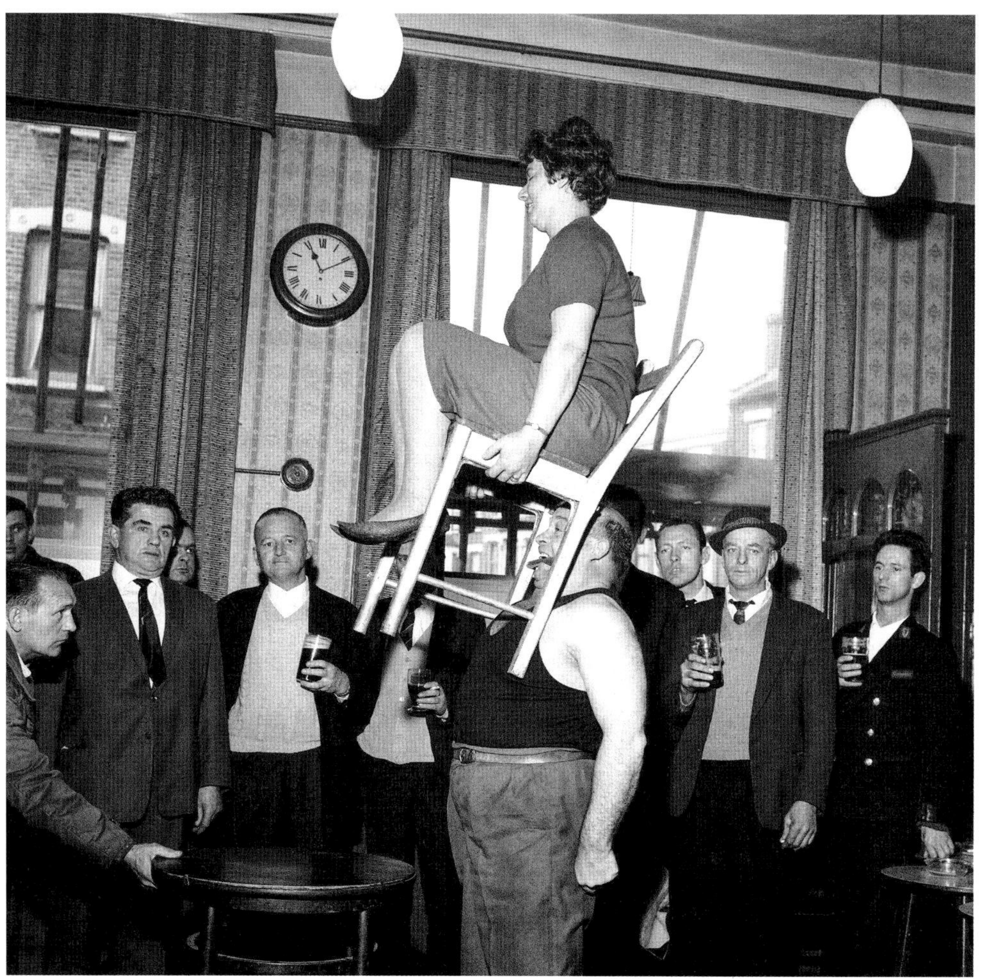

Publican (and ex-circus strong man), Butty Sugrue, lifts a barmaid
at the Admiral Nelson (now demolished). *Kilburn, 1965*

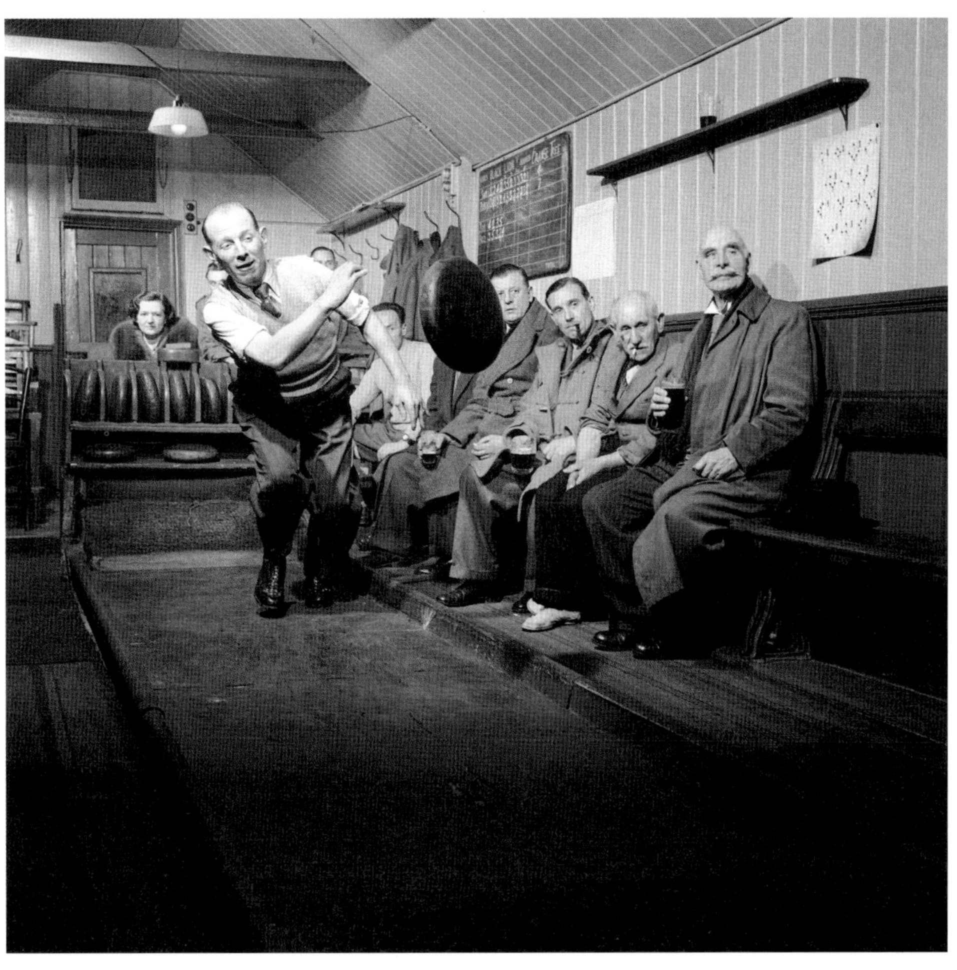

Games were such an integral part of pubs that many built their own skittle alleys. Players would knock down pins with a wooden 'cheese'. The Black Lion. *London, c.1955*

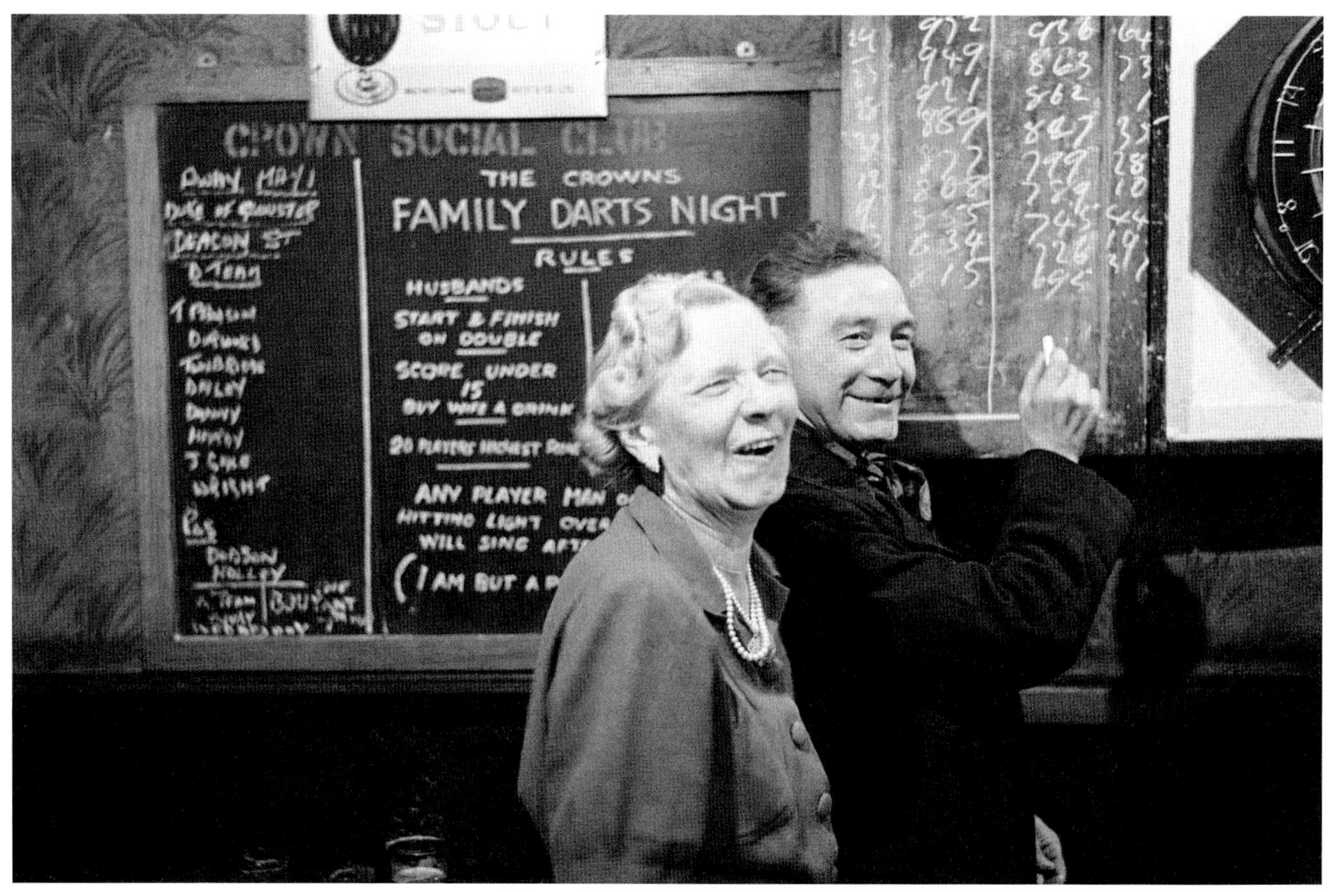

Scoring darts at The Crown during celebrations for the wedding of Elizabeth II. *Southwark, 1947*

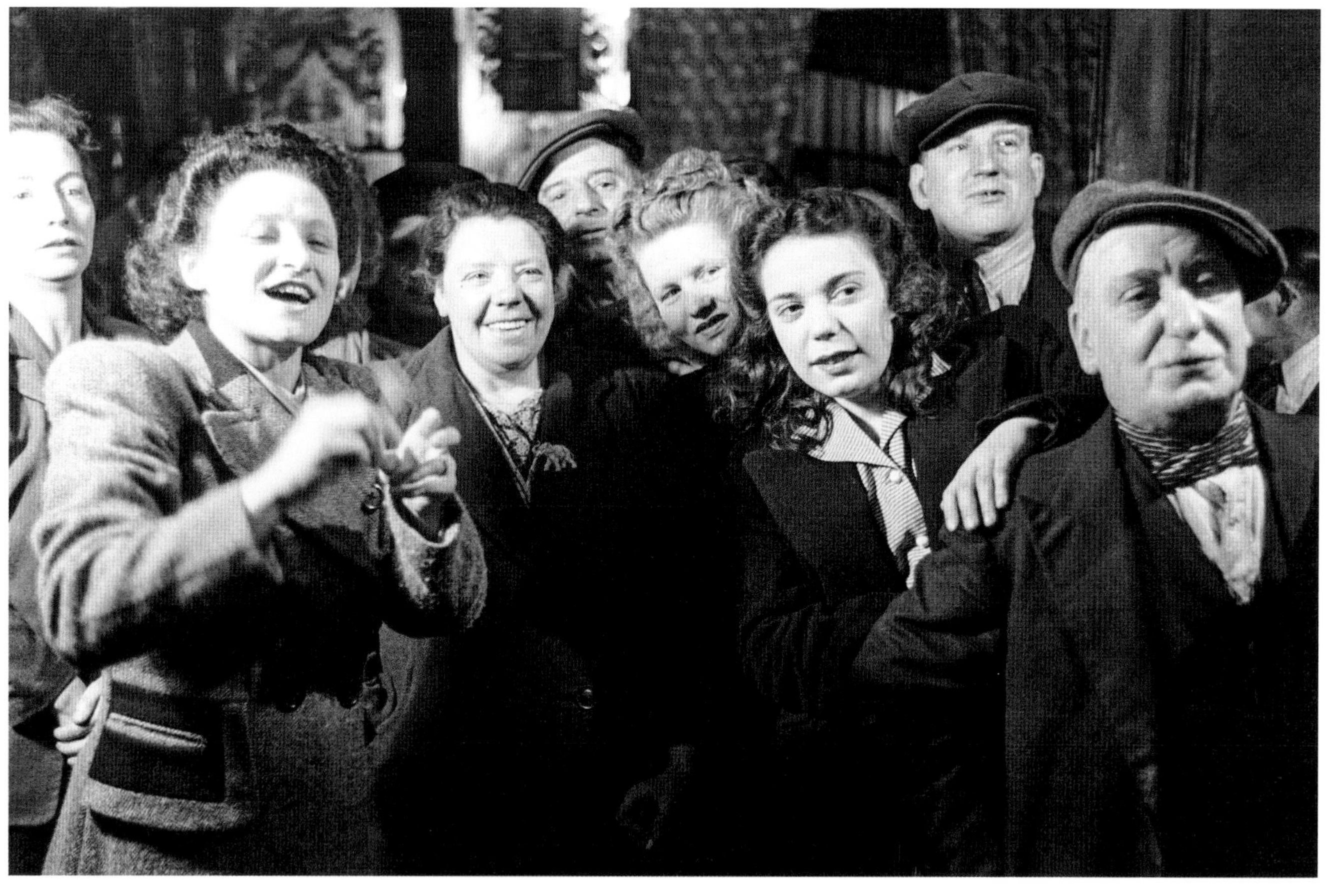

Celebrations continue at The Crown. *Southwark, 1947*

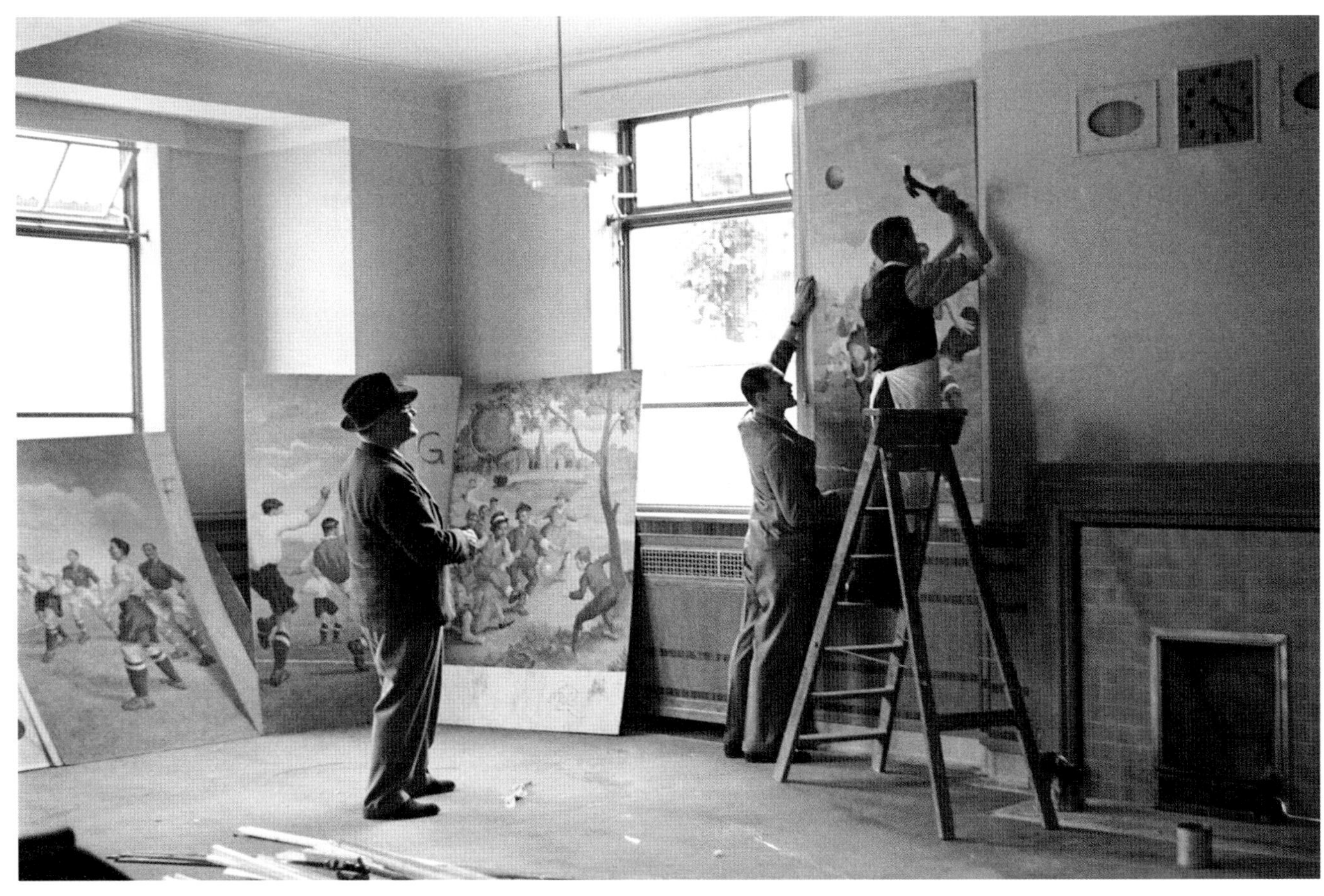

Paintings of Tottenham Hotspur FC for the walls of The Spurs (now demolished). Any pub is a reflection of the community it serves and this one was a shrine to the local football team. *Tottenham, 1939*

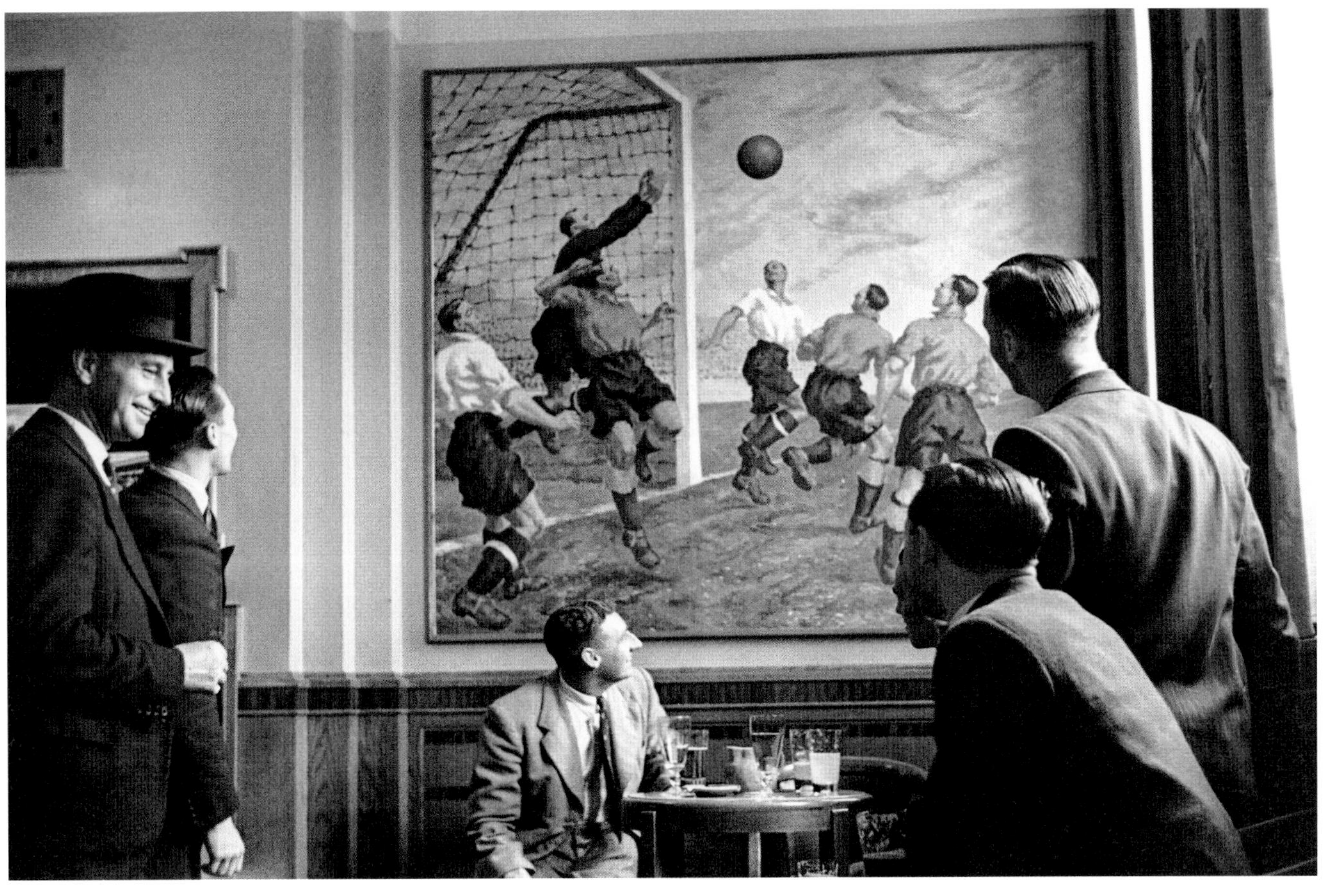

Members of Tottenham Hotspur FC admire the paintings at The Spurs. *Tottenham, 1939*

When TVs began appearing in pubs in the 1960s, many households didn't have their own set. By the end of the decade most houses did, but the pub was still the best place to watch important events together. *Old Kent Road, 1962*

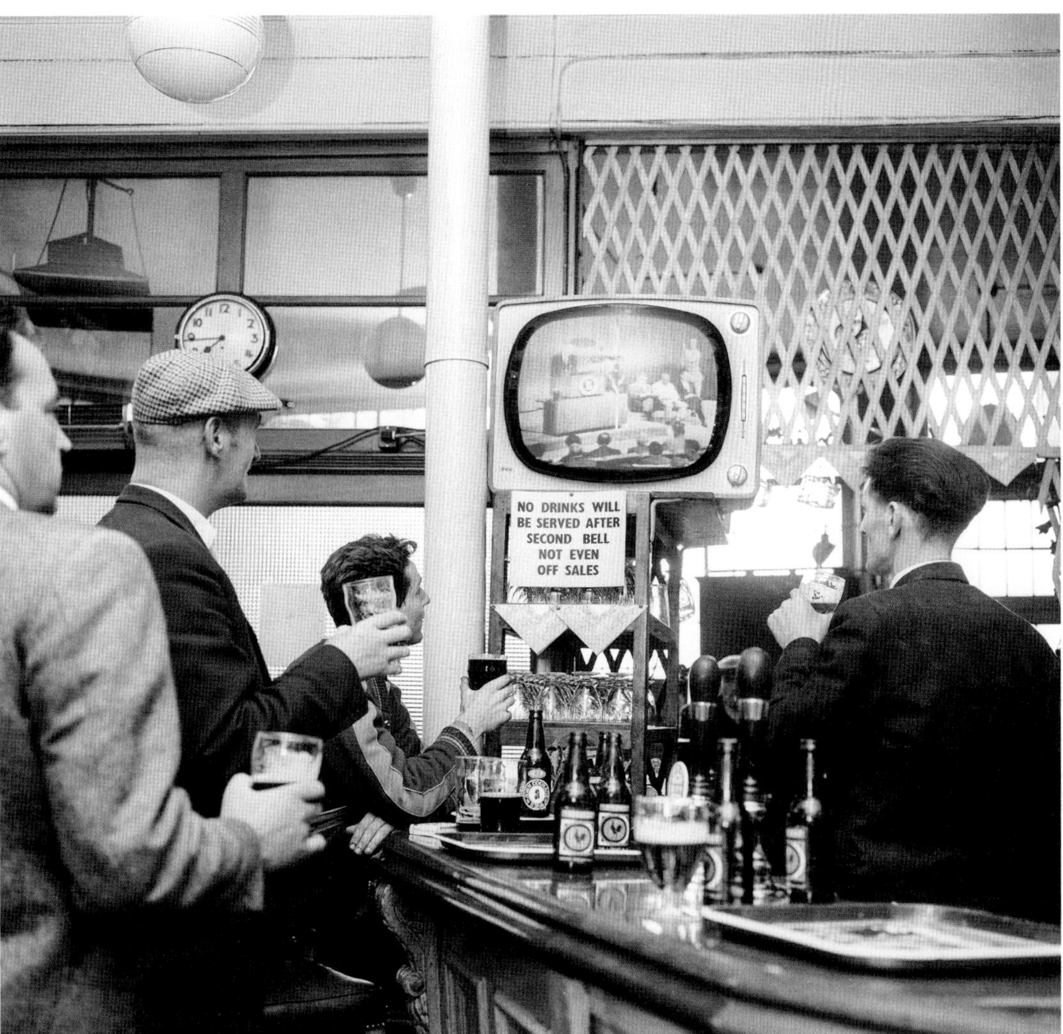

NO DRINKS WILL
BE SERVED AFTER
SECOND BELL
NOT EVEN
OFF SALES

Watching a broadcast of Prime Minister Sir Anthony Eden
during the Suez Crisis. *London, 1956*

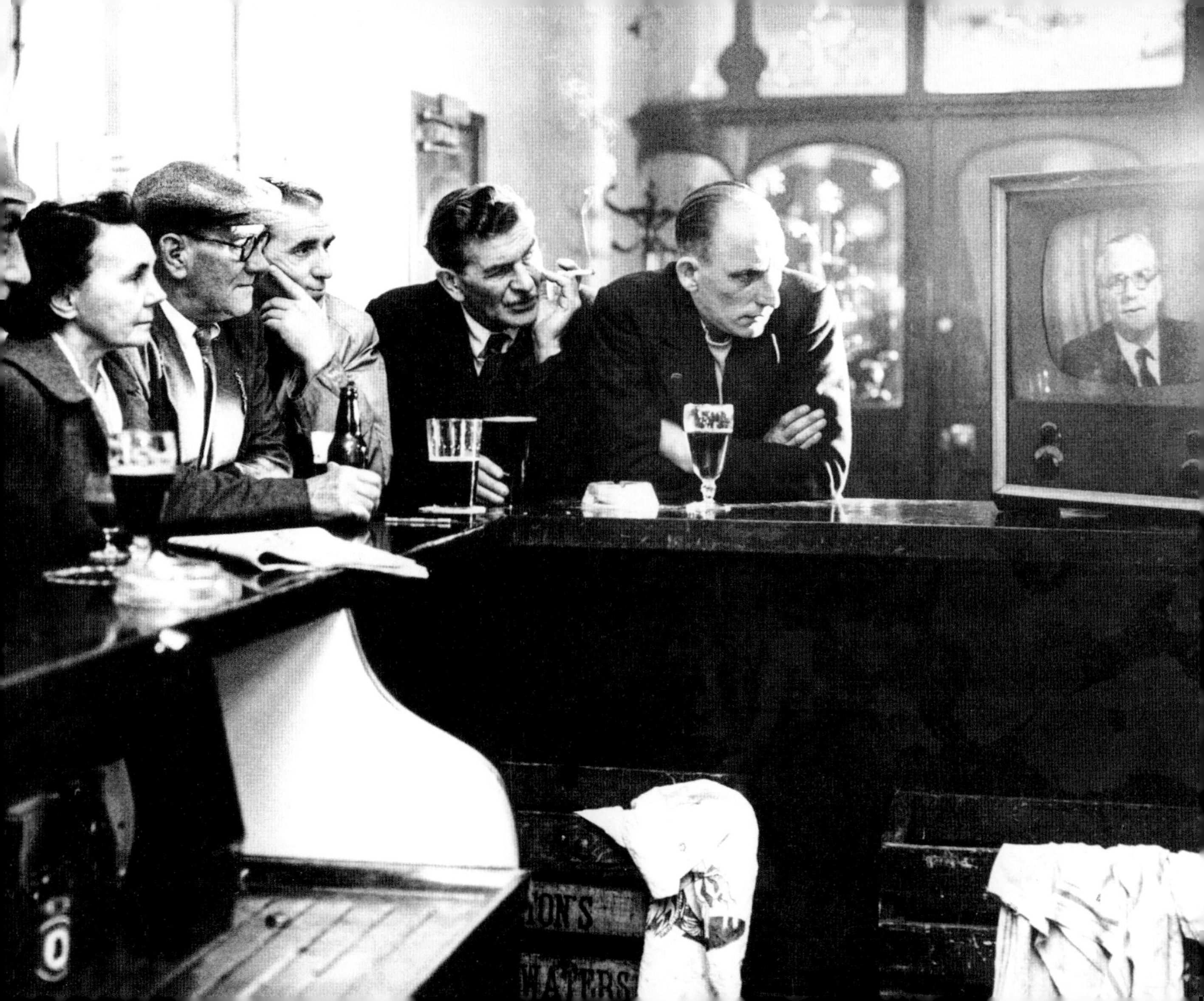

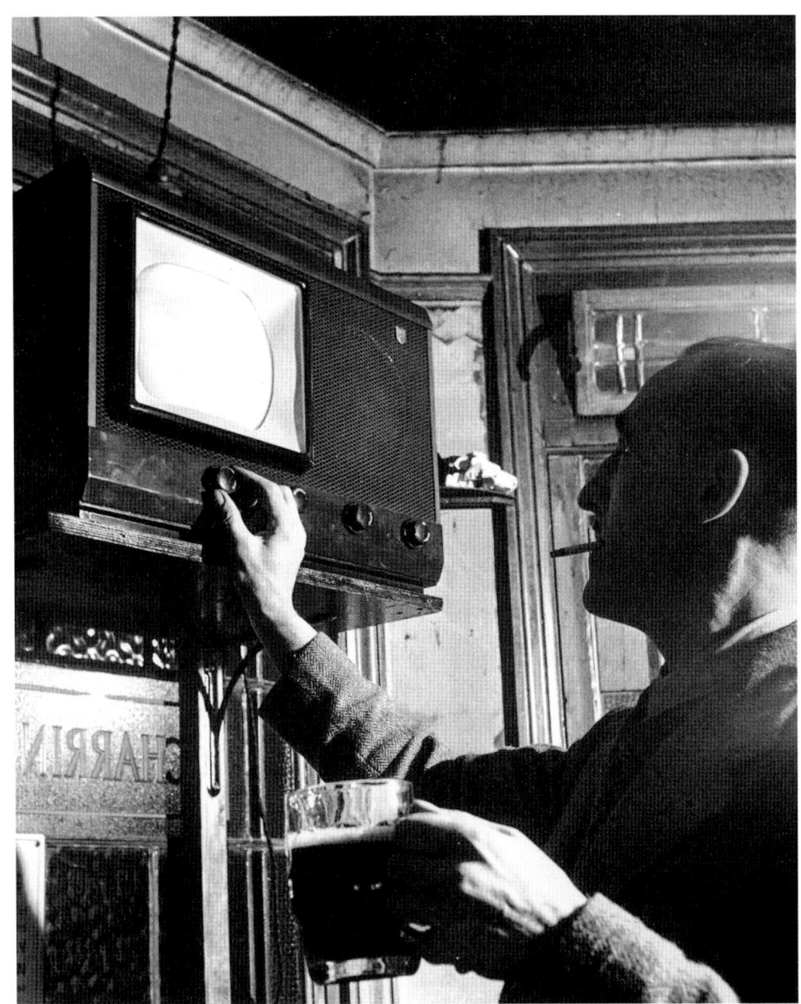

The Leigham Arms. *Streatham, 1948*

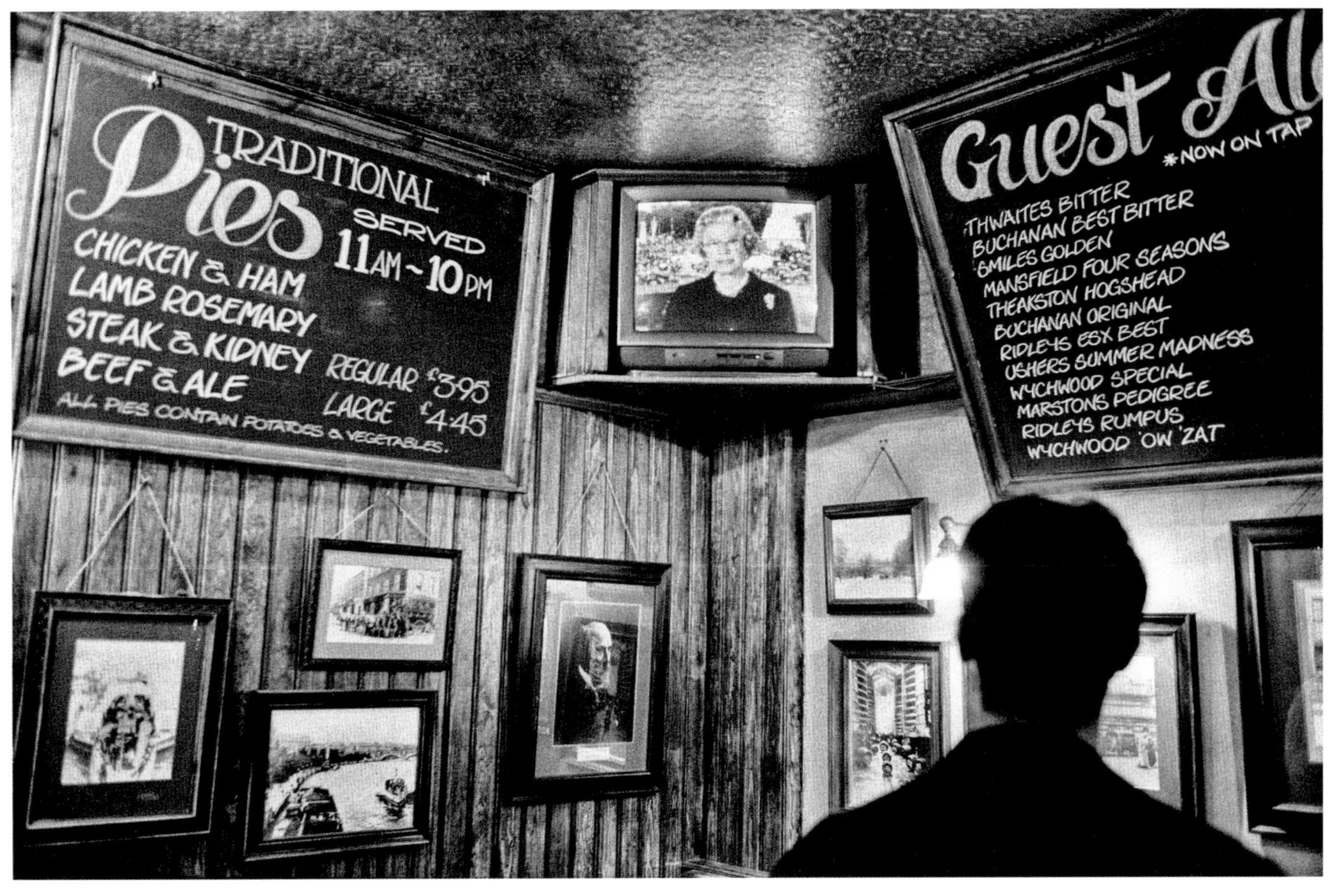

Queen Elizabeth II gives a speech during the public funeral of Princess Diana. *London, 1997*

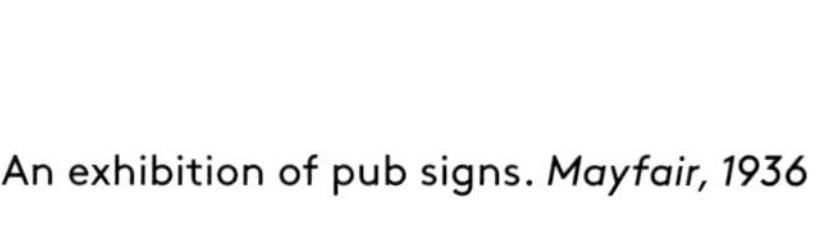
An exhibition of pub signs. *Mayfair, 1936*

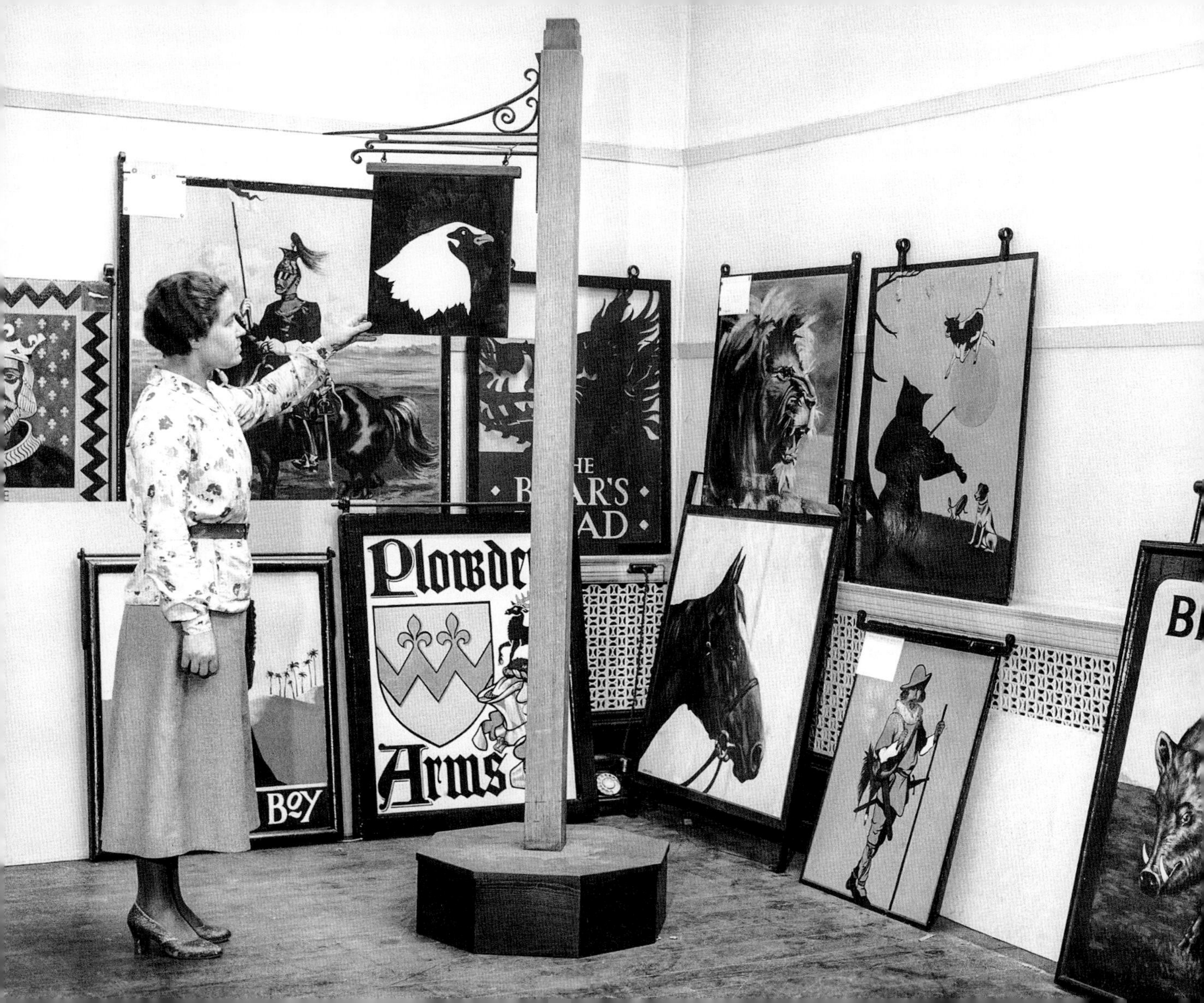
THE BOAR'S HEAD
Plowden
Arms
Boy

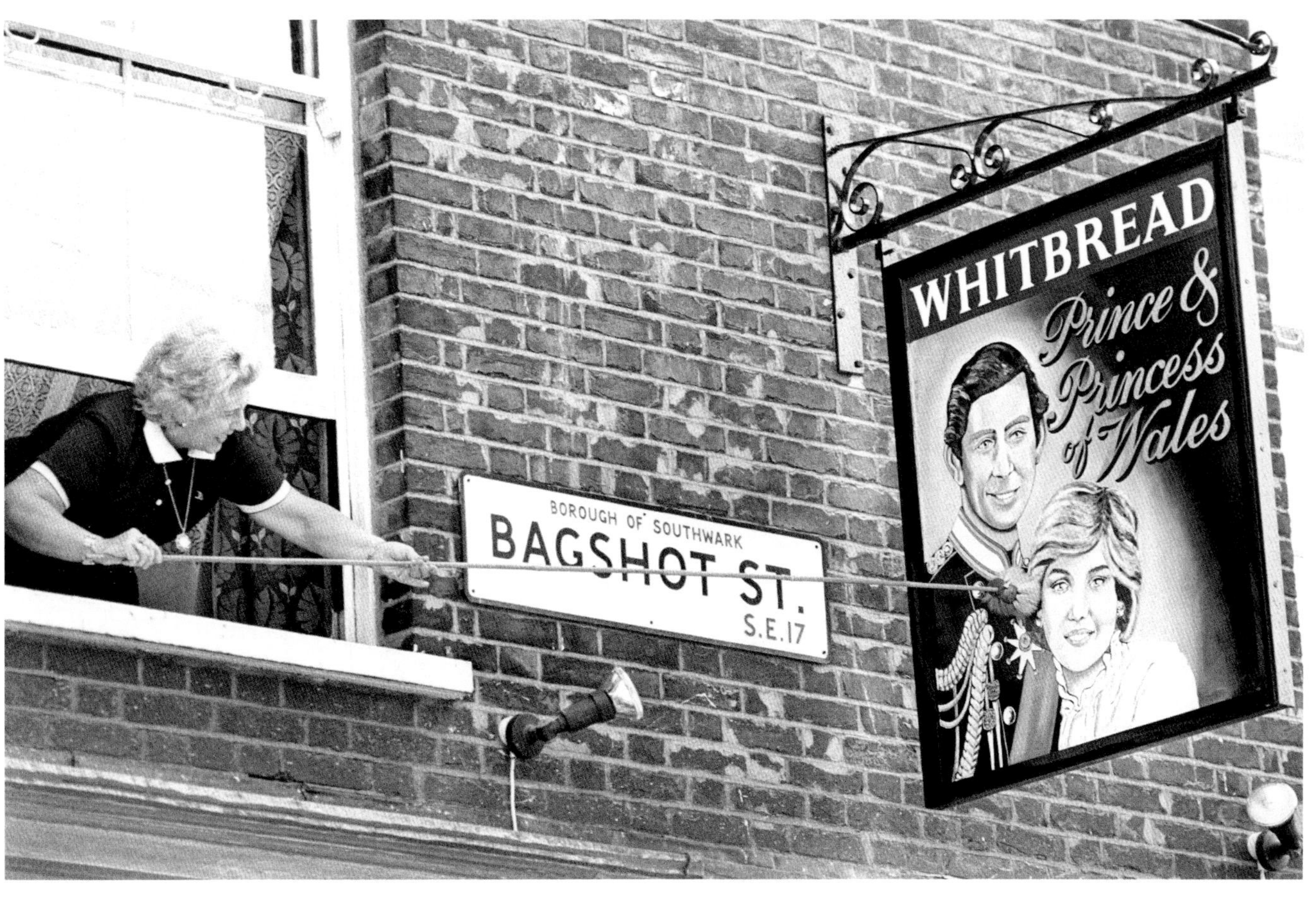

In the Middle Ages, hanging signs were common to any commercial establishment. In pubs, they stuck around. A pub might be named after a royal for centuries, with the sign changing to reflect the individual holding the title. Prince and Princess of Wales (now closed). *Southwark, 1981*

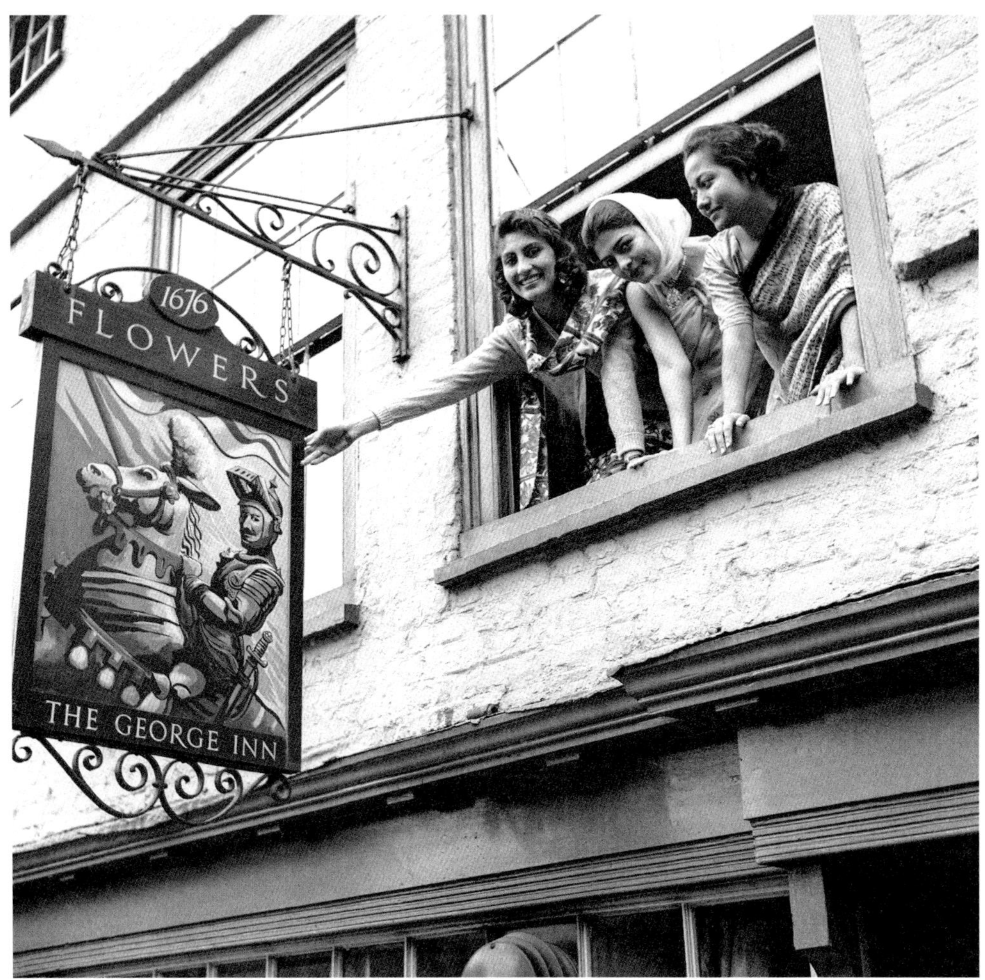

The George is London's last surviving galleried coaching inn (a galleried inn has distinctive multi-storey guest rooms). *Southwark, 1962*

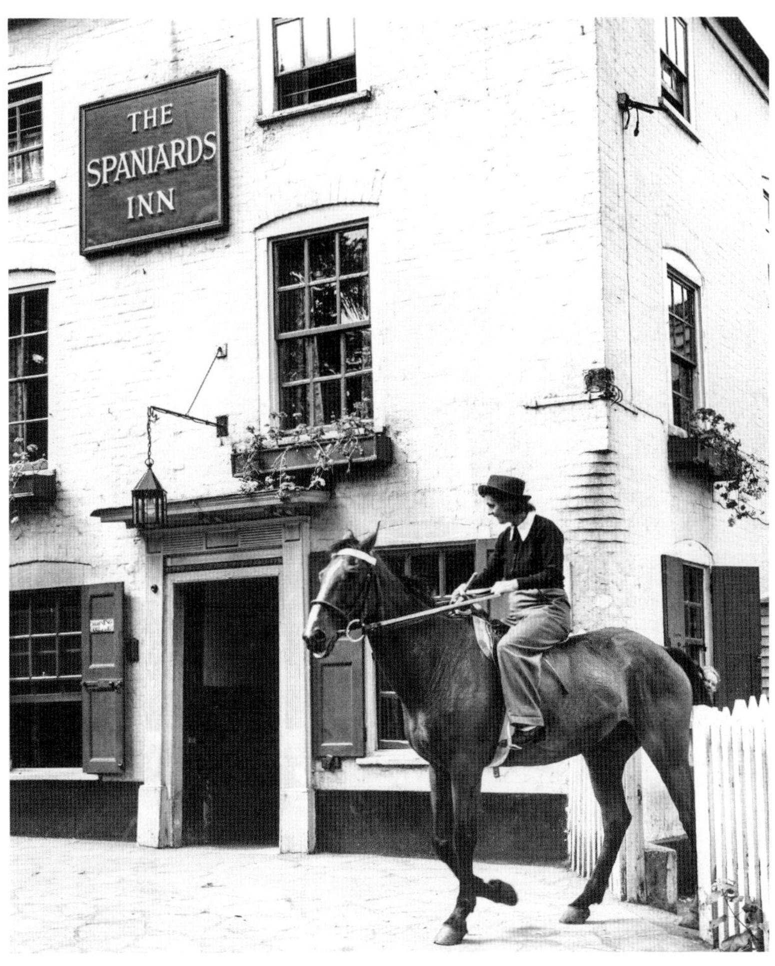

Built in 1585 as a tollgate, The Spaniards Inn was named after the Spanish ambassador to King James I. It also claims to be the birthplace and favourite haunt of Dick Turpin. *Hampstead, 1952*

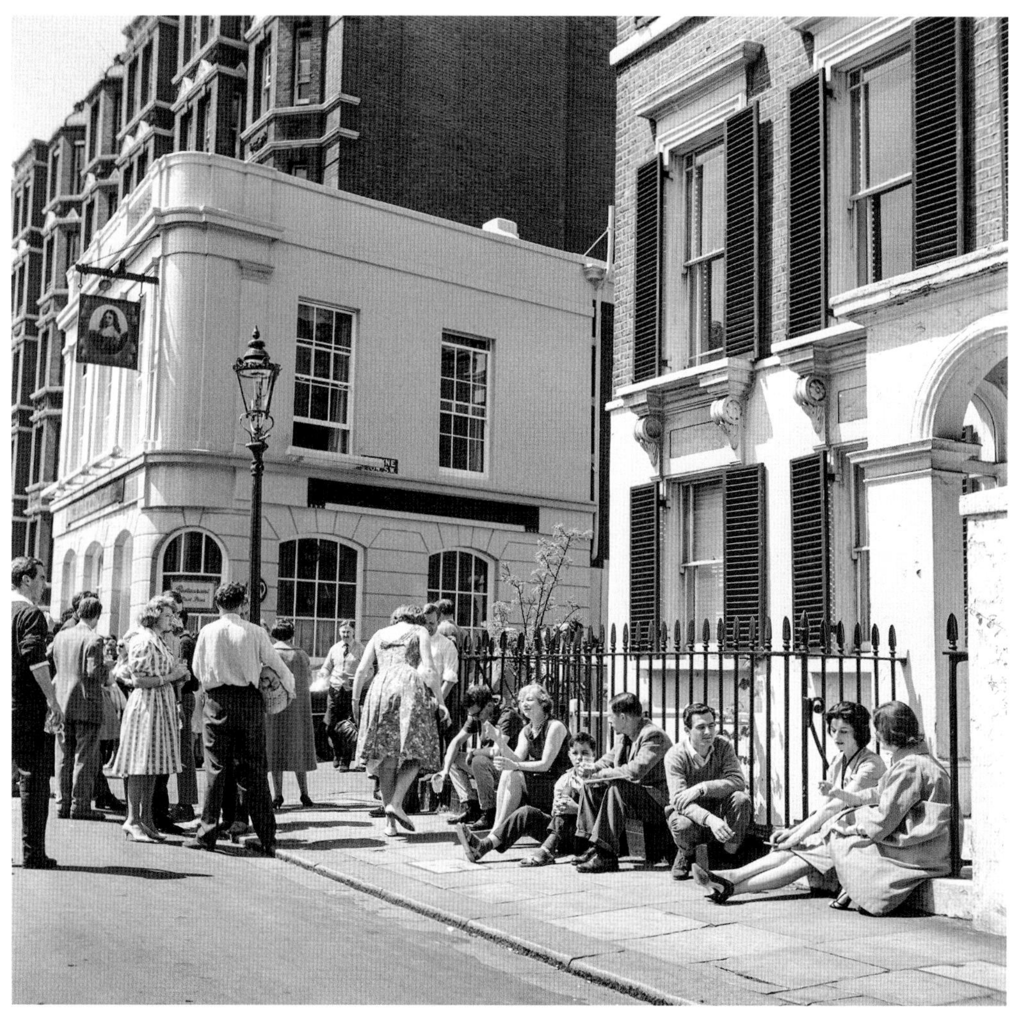

Sunday morning at The King's Head and Eight Bells (now closed). *Chelsea, 1959*

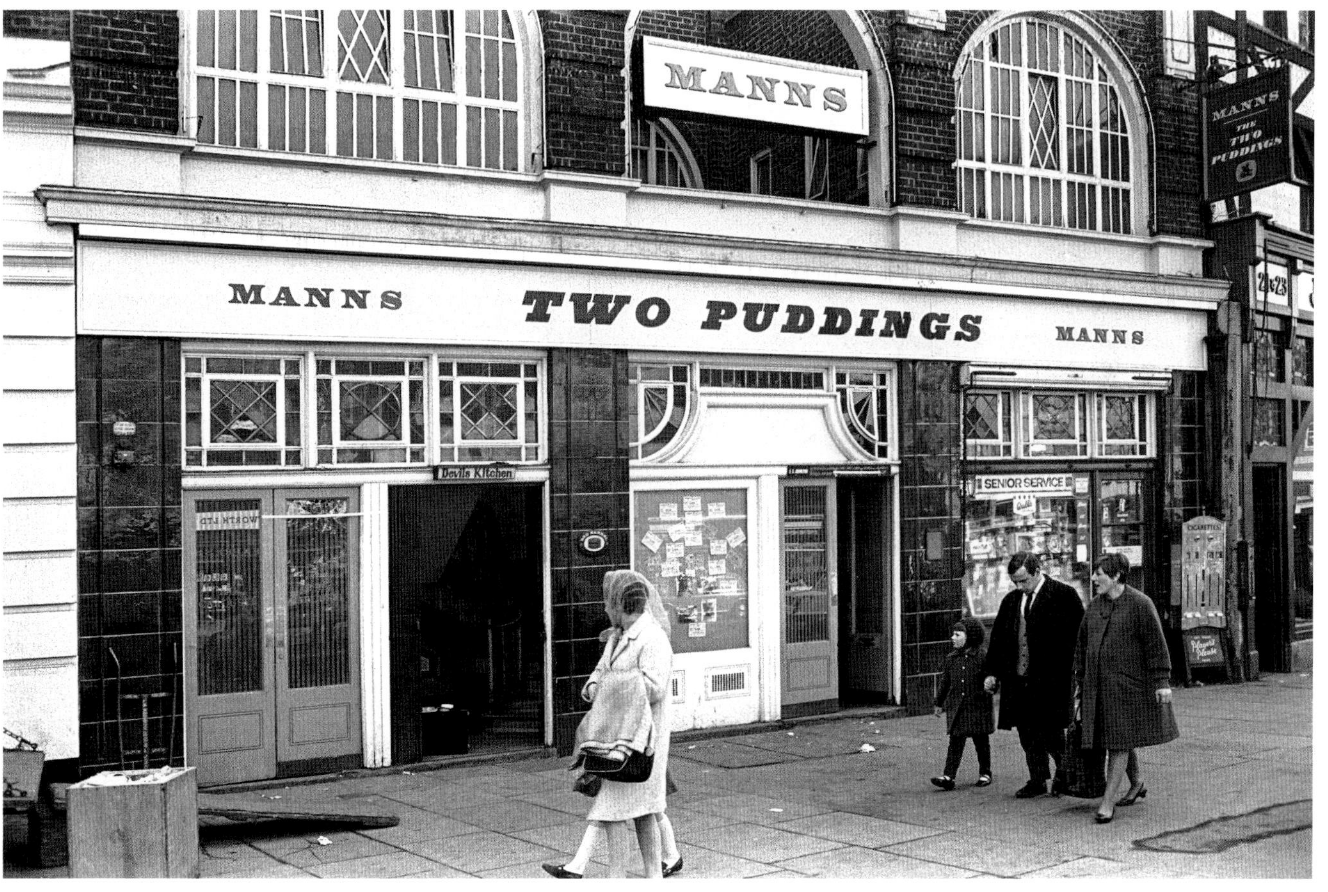

The Two Puddings was a legendary East End pub (now closed), so rough it was nicknamed 'The Butcher's Shop'. *Stratford, c.1960*

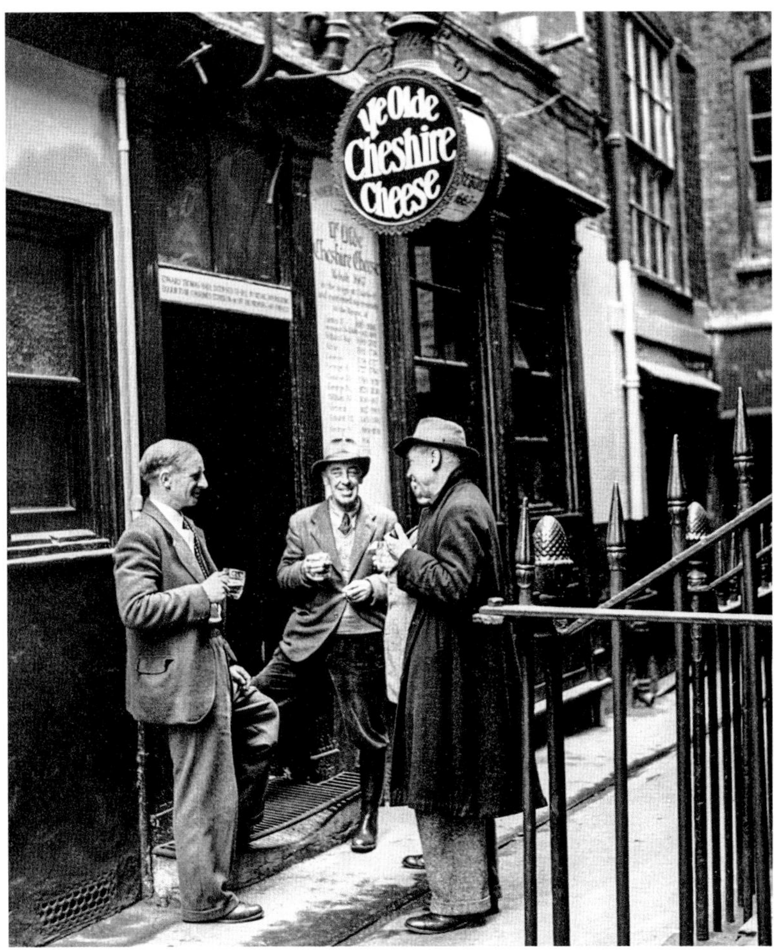

Ye Olde Cheshire Cheese claims to be London's oldest pub. It's certainly one of the city's most literary haunts. Samuel Johnson probably drank here. Charles Dickens, Mark Twain and PG Wodehouse definitely did. *City of London, c.1930*

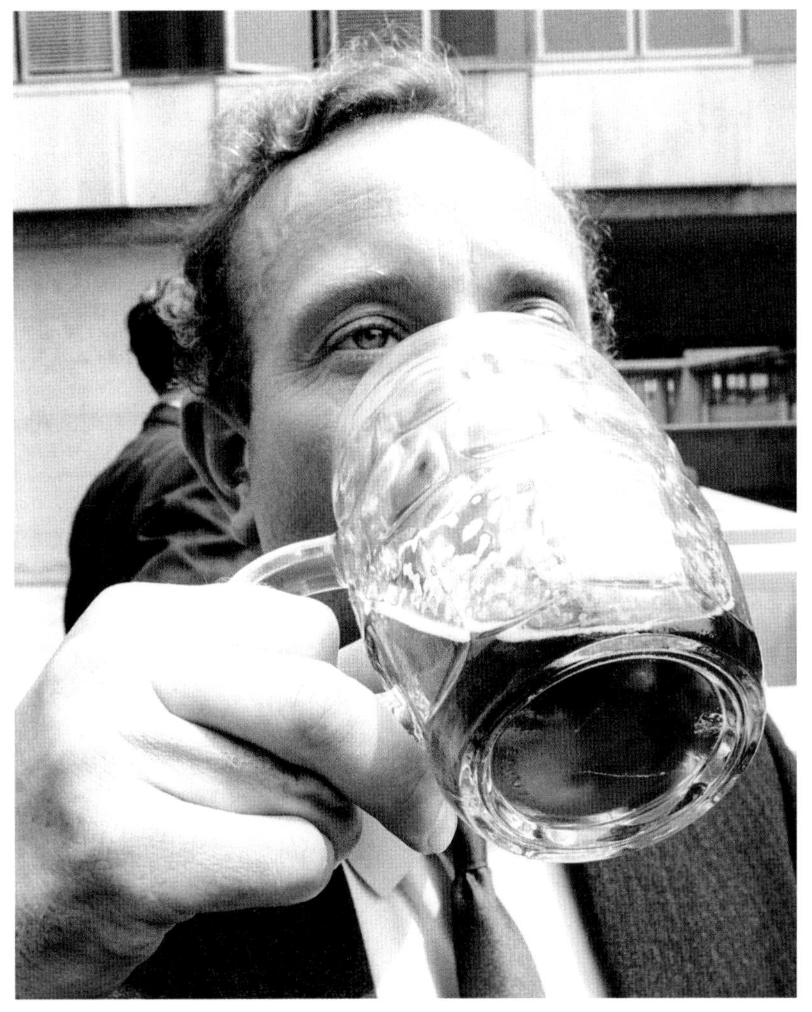

Lunchtime pint during a heatwave. *London, 1969*

Outside the pub on a bank holiday. *London, 1947*

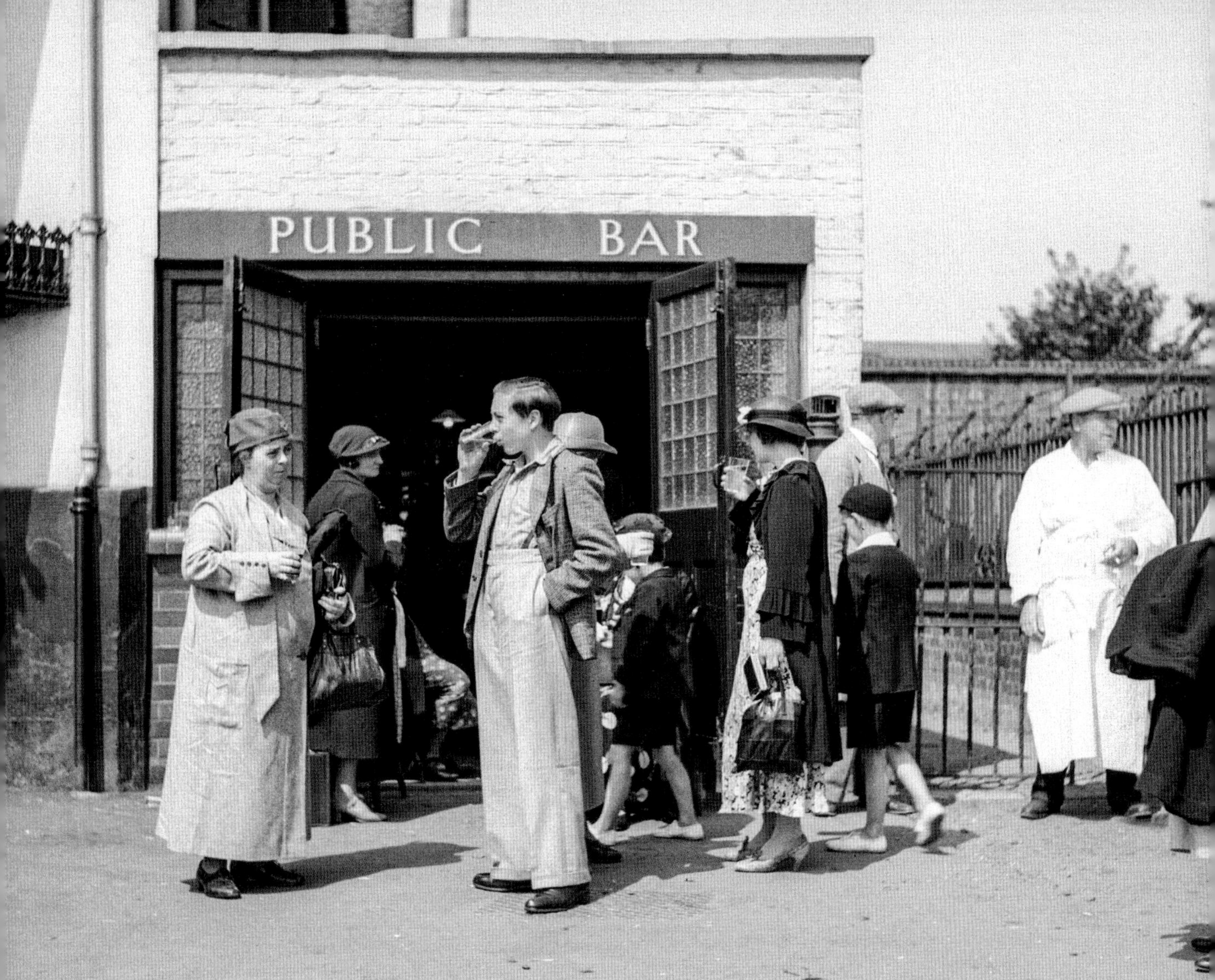

PUBLIC   BAR

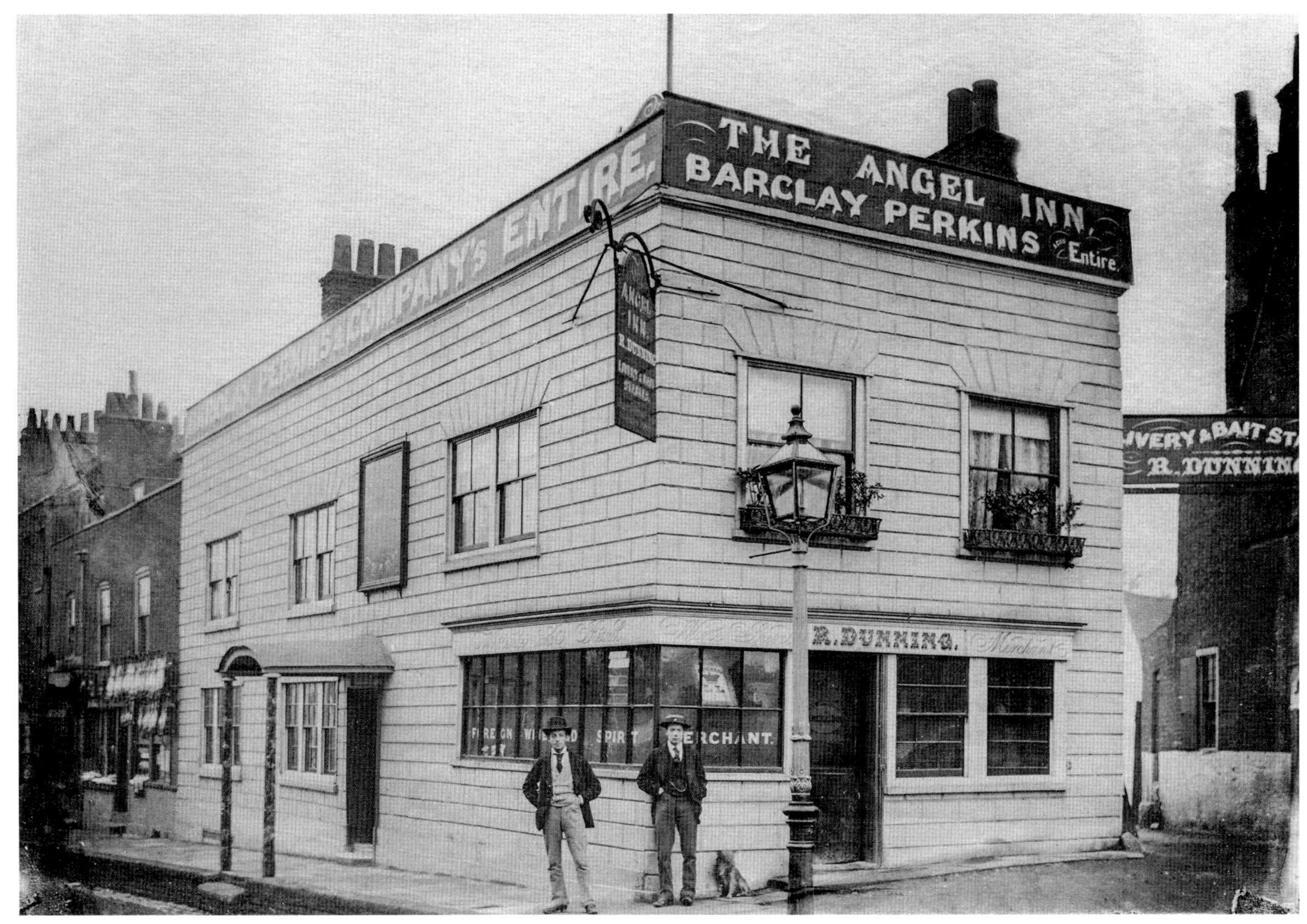

The Angel Inn. *Highgate, 1874*

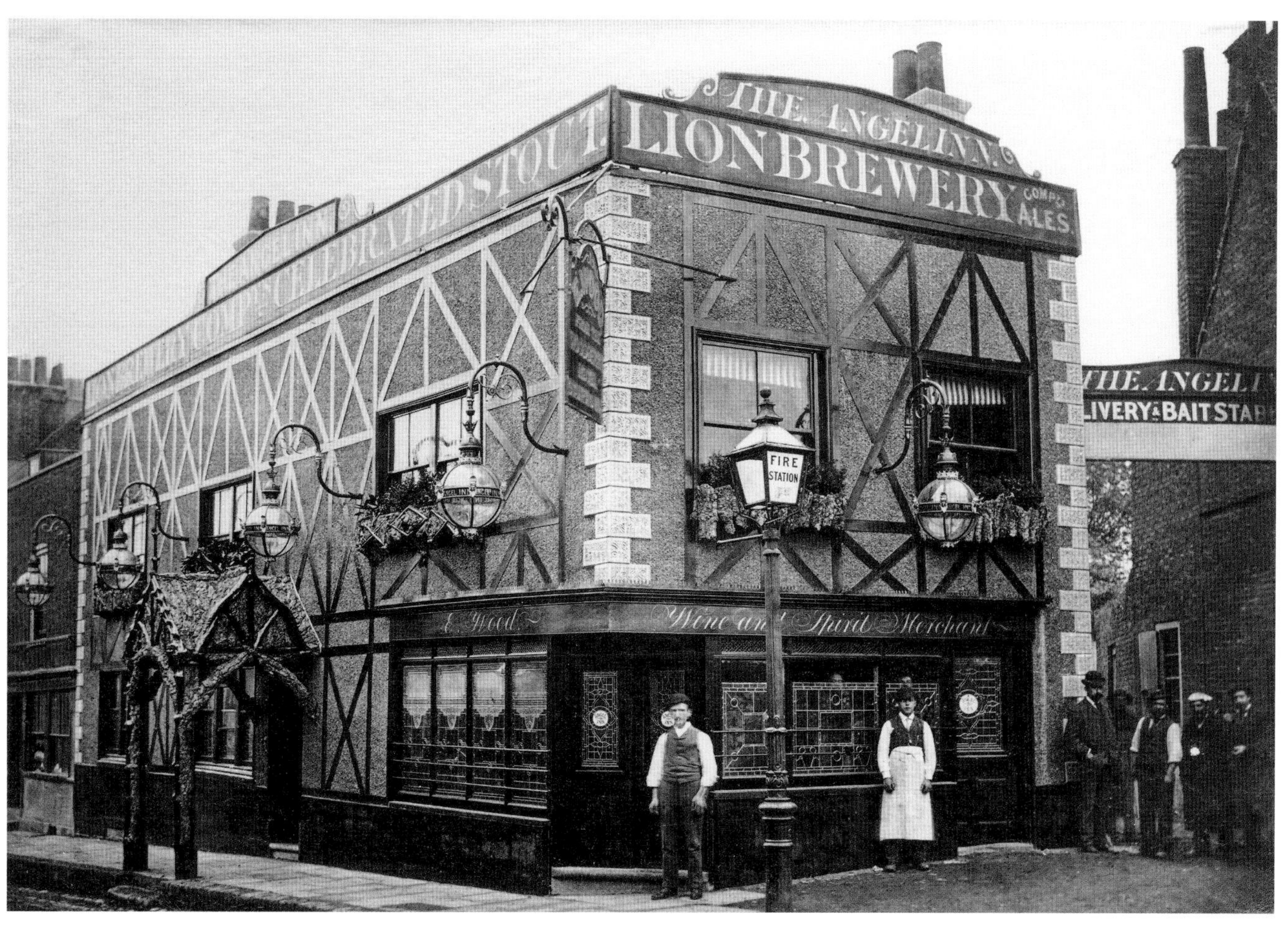

The Angel Inn was a coaching inn, but when railways made stagecoaches obsolete, inns had to adapt or die. In the 1880s, Lion Brewery added gas lamps and other ornamentations to transform the inn into a gin palace. *Highgate, 1882*

The Crown and The Greyhound were originally two separate pubs across the road from each other in Dulwich. The Crown catered to agricultural workers, while The Greyhound had a more middle-class clientele. In 1897, the two pubs were combined and became The Crown and Greyhound. *Dulwich, c.1905*

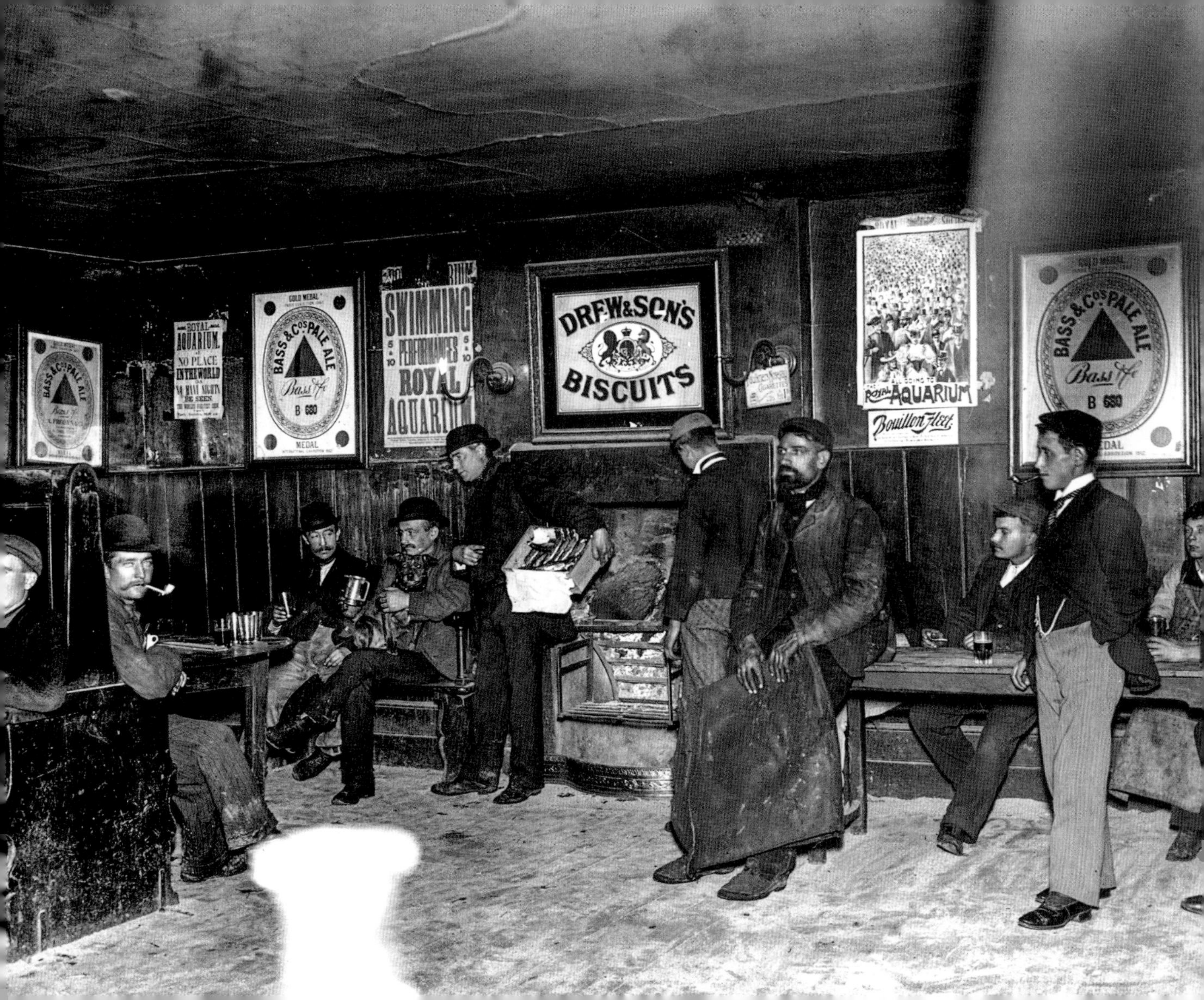
BASS & Co's PALE ALE
Bass & Co
ROYAL AQUARIUM
NO PLACE IN THE WORLD
SO MANY SIGHTS
BE SEEN
GOLD MEDAL
BASS & Co's PALE ALE
Bass & Co
B 680
MEDAL
SWIMMING
PERFORMANCES
ROYAL AQUARIUM
DREW & SON'S
BISCUITS
ROYAL AQUARIUM
Bouillon Fleet
GOLD MEDAL
BASS & Co's PALE ALE
Bass & Co
B 680

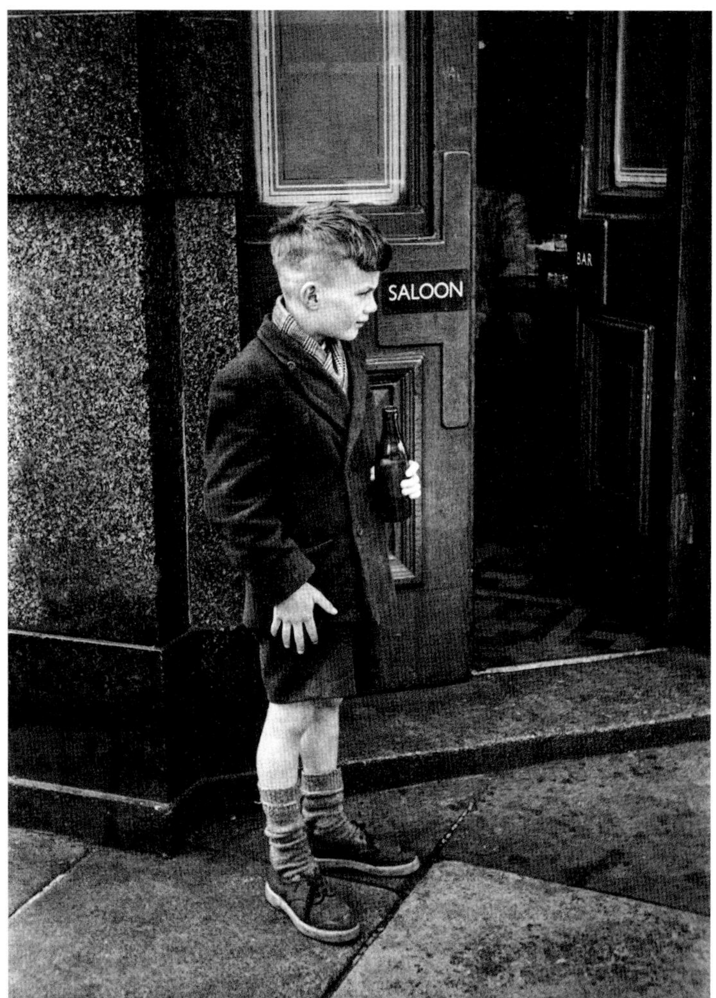

London, 1900

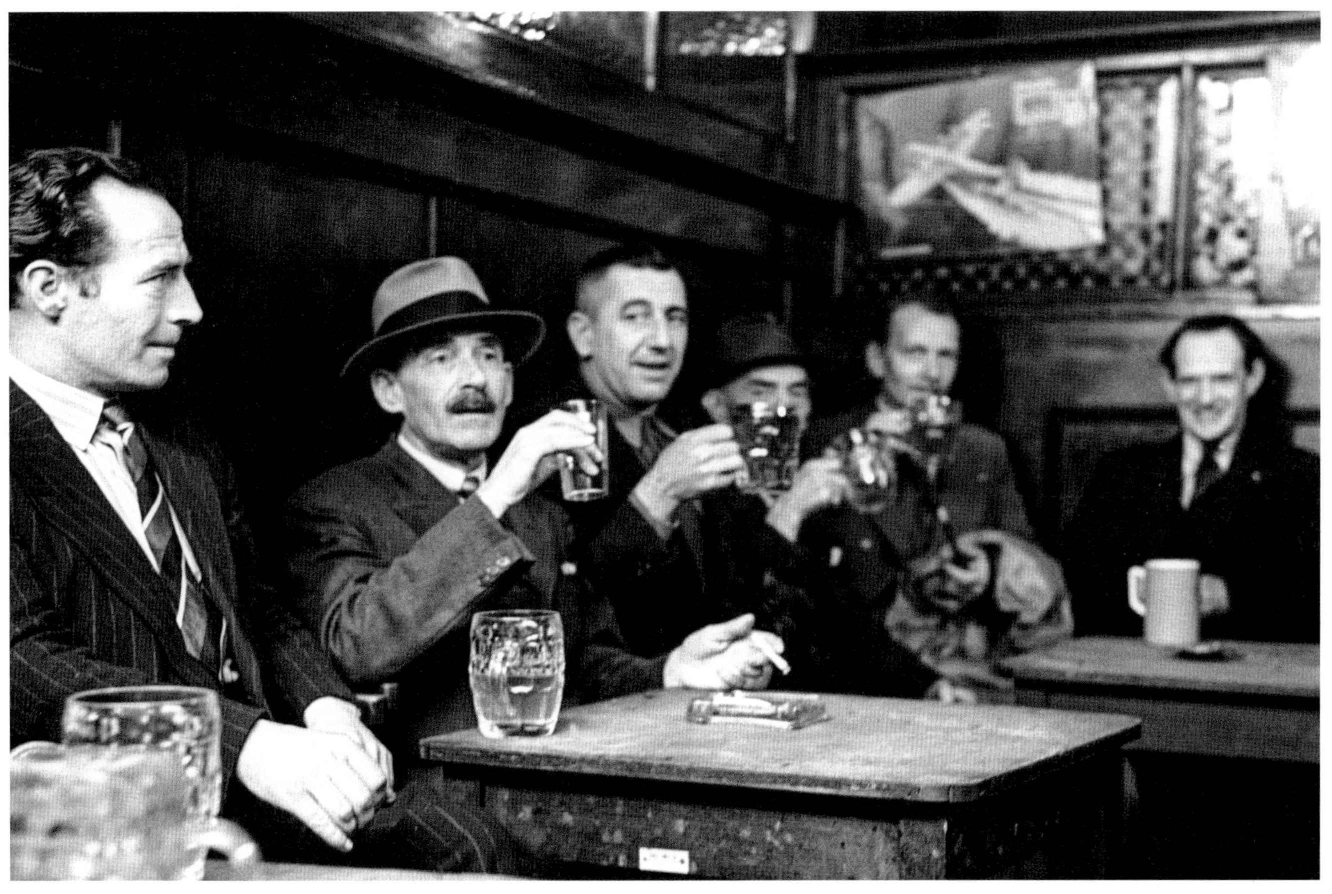

Traditionally cider was a drink for rural workers while beer was more urban.
It was quite unusual for London to have a dedicated cider house.
The Cider House (now demolished). *Maida Hill, c.1946*

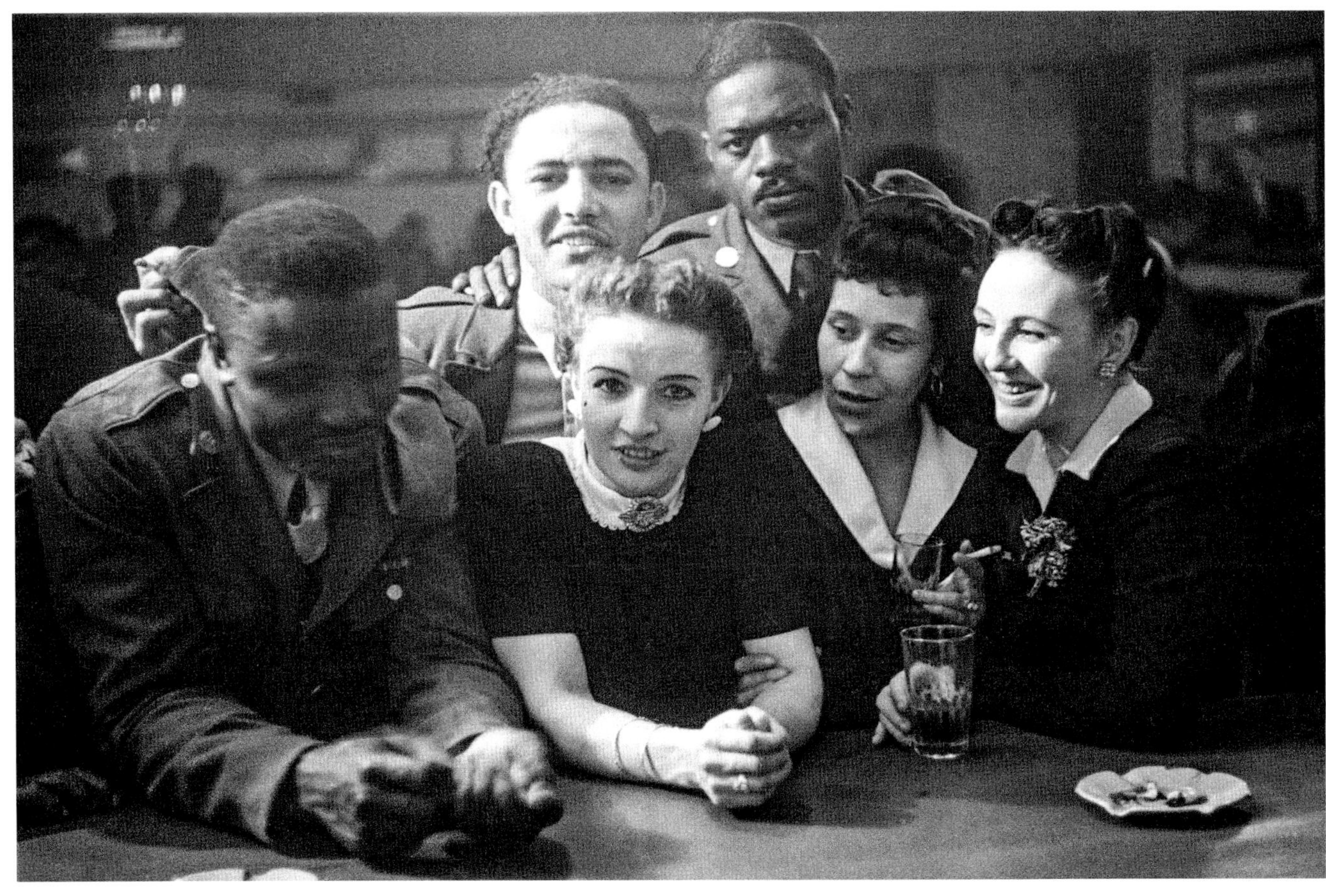

American troops during WWII. *London, 1943*

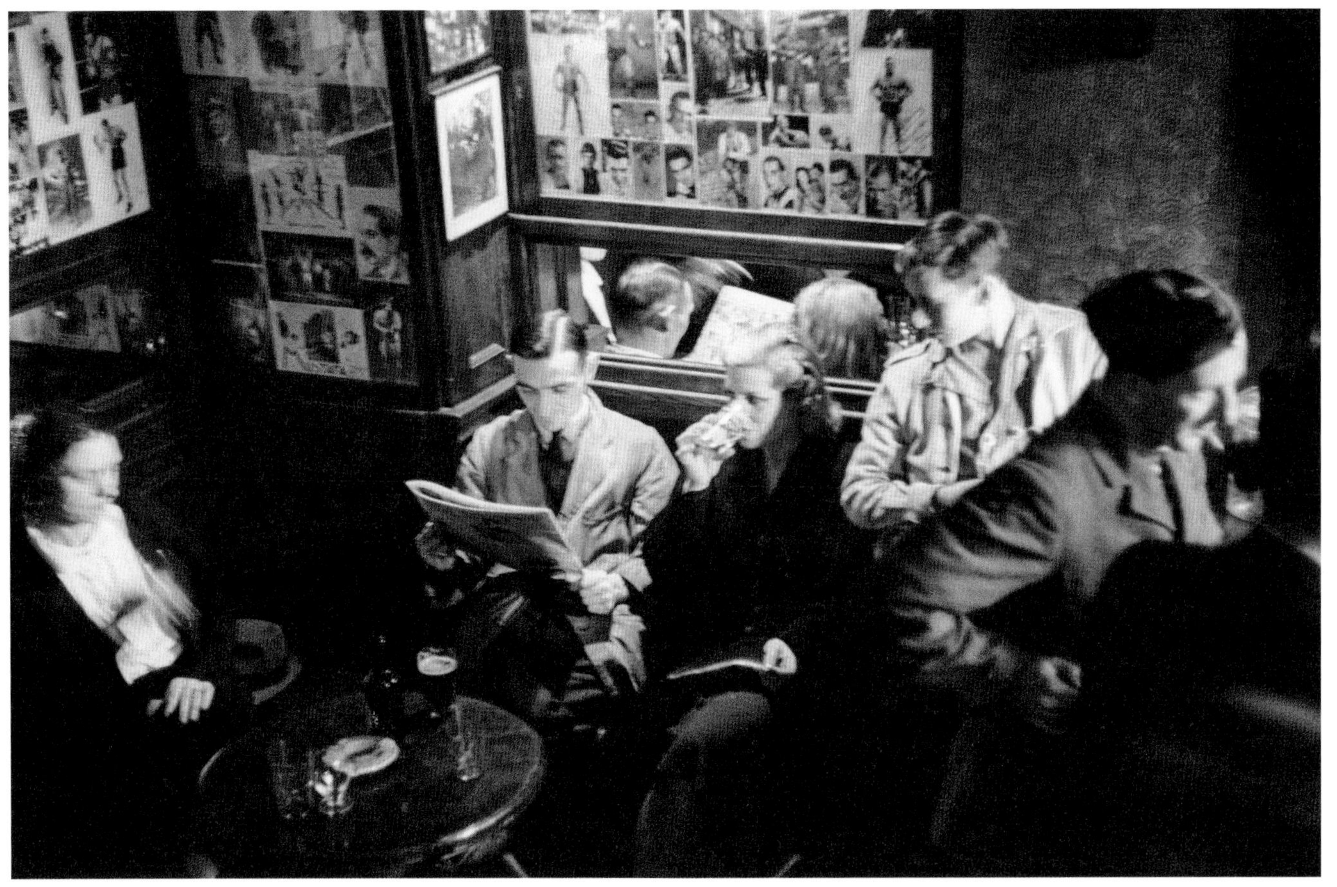

The French House. *Soho, 1941*

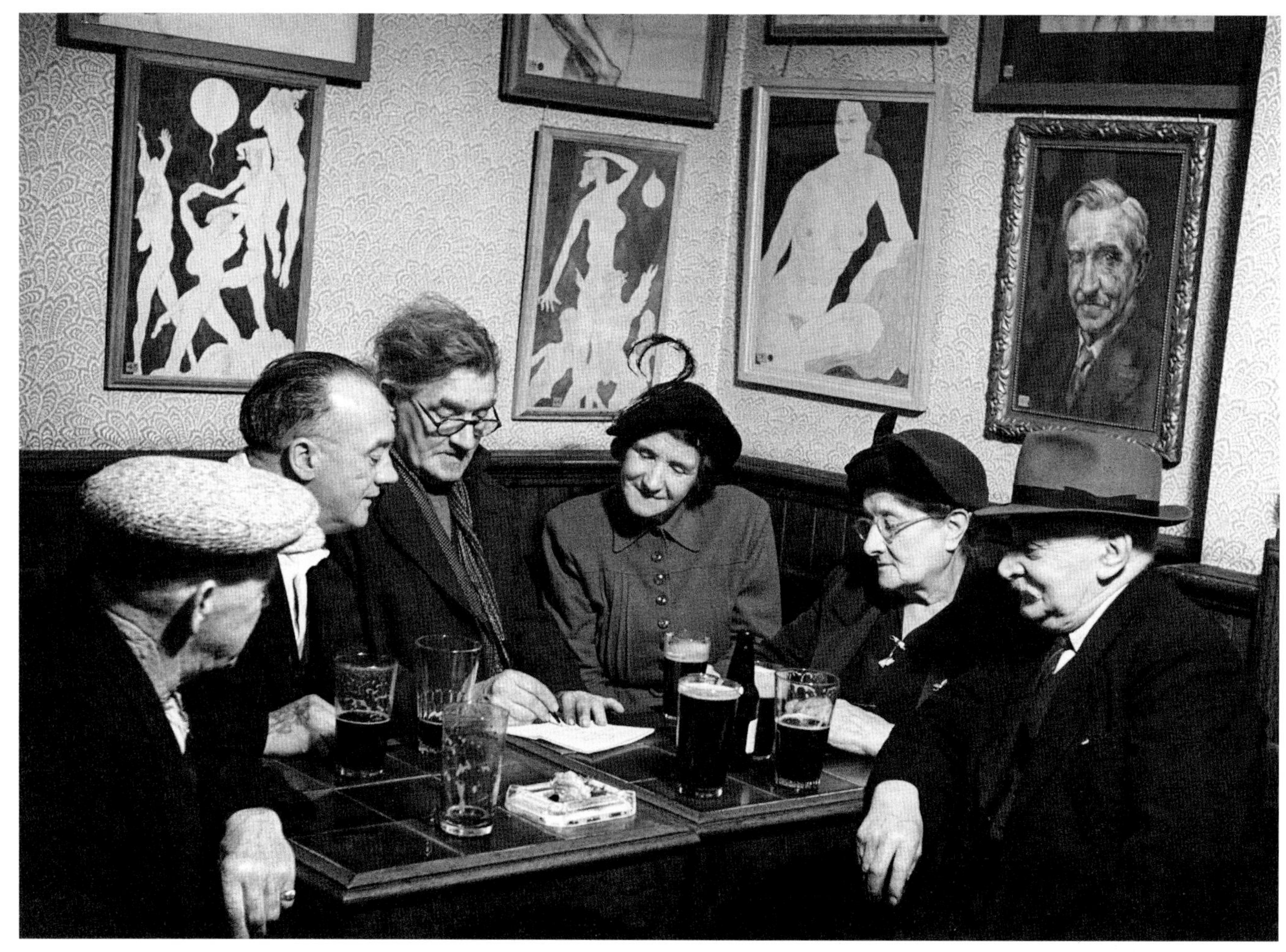

Painter and occultist Austin Osman Spare with friends. *London, 1953*

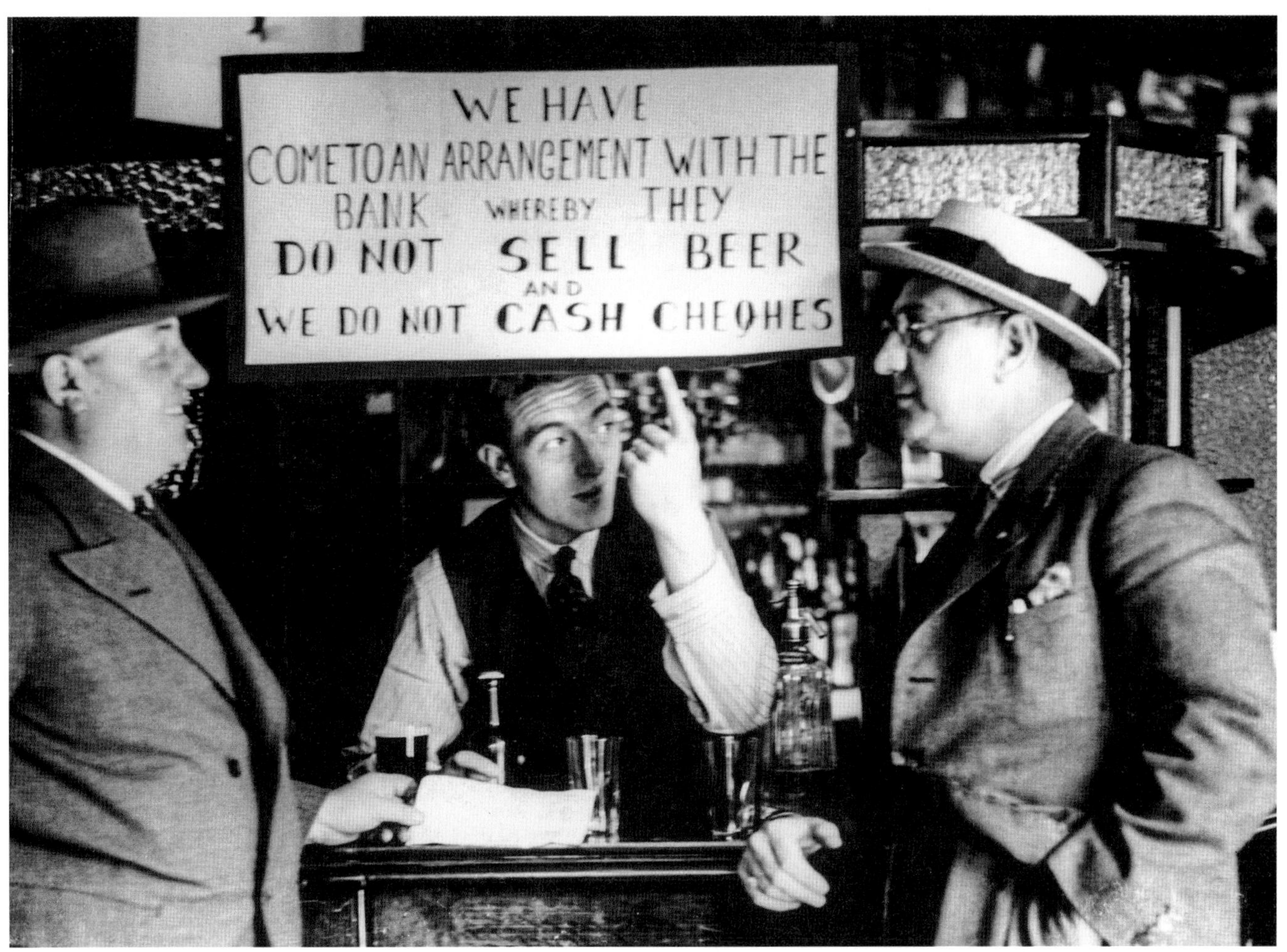

Landlord makes it clear that draughts, not overdrafts, are available behind the bar. *London*

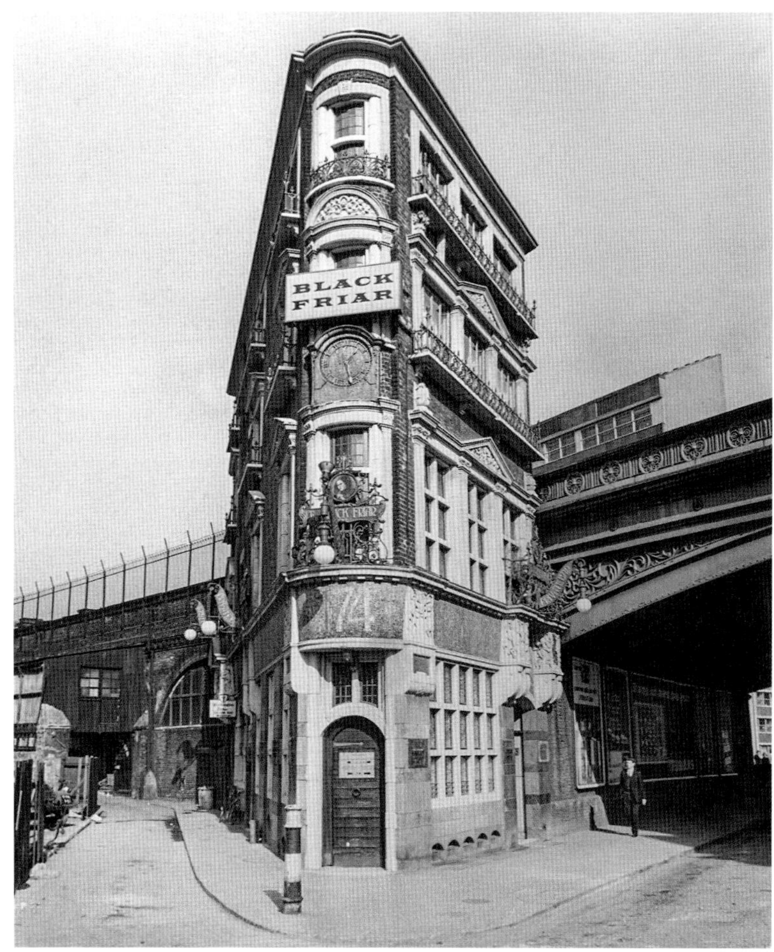

The Blackfrair is one of London's most distinctive pubs.
The eccentric interior, full of sculpture, was designed by
architect Herbert Fuller-Clark. *Blackfriars, 1966*

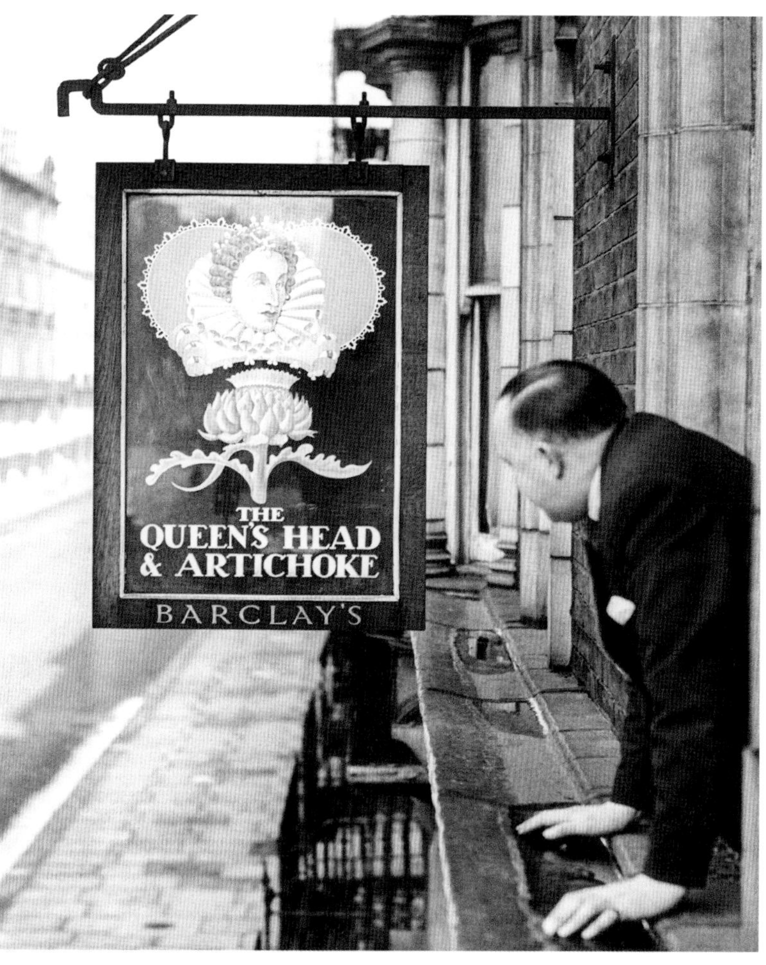

Pubs often have odd juxtapositions in their names, and a good story behind them. In this case, the pub was once owned by a royal gardener and named after a princess's favourite vegetable. *Near Regent's Park, 1953*

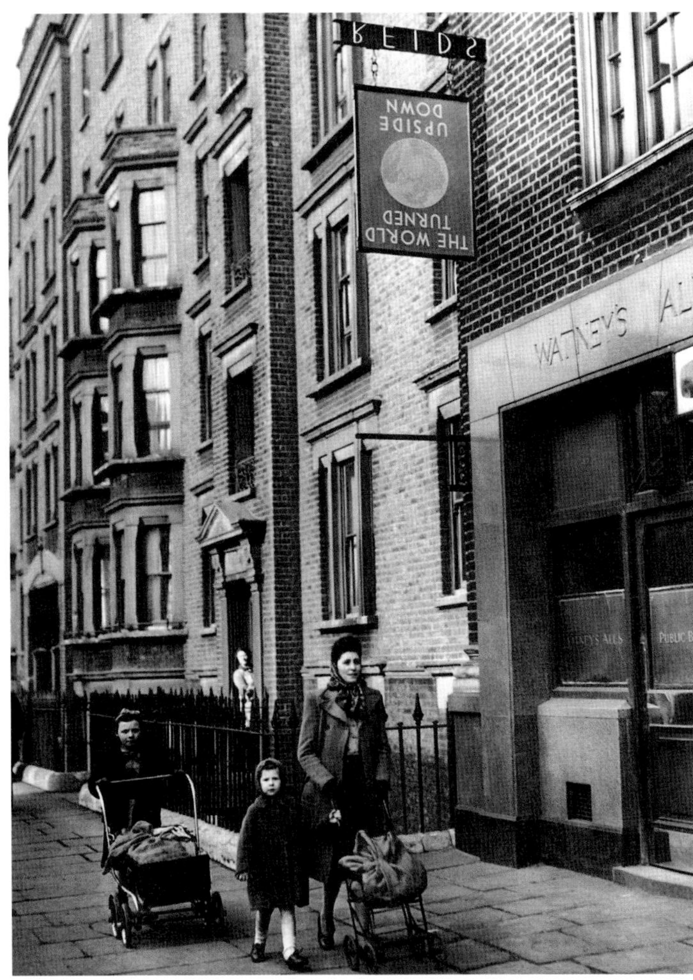

The World Turned Upside Down (now closed)
on the Old Kent Road. *Bermondsey, 1947*

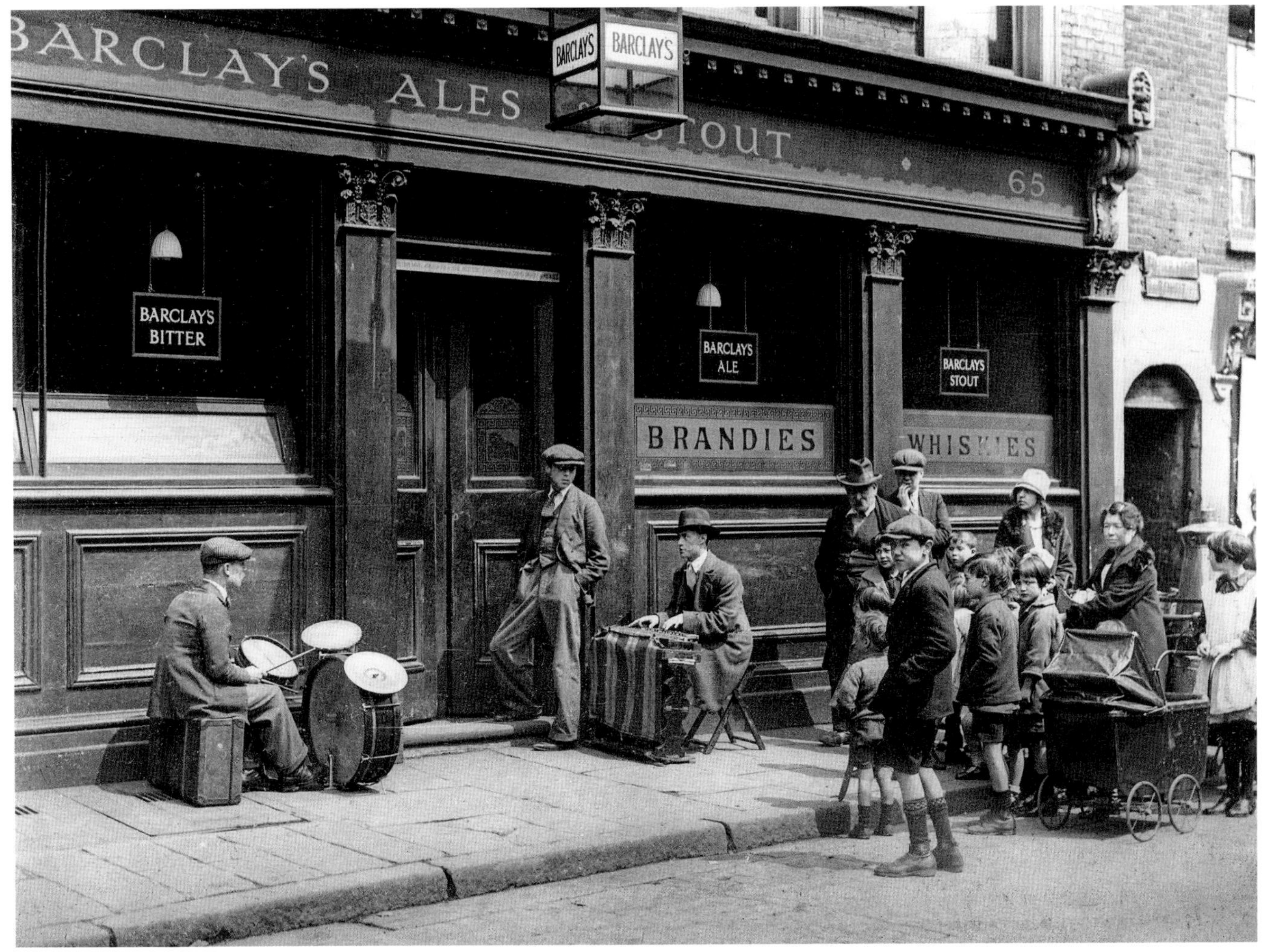

Street band playing in front of a pub. *London, c.1930*

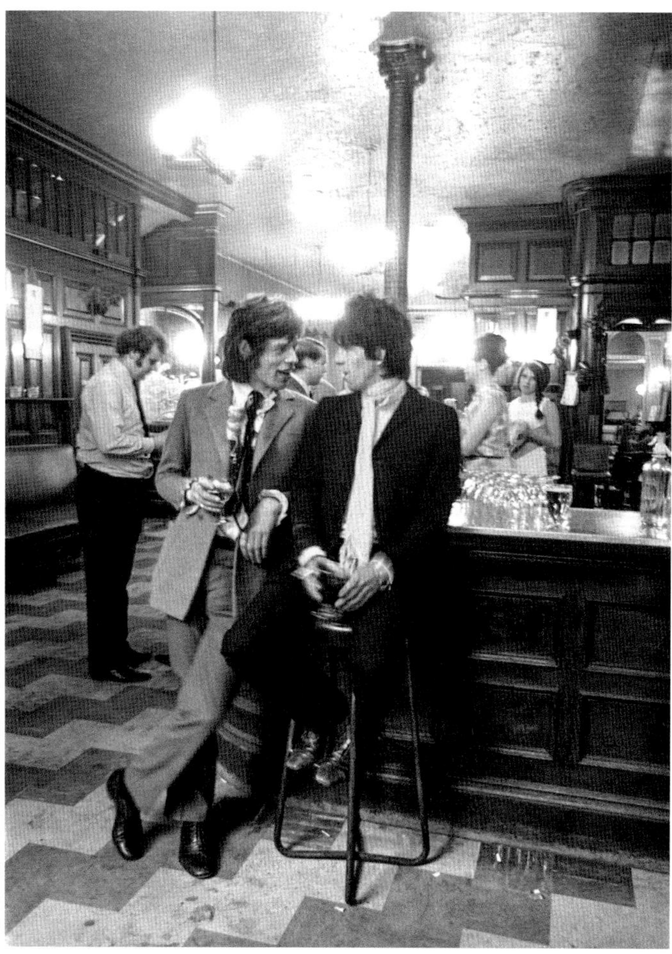

Keith Richards and Mick Jagger have a drink at The Feathers (now closed) near Fleet Street while out on bail after being arrested for drug possession. *City of London, 1967*

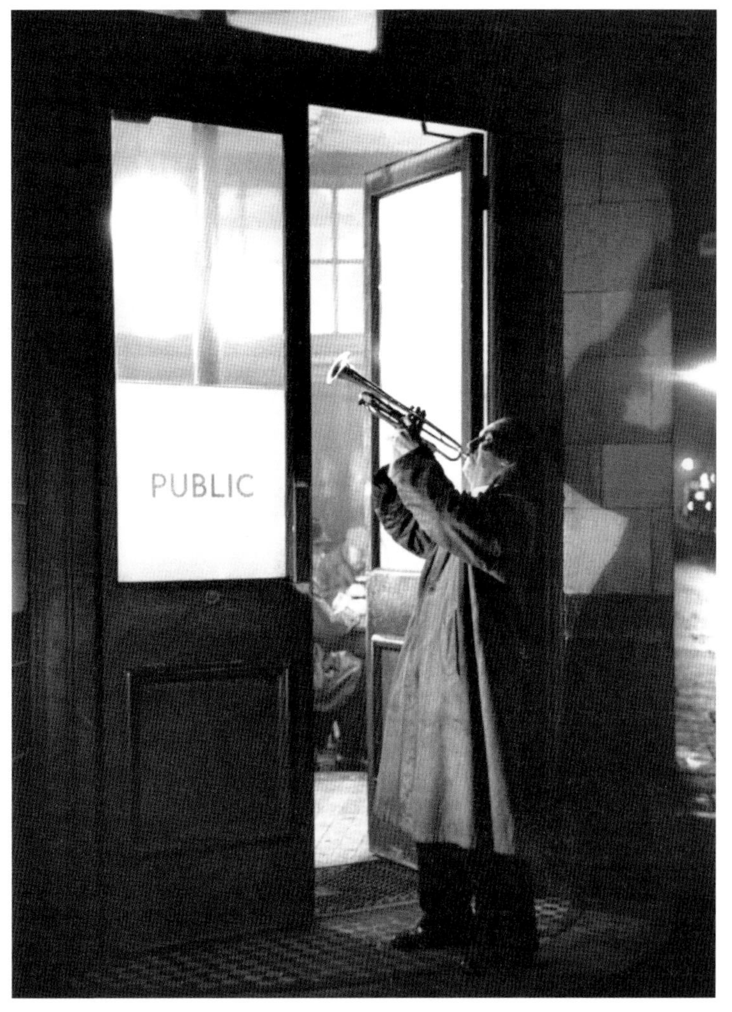

Street musician busks outside a pub. *Elephant and Castle, 1949*

Peggy Seeger playing at The Enterprise. Music has always been a feature of London pubs; countless acts from the Rolling Stones to Madness began their careers playing in pubs. Tomorrow's stars are probably there right now. *Covent Garden, c.1960*

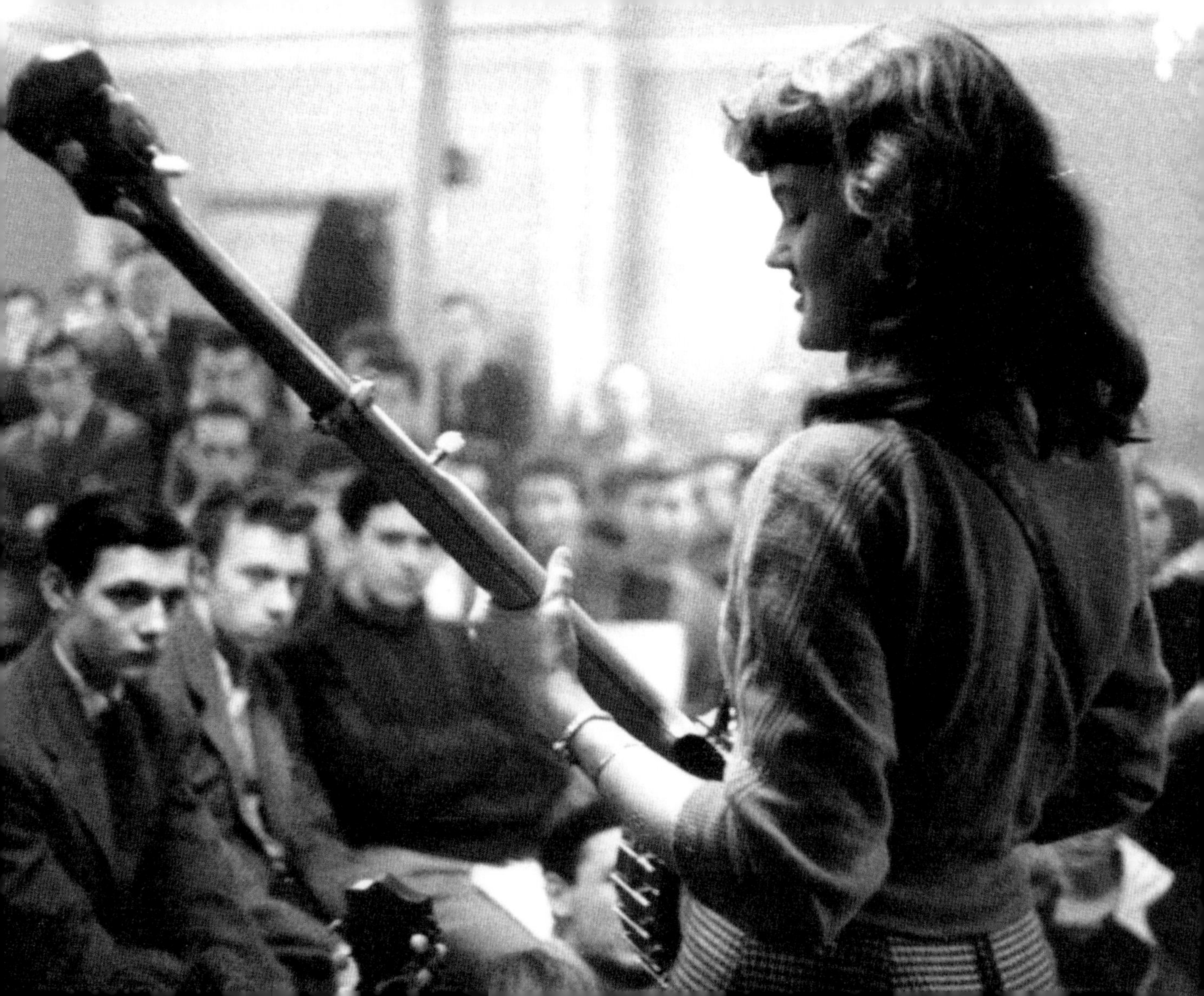

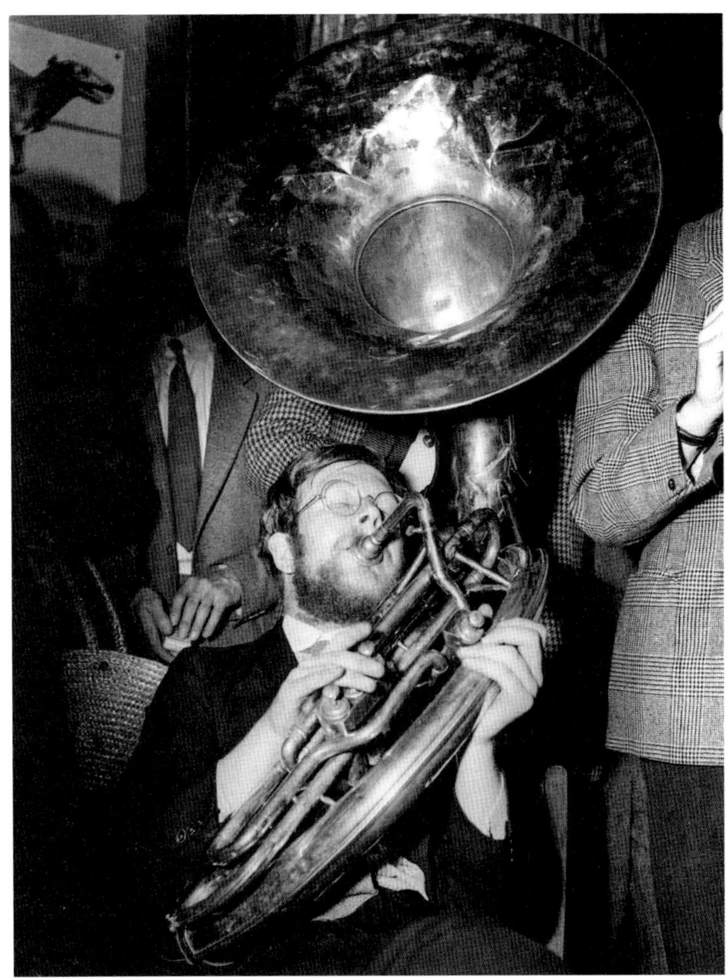

A member of the Fleet Street Jazz Club plays
the sousaphone at a pub. *London, 1954*

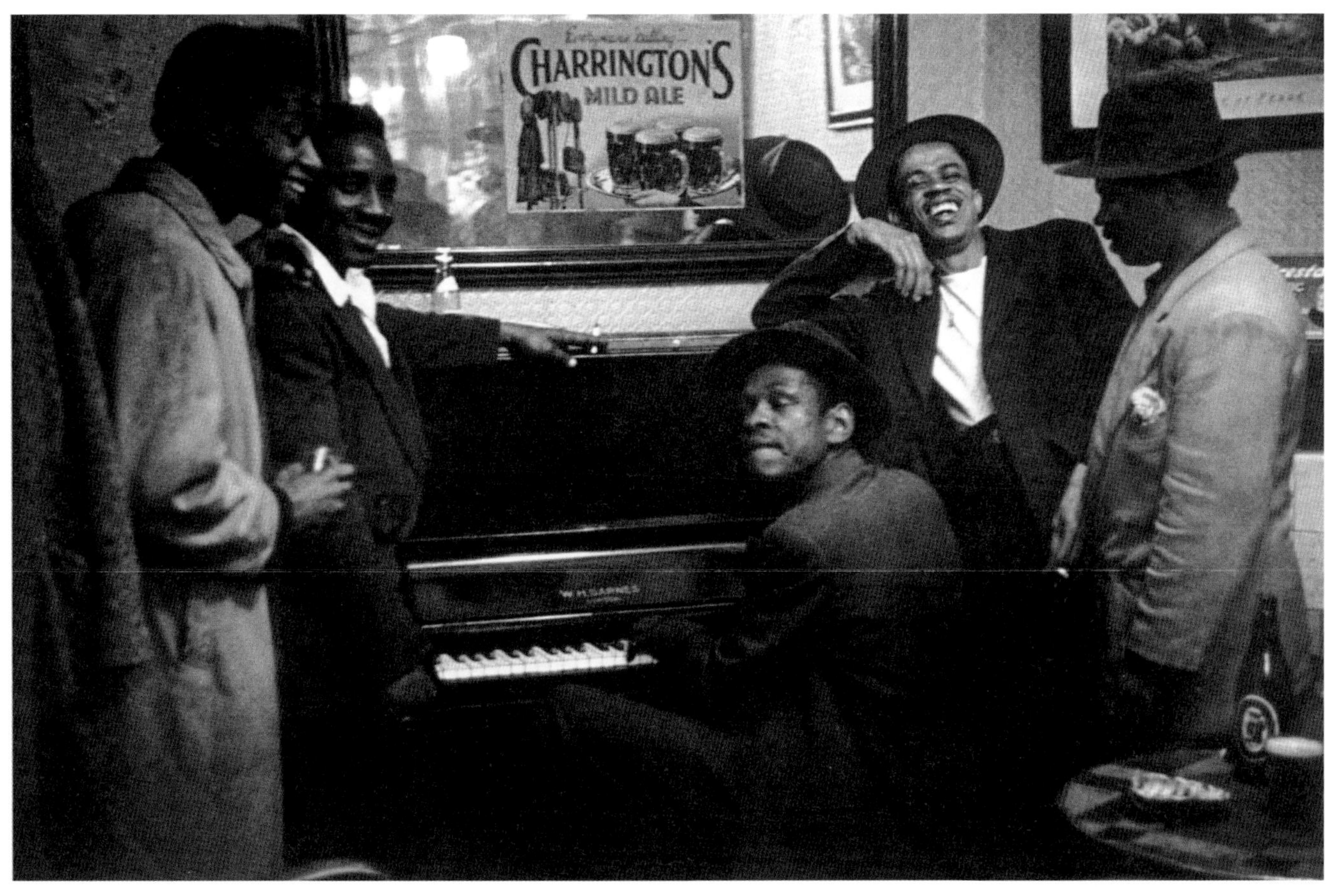

Stepney, 1949

A drag artist performs at the Royal Vauxhall Tavern,
South London's oldest surviving gay venue. *Vauxhall, c.1977*

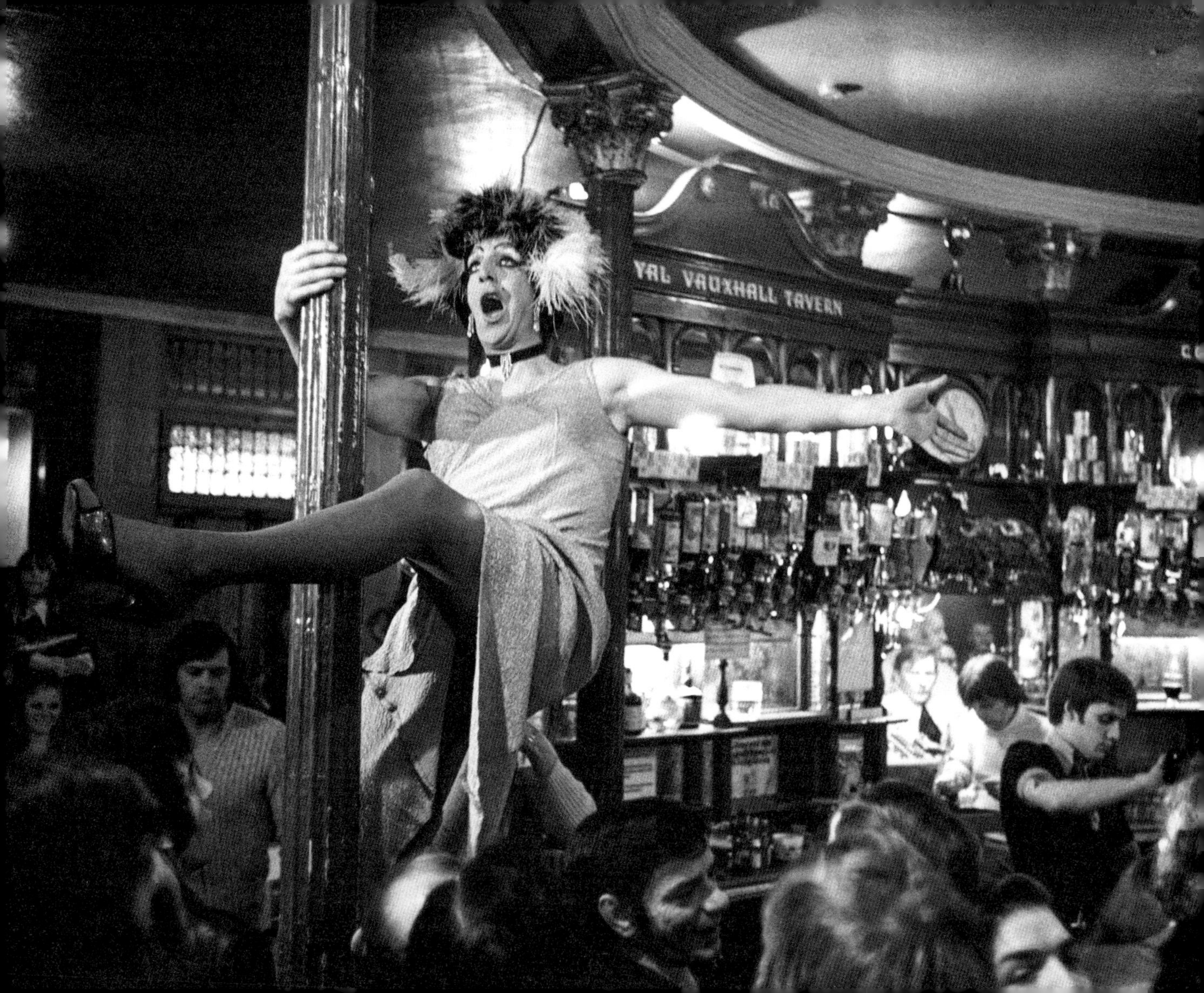
ROYAL VAUXHALL TAVERN

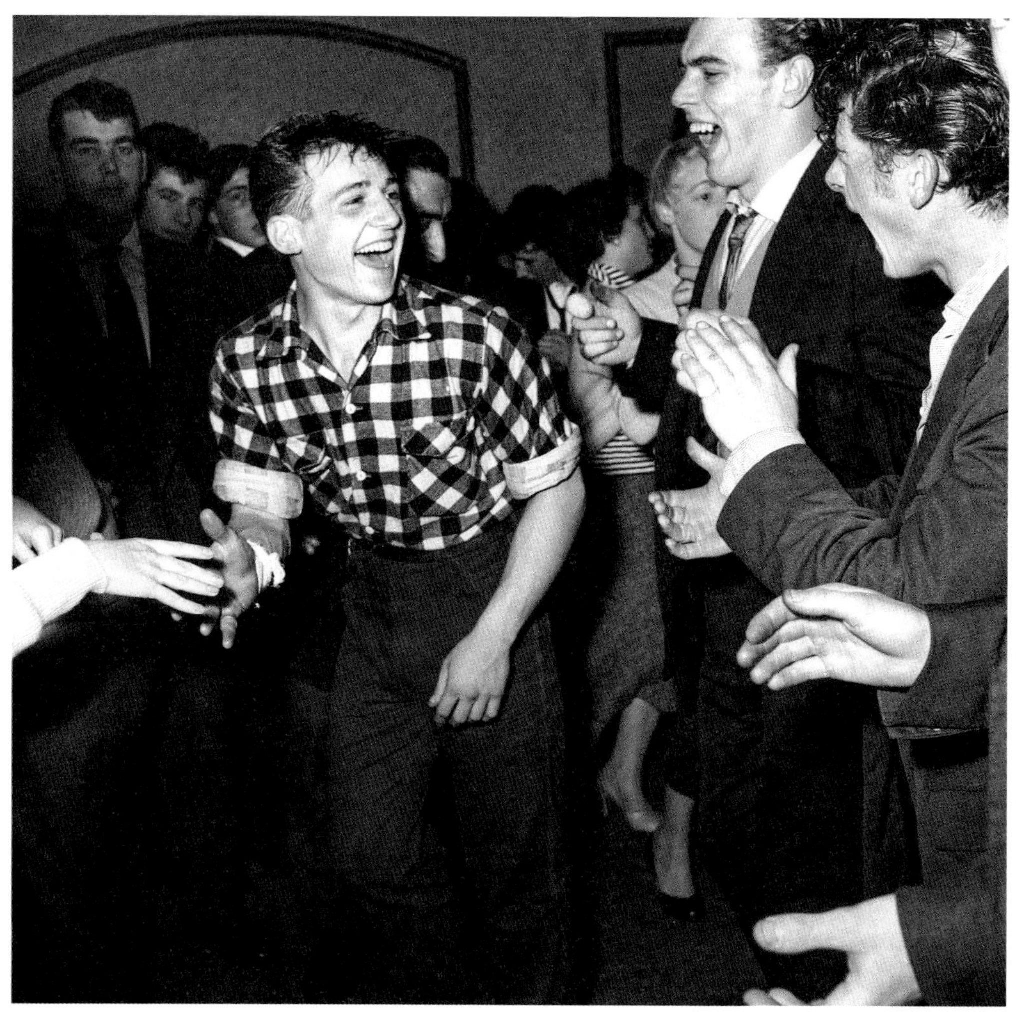

The Crown and Anchor, one of the first rock 'n' roll clubs in Britain. *Brixton, 1956*

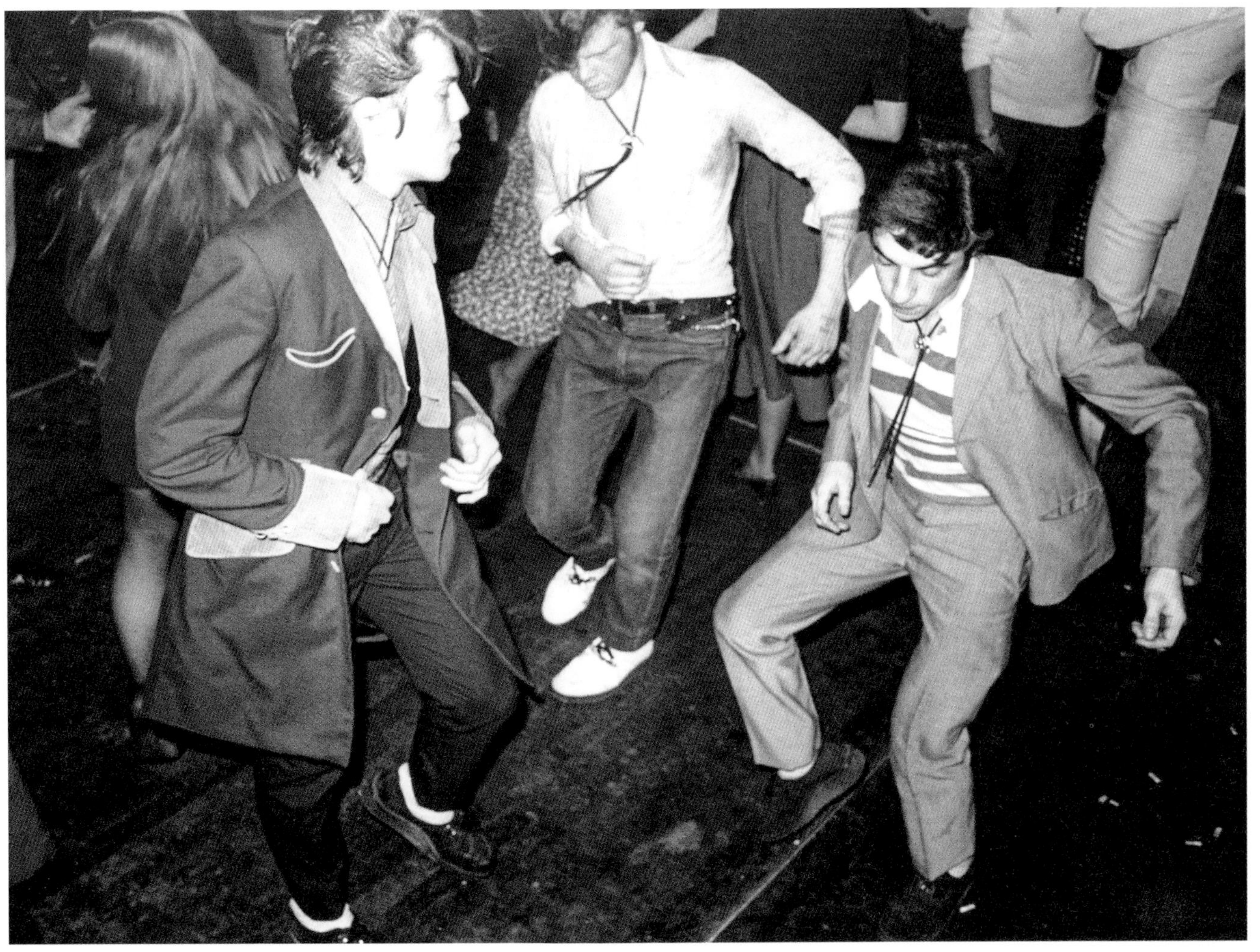

Teddy Boys at the Adam and Eve pub. *Homerton, 1976*

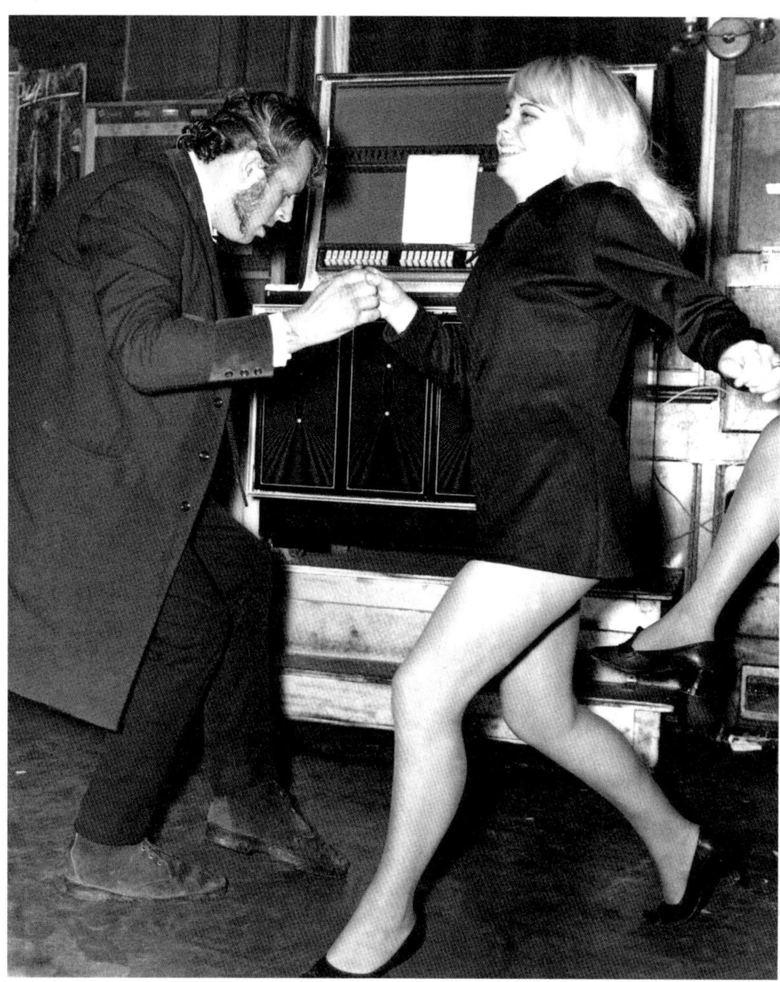

Teddy Boys return to dance at the Black Raven during
the subculture's revival (now closed). *Bishopsgate, 1970*

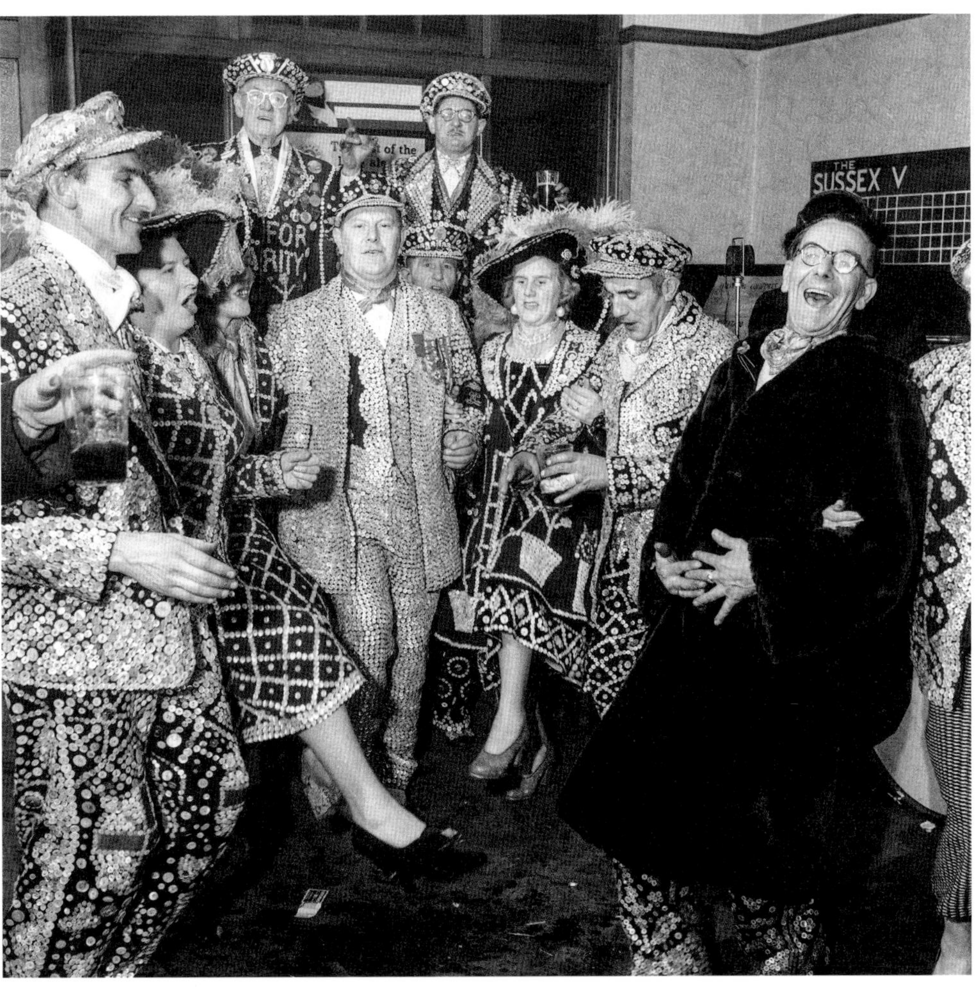

Pearly Kings and Queens at a pub. A beloved working-class tradition focused on raising money for hospitals, orphanages and other charities. *Hackney, 1955*

Sailors from the Naval Reserve enjoying a drink
while the threat of war looms. *London, 1939*

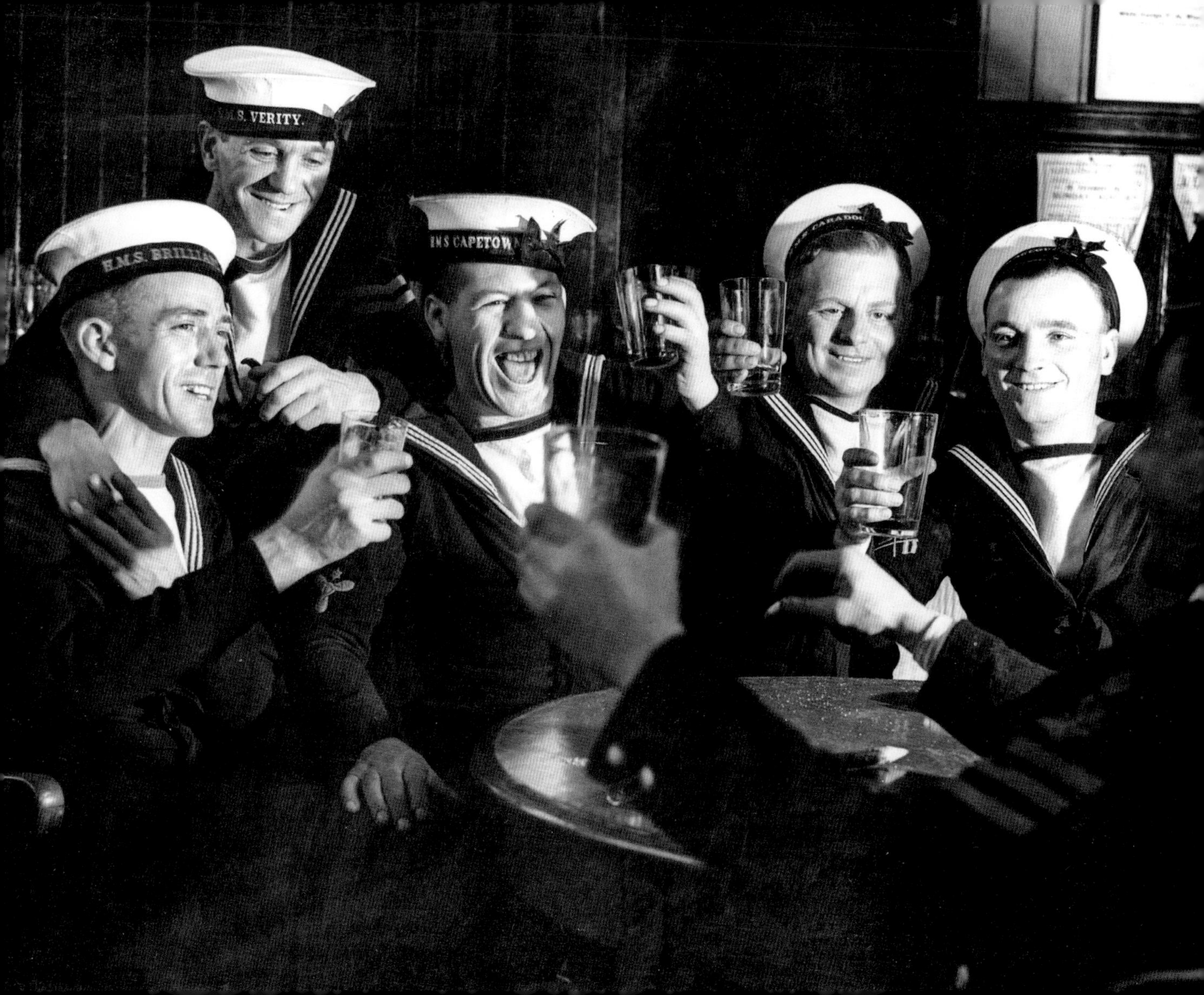
H.M.S. VERITY.
H.M.S. BRILLIA
H.M.S CAPETOW
CARADO

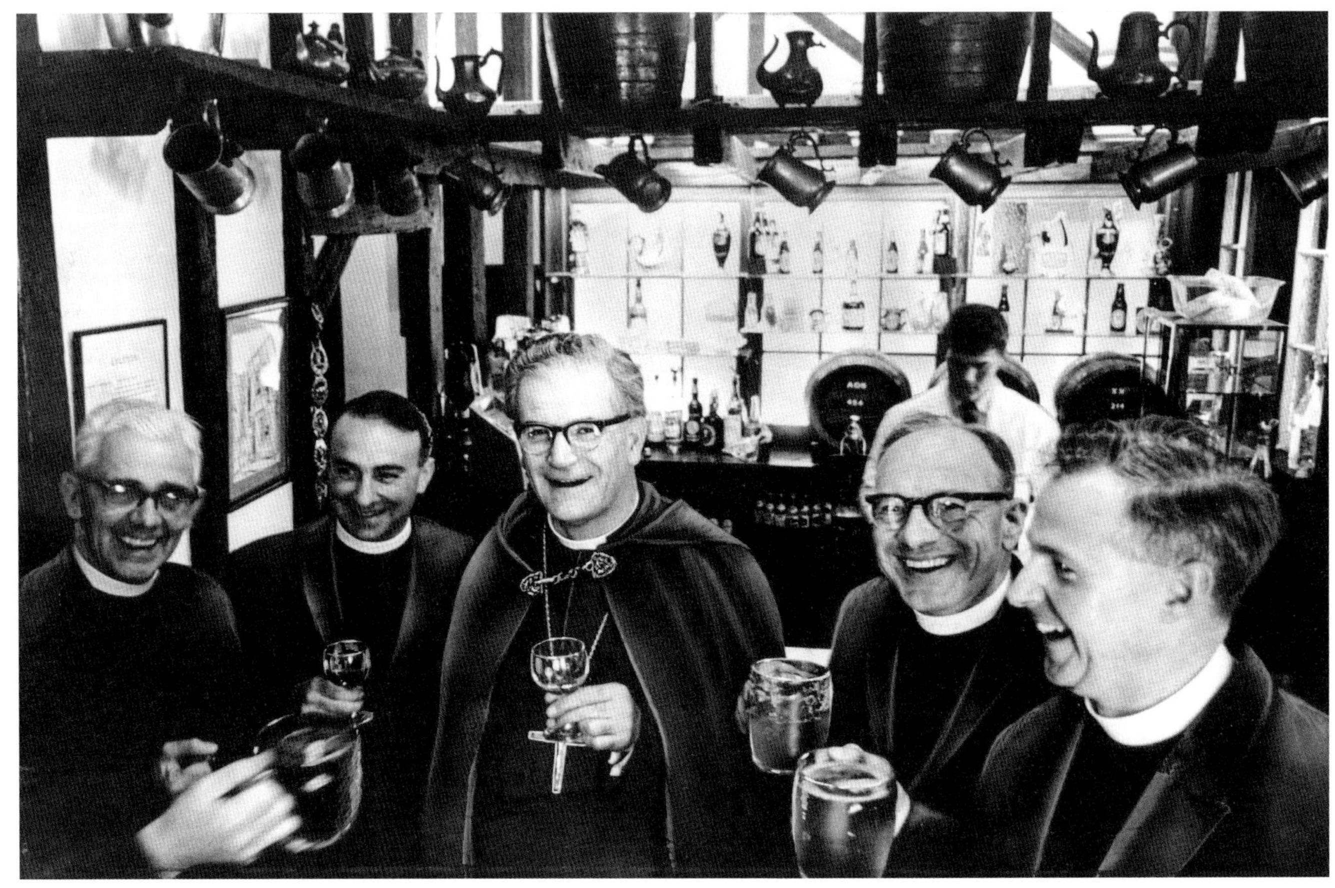

Newly-appointed clergymen drink with the
Bishop of Southwark at a pub. *Southwark, c.1965*

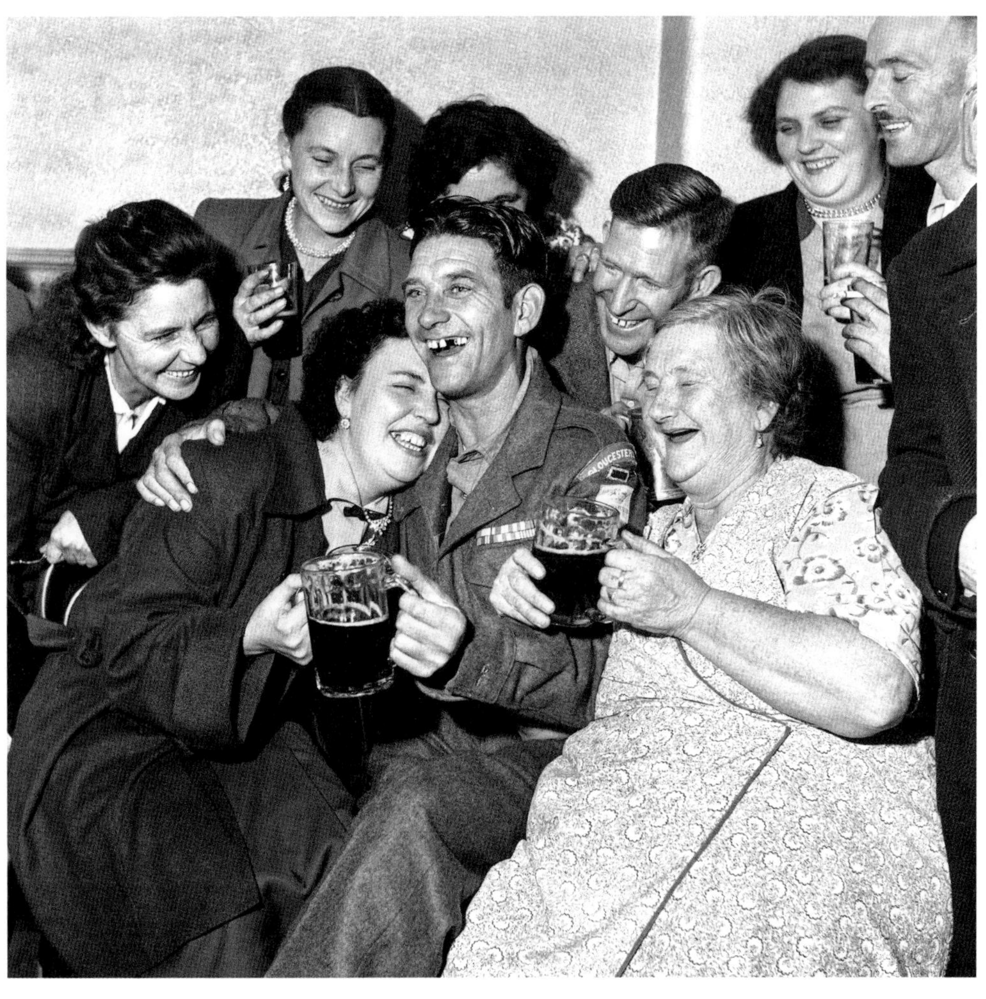

Private Thomas Nugent celebrates finally returning home from a PoW camp in Korea. *Edmonton, 1953*

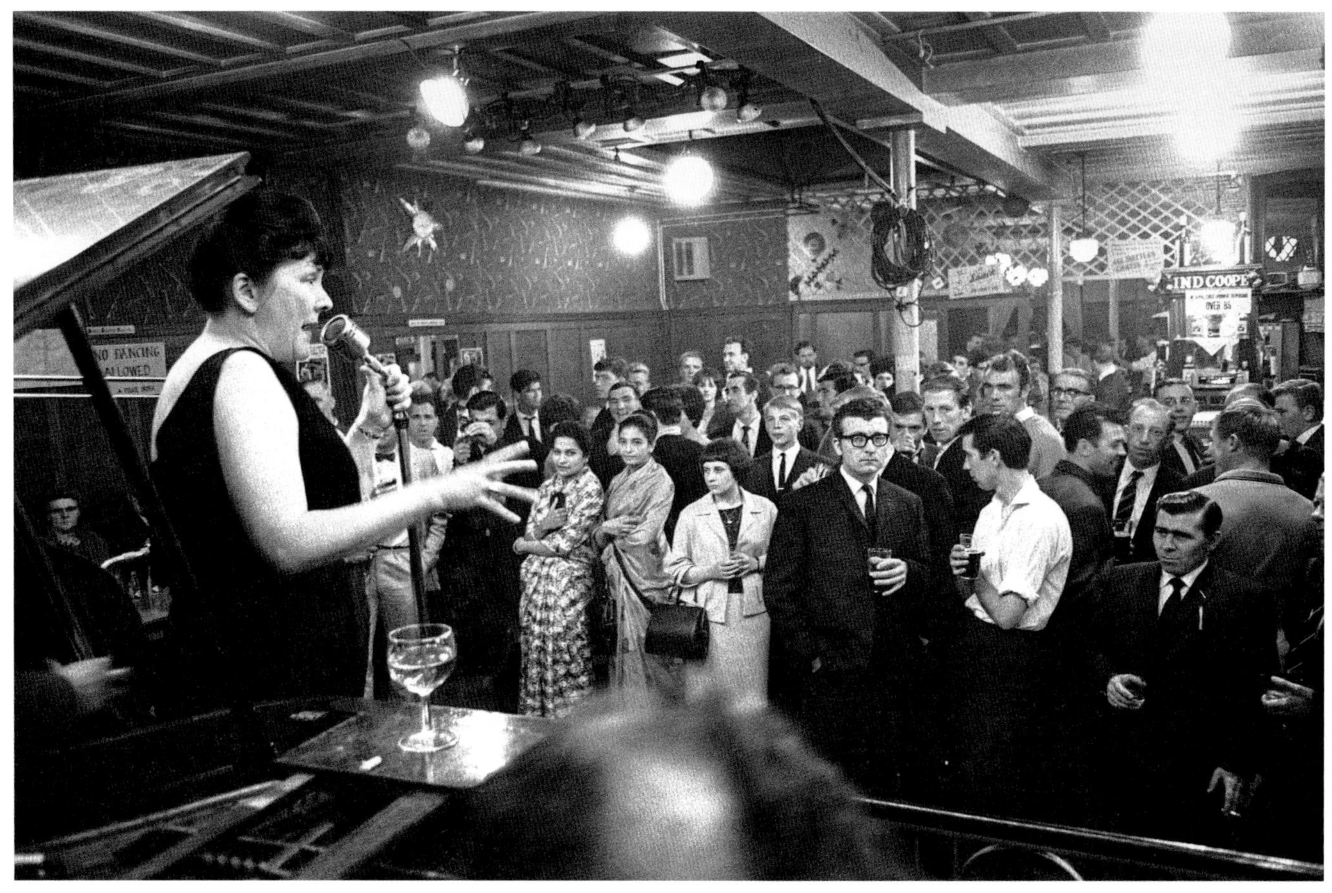

Cabaret singer at a pub on a Saturday night. Singing became so popular that some pubs sported purpose-built concert rooms. In male-dominated venues, the Saturday night 'turn' was a chance for wives and girlfriends to come along. *East End, 1963*

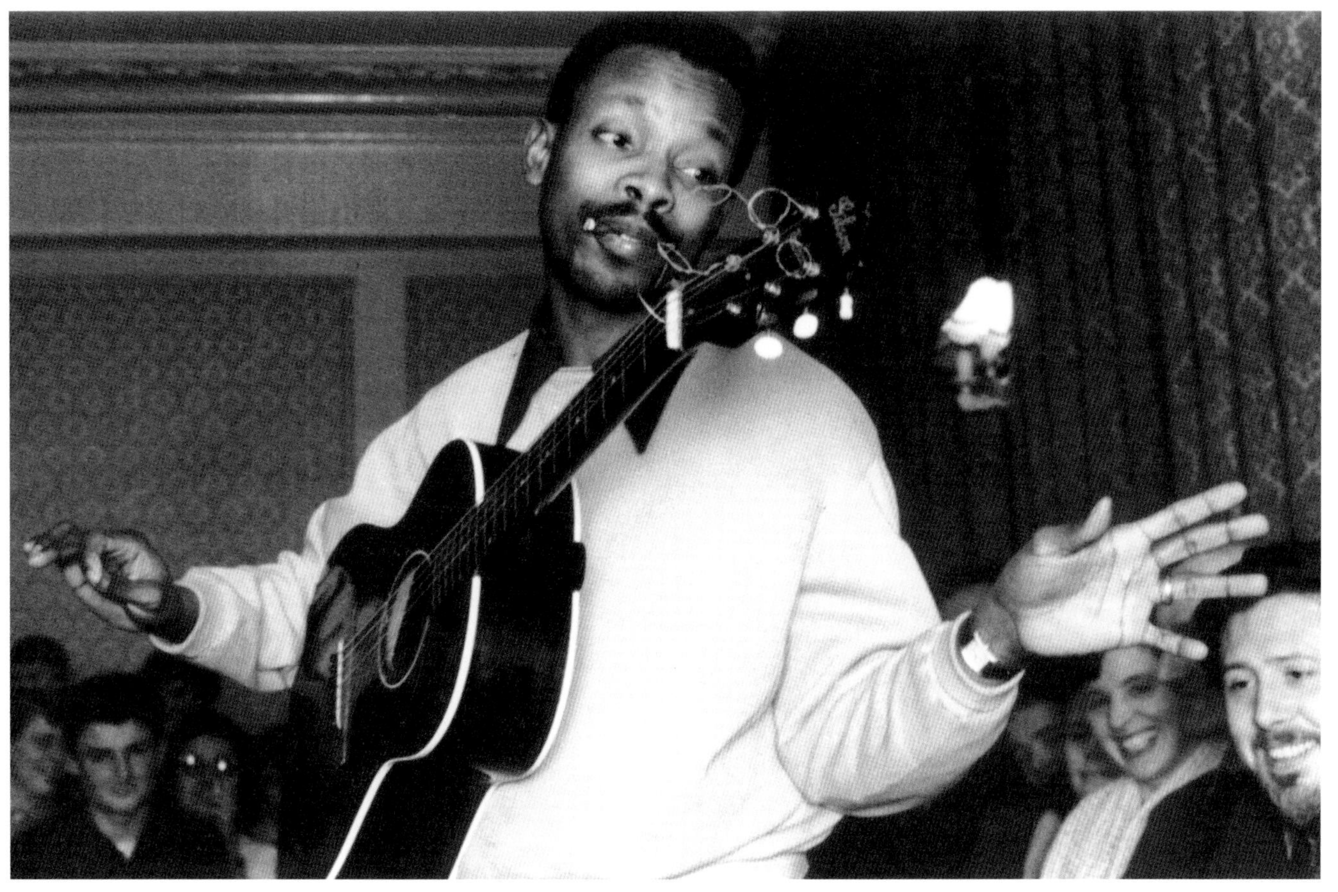

Fitzroy Coleman and Ewan MacColl at The Enterprise. *Covent Garden, c.1960*

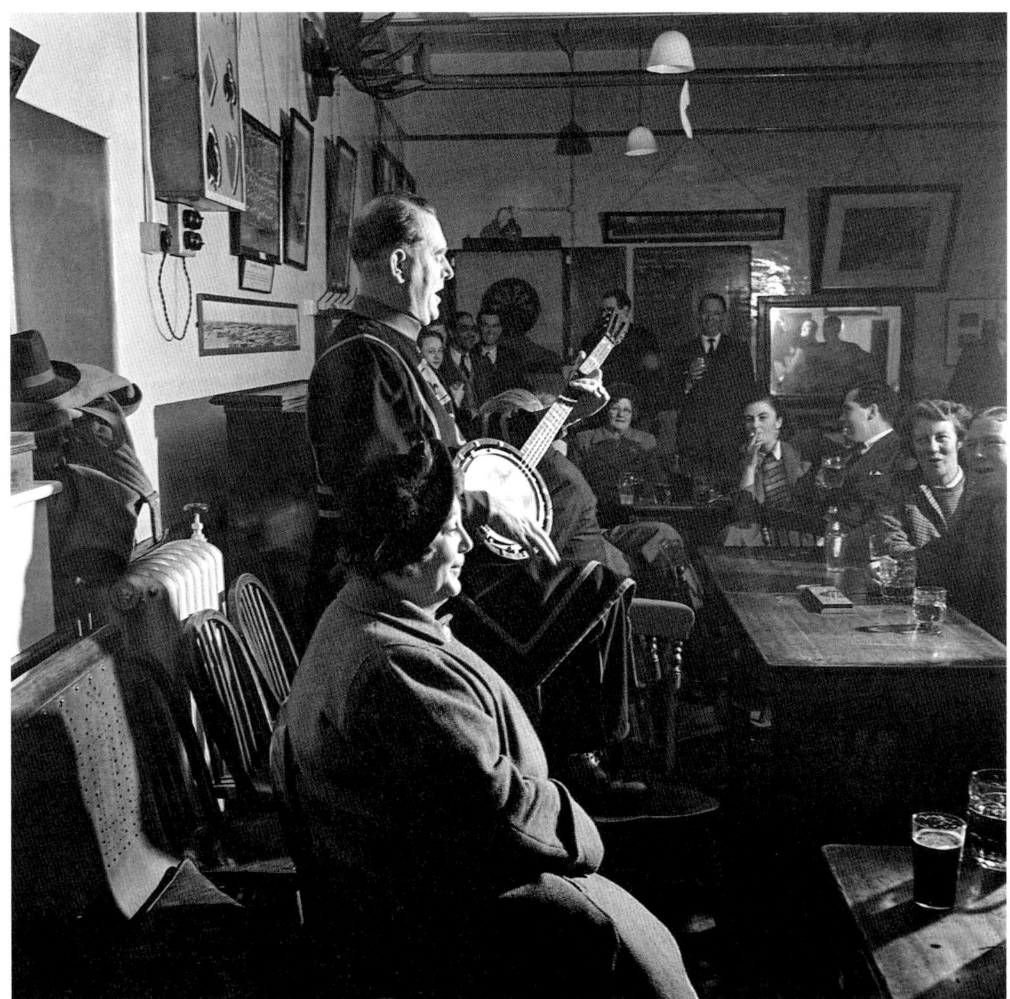

Tower Hill, 1951

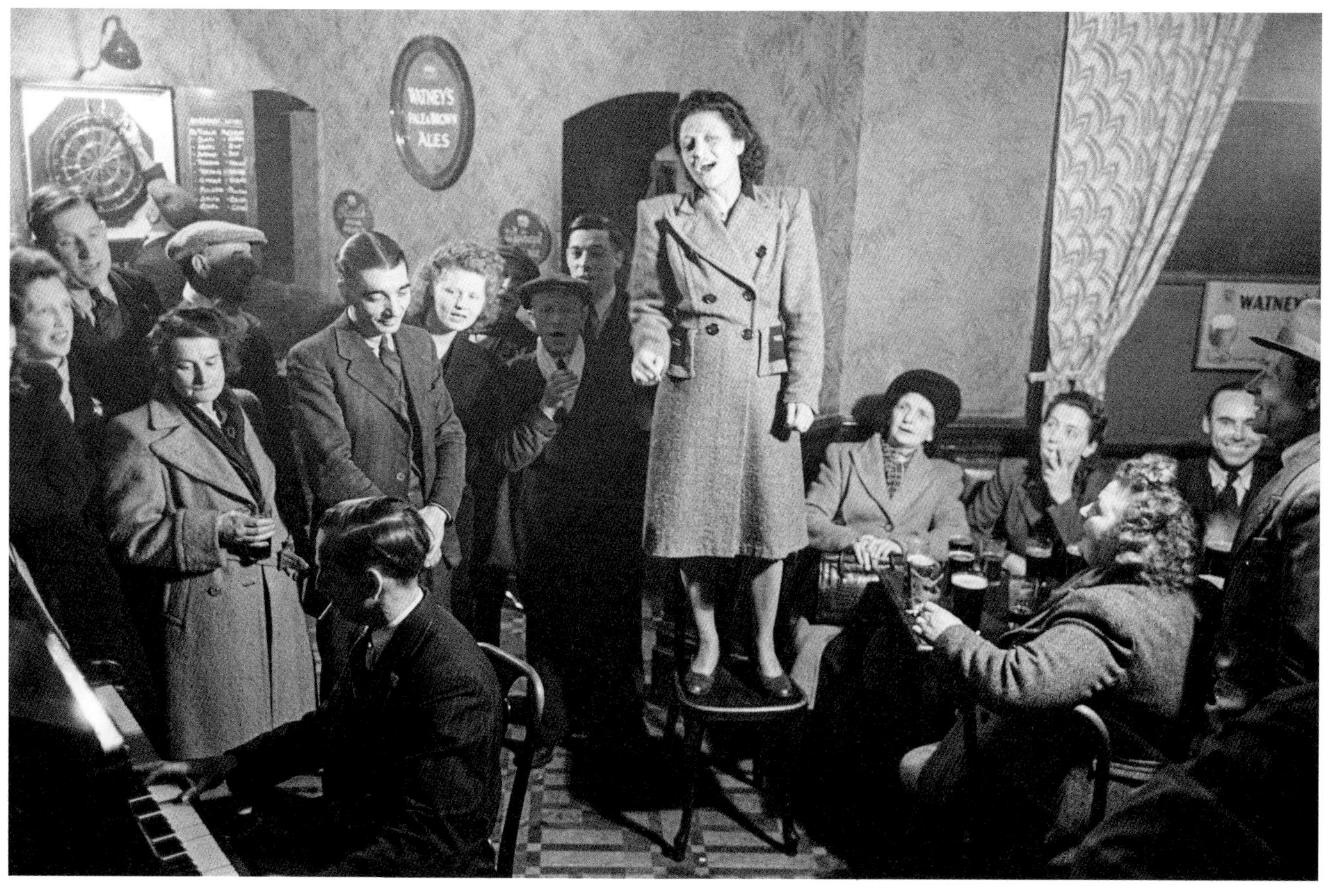

Pub singing began with the 'free and easy', with regular 'turns' getting up and doing their party piece in front of friends. The Crown. *Southwark, 1947*

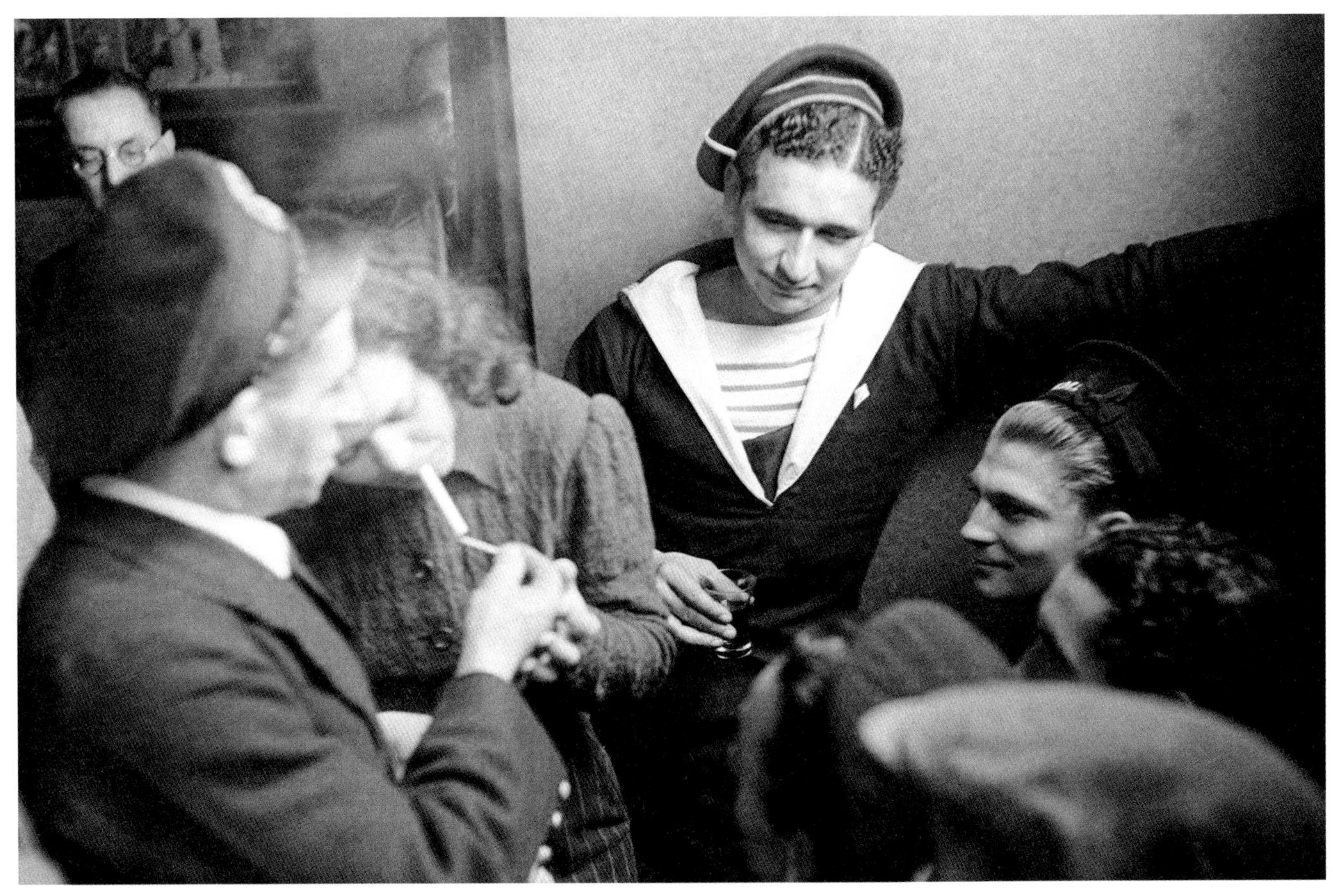

Sailors of Free France (serving under the French government-in-exile, during Nazi occupation) at The French House. *Soho, 1941*

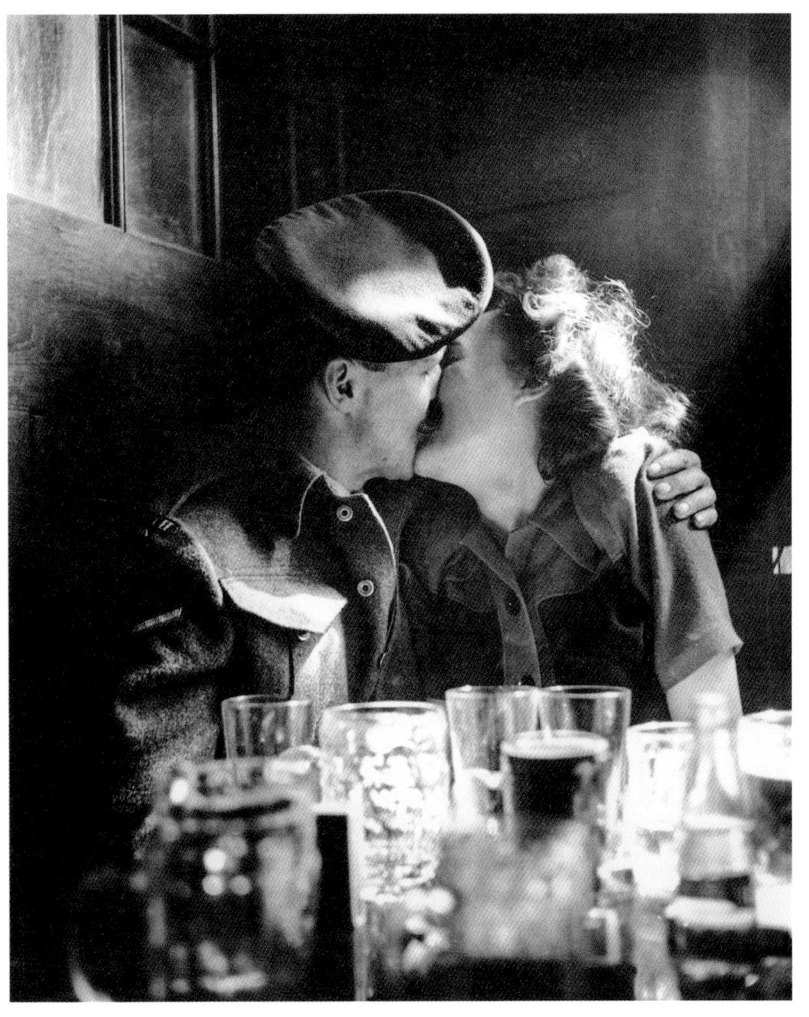

V-E Day at a pub. *London, 1945*

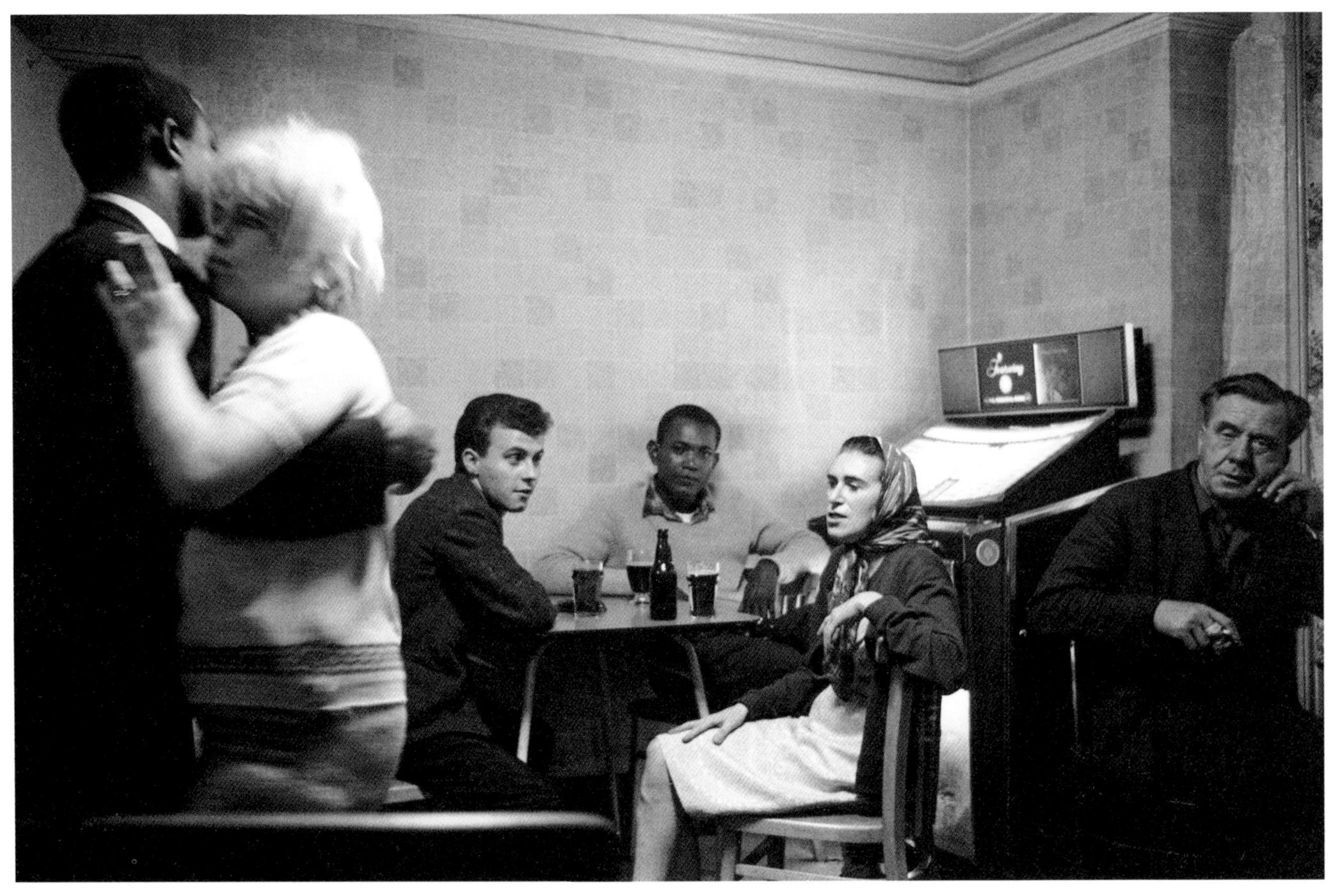

The jukebox was an increasingly popular fixture from the 1950s onwards, allowing drinkers to create their own soundtracks. *London, 1966*

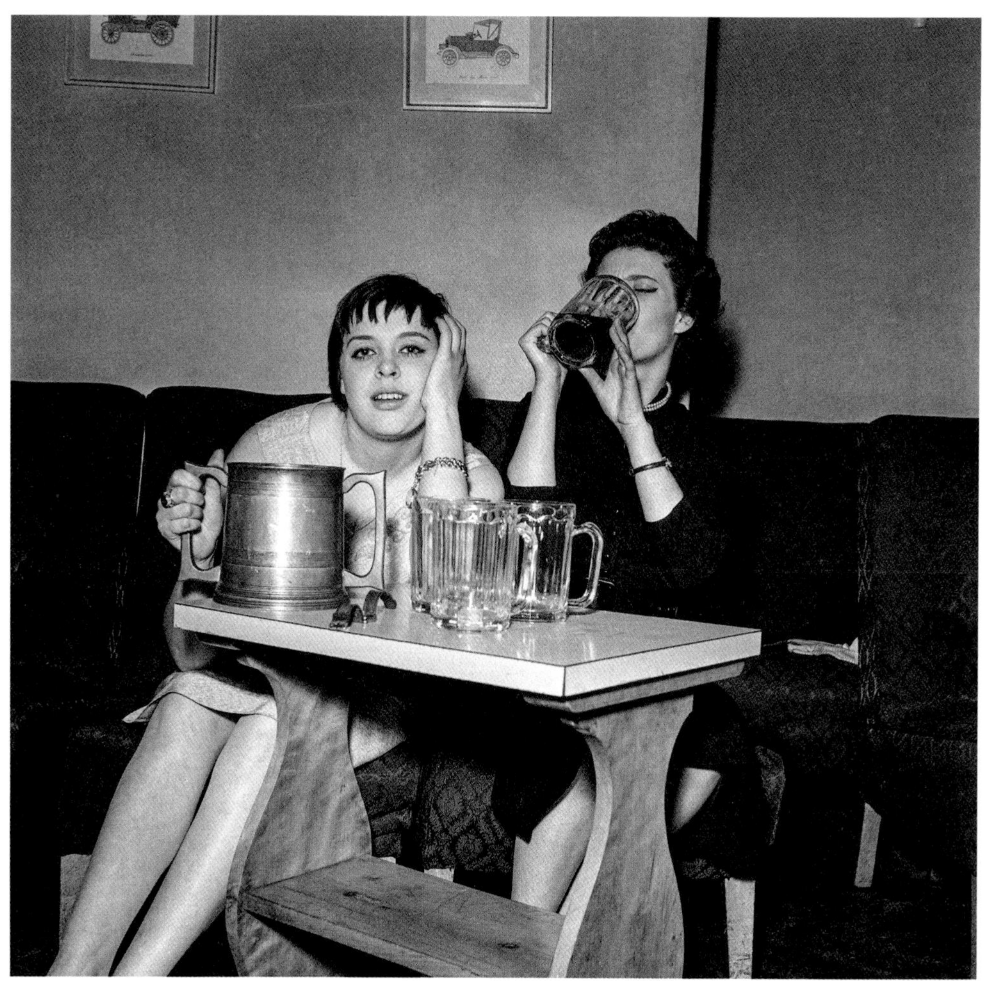

A beer drinking contest. The winners, pictured here, drank a yard and
a half of beer (over three pints) in two minutes. *Mayfair, 1957*

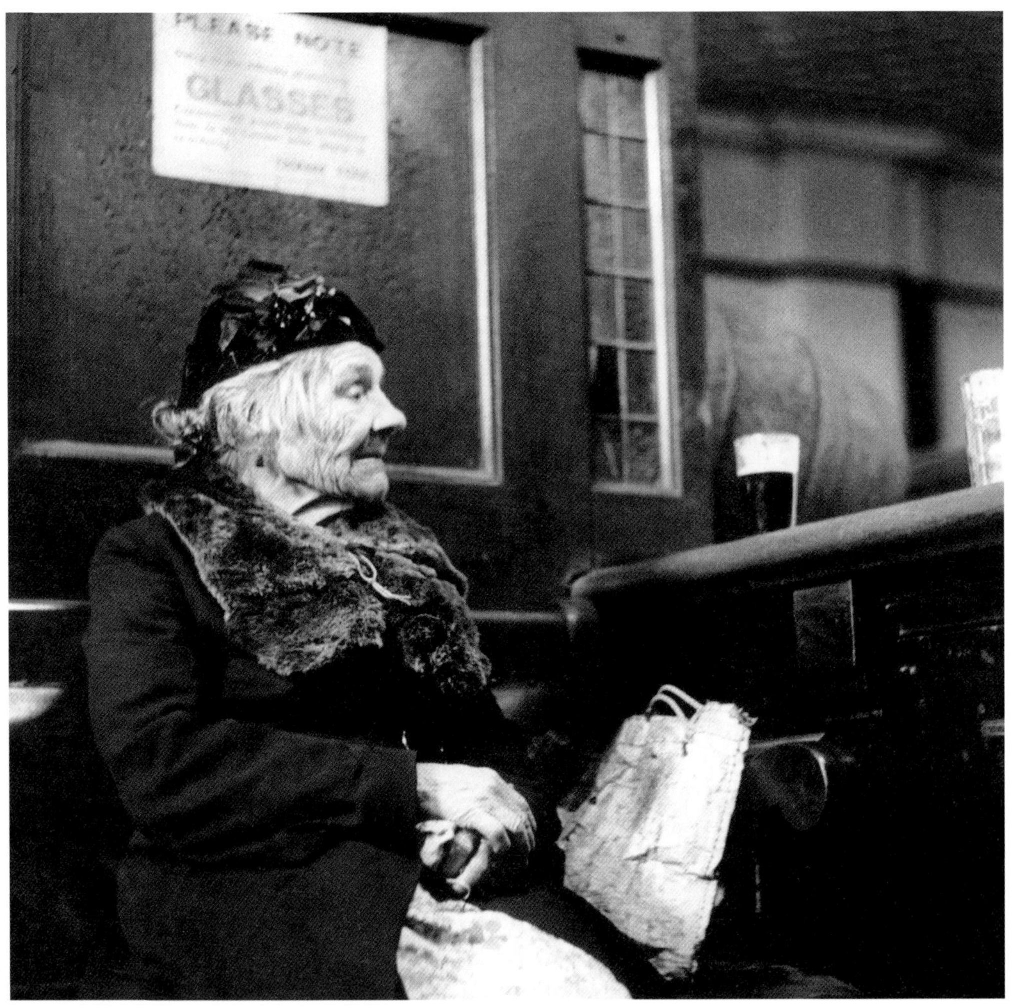

The Green Man (now closed). *Bethnal Green, c.1950*

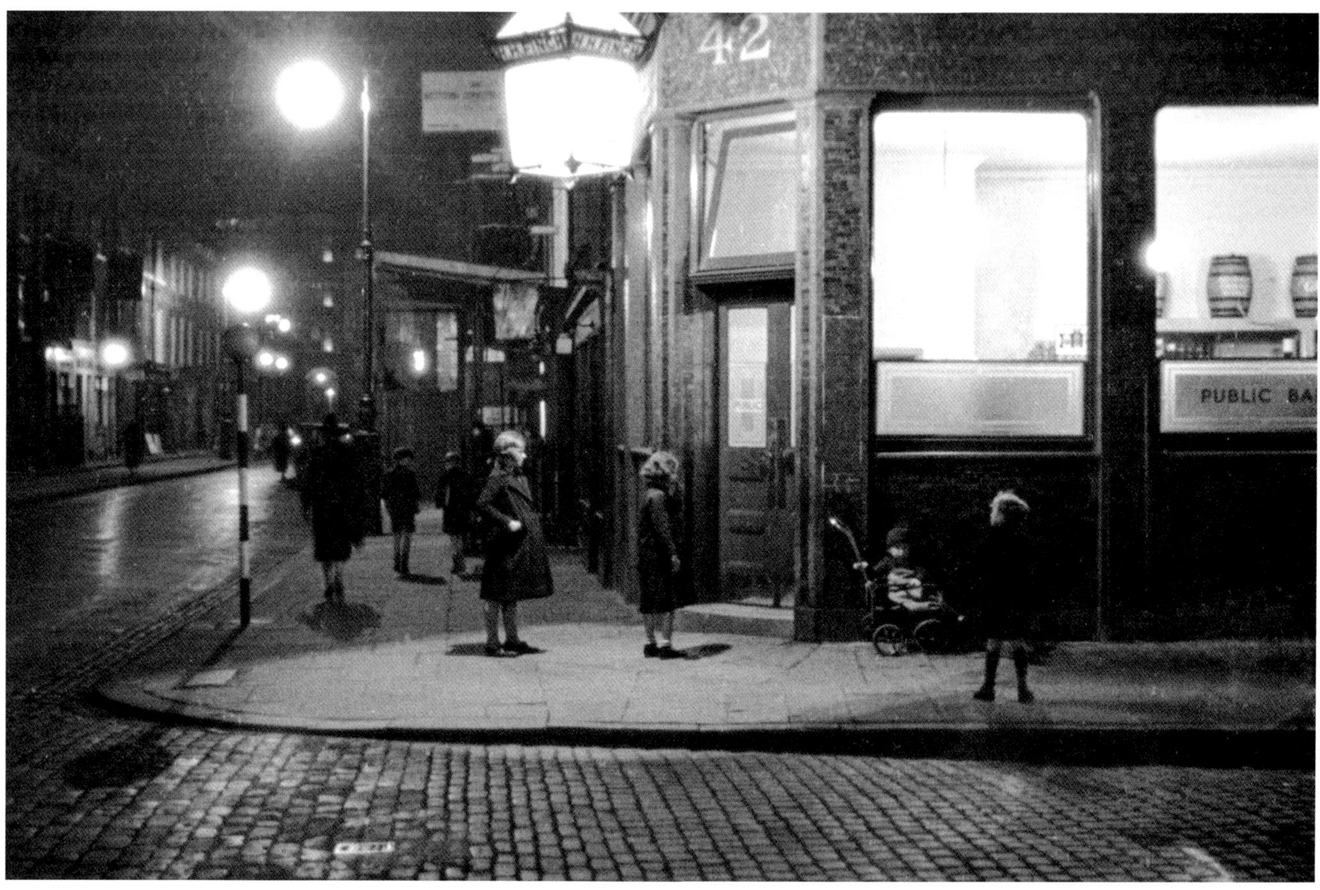

Children wait outside a pub for their parents. *London, 1938*

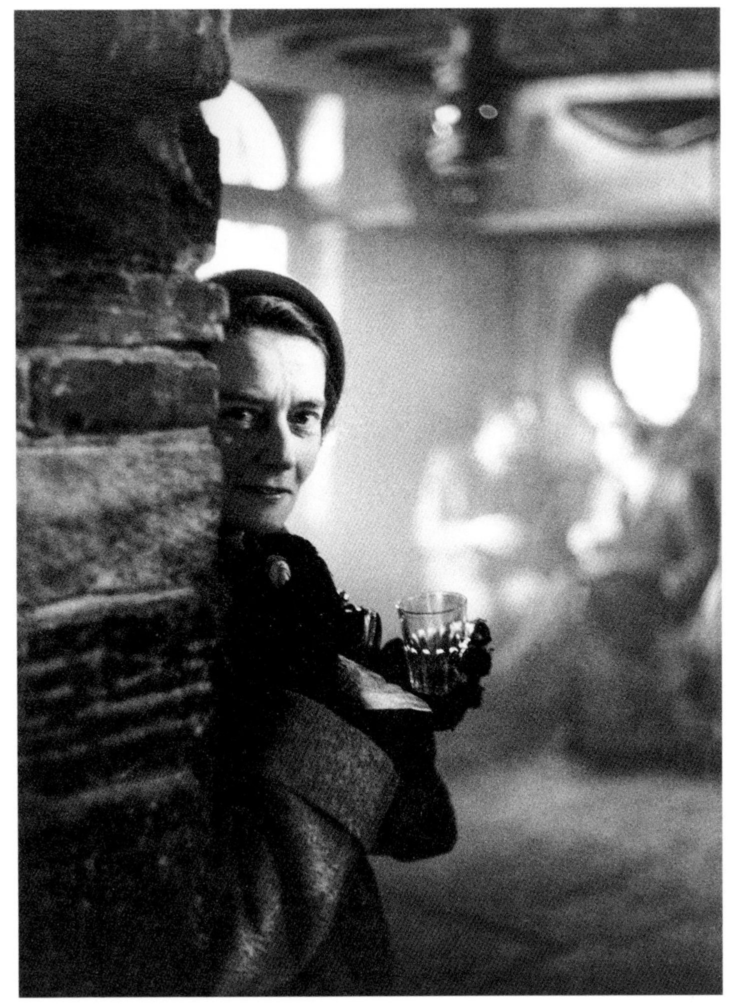

London, 1955

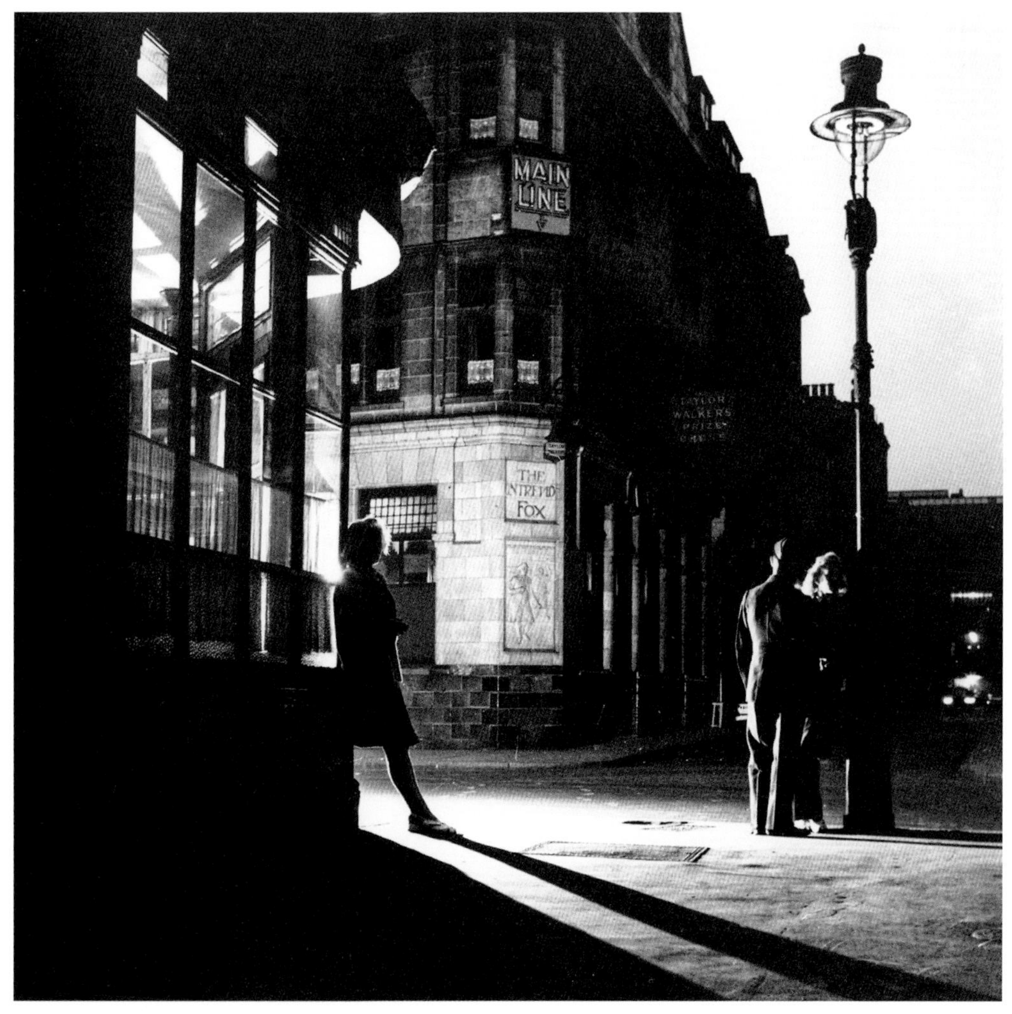

The Intrepid Fox (now closed) on Wardour Street. *Soho, 1947*

The London Pub

First edition, published 2022
by Hoxton Mini Press, London
Book design copyright © Hoxton Mini Press 2022
All rights reserved

Design and sequence by Friederike Huber
Introduction by Pete Brown
Copy-editing by Octavia Stocker
Additional design by Richard Mason
Production by Sarah-Louise Deazley

A CIP catalogue record for this book is available from the British
Library. No part of this publication may be reproduced, stored in a
retrieval system, or transmitted in any form or by any means, electronic,
mechanical, photocopying, recording or otherwise, without the prior
written permission of the copyright owner.

ISBN: 978-1-914314-28-5

Printed and bound by OZGraf, Poland

Hoxton Mini Press is an environmentally conscious publisher,
committed to offsetting our carbon footprint. The offset for this book
was purchased from Stand For Trees.

For every book you buy from our website, we plant a tree:
www.hoxtonminipress.com

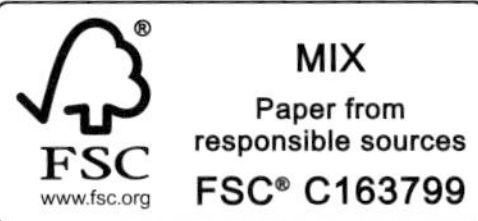